FREE Test Taking Tips DVD Offer

To help us better serve you, we have developed a Test Taking Tips DVD that we would like to give you for FREE. **This DVD covers world-class test taking tips that you can use to be even more successful when you are taking your test.**

All that we ask is that you email us your feedback about your study guide. Please let us know what you thought about it – whether that is good, bad or indifferent.

To get your **FREE Test Taking Tips DVD**, email freedvd@studyguideteam.com with "FREE DVD" in the subject line and the following information in the body of the email:

a. The title of your study guide.

b. Your product rating on a scale of 1-5, with 5 being the highest rating.

c. Your feedback about the study guide. What did you think of it?

d. Your full name and shipping address to send your free DVD.

If you have any questions or concerns, please don't hesitate to contact us at freedvd@studyguideteam.com.

Thanks again!

Series 7 Exam Prep

FINRA Series 7 Study Guide and Practice Exam Questions
[Updated for the New Official Outline]

TPB Publishing

Written and edited by TPB Publishing.

ISBN 13: 9781628458978
ISBN 10: 1628458976

Table of Contents

Quick Overview

As you draw closer to taking your exam, effective preparation becomes more and more important. Thankfully, you have this study guide to help you get ready. Use this guide to help keep your studying on track and refer to it often.

This study guide contains several key sections that will help you be successful on your exam. The guide contains tips for what you should do the night before and the day of the test. Also included are test-taking tips. Knowing the right information is not always enough. Many well-prepared test takers struggle with exams. These tips will help equip you to accurately read, assess, and answer test questions.

A large part of the guide is devoted to showing you what content to expect on the exam and to helping you better understand that content. In this guide are practice test questions so that you can see how well you have grasped the content. Then, answer explanations are provided so that you can understand why you missed certain questions.

Don't try to cram the night before you take your exam. This is not a wise strategy for a few reasons. First, your retention of the information will be low. Your time would be better used by reviewing information you already know rather than trying to learn a lot of new information. Second, you will likely become stressed as you try to gain a large amount of knowledge in a short amount of time. Third, you will be depriving yourself of sleep. So be sure to go to bed at a reasonable time the night before. Being well-rested helps you focus and remain calm.

Be sure to eat a substantial breakfast the morning of the exam. If you are taking the exam in the afternoon, be sure to have a good lunch as well. Being hungry is distracting and can make it difficult to focus. You have hopefully spent lots of time preparing for the exam. Don't let an empty stomach get in the way of success!

When travelling to the testing center, leave earlier than needed. That way, you have a buffer in case you experience any delays. This will help you remain calm and will keep you from missing your appointment time at the testing center.

Be sure to pace yourself during the exam. Don't try to rush through the exam. There is no need to risk performing poorly on the exam just so you can leave the testing center early. Allow yourself to use all of the allotted time if needed.

Remain positive while taking the exam even if you feel like you are performing poorly. Thinking about the content you should have mastered will not help you perform better on the exam.

Once the exam is complete, take some time to relax. Even if you feel that you need to take the exam again, you will be well served by some down time before you begin studying again. It's often easier to convince yourself to study if you know that it will come with a reward!

Test-Taking Strategies

1. Predicting the Answer

When you feel confident in your preparation for a multiple-choice test, try predicting the answer before reading the answer choices. This is especially useful on questions that test objective factual knowledge. By predicting the answer before reading the available choices, you eliminate the possibility that you will be distracted or led astray by an incorrect answer choice. You will feel more confident in your selection if you read the question, predict the answer, and then find your prediction among the answer choices. After using this strategy, be sure to still read all of the answer choices carefully and completely. If you feel unprepared, you should not attempt to predict the answers. This would be a waste of time and an opportunity for your mind to wander in the wrong direction.

2. Reading the Whole Question

Too often, test takers scan a multiple-choice question, recognize a few familiar words, and immediately jump to the answer choices. Test authors are aware of this common impatience, and they will sometimes prey upon it. For instance, a test author might subtly turn the question into a negative, or he or she might redirect the focus of the question right at the end. The only way to avoid falling into these traps is to read the entirety of the question carefully before reading the answer choices.

3. Looking for Wrong Answers

Long and complicated multiple-choice questions can be intimidating. One way to simplify a difficult multiple-choice question is to eliminate all of the answer choices that are clearly wrong. In most sets of answers, there will be at least one selection that can be dismissed right away. If the test is administered on paper, the test taker could draw a line through it to indicate that it may be ignored; otherwise, the test taker will have to perform this operation mentally or on scratch paper. In either case, once the obviously incorrect answers have been eliminated, the remaining choices may be considered. Sometimes identifying the clearly wrong answers will give the test taker some information about the correct answer. For instance, if one of the remaining answer choices is a direct opposite of one of the eliminated answer choices, it may well be the correct answer. The opposite of obviously wrong is obviously right! Of course, this is not always the case. Some answers are obviously incorrect simply because they are irrelevant to the question being asked. Still, identifying and eliminating some incorrect answer choices is a good way to simplify a multiple-choice question.

4. Don't Overanalyze

Anxious test takers often overanalyze questions. When you are nervous, your brain will often run wild, causing you to make associations and discover clues that don't actually exist. If you feel that this may be a problem for you, do whatever you can to slow down during the test. Try taking a deep breath or counting to ten. As you read and consider the question, restrict yourself to the particular words used by the author. Avoid thought tangents about what the author *really* meant, or what he or she was *trying* to say. The only things that matter on a multiple-choice test are the words that are actually in the question. You must avoid reading too much into a multiple-choice question, or supposing that the writer meant something other than what he or she wrote.

5. No Need for Panic

It is wise to learn as many strategies as possible before taking a multiple-choice test, but it is likely that you will come across a few questions for which you simply don't know the answer. In this situation, avoid panicking. Because most multiple-choice tests include dozens of questions, the relative value of a single wrong answer is small. As much as possible, you should compartmentalize each question on a multiple-choice test. In other words, you should not allow your feelings about one question to affect your success on the others. When you find a question that you either don't understand or don't know how to answer, just take a deep breath and do your best. Read the entire question slowly and carefully. Try rephrasing the question a couple of different ways. Then, read all of the answer choices carefully. After eliminating obviously wrong answers, make a selection and move on to the next question.

6. Confusing Answer Choices

When working on a difficult multiple-choice question, there may be a tendency to focus on the answer choices that are the easiest to understand. Many people, whether consciously or not, gravitate to the answer choices that require the least concentration, knowledge, and memory. This is a mistake. When you come across an answer choice that is confusing, you should give it extra attention. A question might be confusing because you do not know the subject matter to which it refers. If this is the case, don't eliminate the answer before you have affirmatively settled on another. When you come across an answer choice of this type, set it aside as you look at the remaining choices. If you can confidently assert that one of the other choices is correct, you can leave the confusing answer aside. Otherwise, you will need to take a moment to try to better understand the confusing answer choice. Rephrasing is one way to tease out the sense of a confusing answer choice.

7. Your First Instinct

Many people struggle with multiple-choice tests because they overthink the questions. If you have studied sufficiently for the test, you should be prepared to trust your first instinct once you have carefully and completely read the question and all of the answer choices. There is a great deal of research suggesting that the mind can come to the correct conclusion very quickly once it has obtained all of the relevant information. At times, it may seem to you as if your intuition is working faster even than your reasoning mind. This may in fact be true. The knowledge you obtain while studying may be retrieved from your subconscious before you have a chance to work out the associations that support it. Verify your instinct by working out the reasons that it should be trusted.

8. Key Words

Many test takers struggle with multiple-choice questions because they have poor reading comprehension skills. Quickly reading and understanding a multiple-choice question requires a mixture of skill and experience. To help with this, try jotting down a few key words and phrases on a piece of scrap paper. Doing this concentrates the process of reading and forces the mind to weigh the relative importance of the question's parts. In selecting words and phrases to write down, the test taker thinks about the question more deeply and carefully. This is especially true for multiple-choice questions that are preceded by a long prompt.

9. Subtle Negatives

One of the oldest tricks in the multiple-choice test writer's book is to subtly reverse the meaning of a question with a word like *not* or *except*. If you are not paying attention to each word in the question, you can easily be led astray by this trick. For instance, a common question format is, "Which of the following is...?" Obviously, if the question instead is, "Which of the following is not...?," then the answer will be quite different. Even worse, the test makers are aware of the potential for this mistake and will include one answer choice that would be correct if the question were not negated or reversed. A test taker who misses the reversal will find what he or she believes to be a correct answer and will be so confident that he or she will fail to reread the question and discover the original error. The only way to avoid this is to practice a wide variety of multiple-choice questions and to pay close attention to each and every word.

10. Reading Every Answer Choice

It may seem obvious, but you should always read every one of the answer choices! Too many test takers fall into the habit of scanning the question and assuming that they understand the question because they recognize a few key words. From there, they pick the first answer choice that answers the question they believe they have read. Test takers who read all of the answer choices might discover that one of the latter answer choices is actually *more* correct. Moreover, reading all of the answer choices can remind you of facts related to the question that can help you arrive at the correct answer. Sometimes, a misstatement or incorrect detail in one of the latter answer choices will trigger your memory of the subject and will enable you to find the right answer. Failing to read all of the answer choices is like not reading all of the items on a restaurant menu: you might miss out on the perfect choice.

11. Spot the Hedges

One of the keys to success on multiple-choice tests is paying close attention to every word. This is never truer than with words like almost, most, some, and sometimes. These words are called "hedges" because they indicate that a statement is not totally true or not true in every place and time. An absolute statement will contain no hedges, but in many subjects, the answers are not always straightforward or absolute. There are always exceptions to the rules in these subjects. For this reason, you should favor those multiple-choice questions that contain hedging language. The presence of qualifying words indicates that the author is taking special care with his or her words, which is certainly important when composing the right answer. After all, there are many ways to be wrong, but there is only one way to be right! For this reason, it is wise to avoid answers that are absolute when taking a multiple-choice test. An absolute answer is one that says things are either all one way or all another. They often include words like *every*, *always*, *best*, and *never*. If you are taking a multiple-choice test in a subject that doesn't lend itself to absolute answers, be on your guard if you see any of these words.

12. Long Answers

In many subject areas, the answers are not simple. As already mentioned, the right answer often requires hedges. Another common feature of the answers to a complex or subjective question are qualifying clauses, which are groups of words that subtly modify the meaning of the sentence. If the question or answer choice describes a rule to which there are exceptions or the subject matter is complicated, ambiguous, or confusing, the correct answer will require many words in order to be expressed clearly and accurately. In essence, you should not be deterred by answer choices that seem excessively long. Oftentimes, the author of the text will not be able to write the correct answer without offering some qualifications and modifications. Your job is to read the answer choices thoroughly and completely and to select the one that most accurately and precisely answers the question.

13. Restating to Understand

Sometimes, a question on a multiple-choice test is difficult not because of what it asks but because of how it is written. If this is the case, restate the question or answer choice in different words. This process serves a couple of important purposes. First, it forces you to concentrate on the core of the question. In order to rephrase the question accurately, you have to understand it well. Rephrasing the question will concentrate your mind on the key words and ideas. Second, it will present the information to your mind in a fresh way. This process may trigger your memory and render some useful scrap of information picked up while studying.

14. True Statements

Sometimes an answer choice will be true in itself, but it does not answer the question. This is one of the main reasons why it is essential to read the question carefully and completely before proceeding to the answer choices. Too often, test takers skip ahead to the answer choices and look for true statements. Having found one of these, they are content to select it without reference to the question above. Obviously, this provides an easy way for test makers to play tricks. The savvy test taker will always read the entire question before turning to the answer choices. Then, having settled on a correct answer choice, he or she will refer to the original question and ensure that the selected answer is relevant. The mistake of choosing a correct-but-irrelevant answer choice is especially common on questions related to specific pieces of objective knowledge. A prepared test taker will have a wealth of factual knowledge at his or her disposal, and should not be careless in its application.

15. No Patterns

One of the more dangerous ideas that circulates about multiple-choice tests is that the correct answers tend to fall into patterns. These erroneous ideas range from a belief that B and C are the most common right answers, to the idea that an unprepared test-taker should answer "A-B-A-C-A-D-A-B-A." It cannot be emphasized enough that pattern-seeking of this type is exactly the WRONG way to approach a multiple-choice test. To begin with, it is highly unlikely that the test maker will plot the correct answers according to some predetermined pattern. The questions are scrambled and delivered in a random order. Furthermore, even if the test maker was following a pattern in the assignation of correct answers, there is no reason why the test taker would know which pattern he or she was using. Any attempt to discern a pattern in the answer choices is a waste of time and a distraction from the real work of taking the test. A test taker would be much better served by extra preparation before the test than by reliance on a pattern in the answers.

FREE DVD OFFER

Don't forget that doing well on your exam includes both understanding the test content and understanding how to use what you know to do well on the test. We offer a completely FREE Test Taking Tips DVD that covers world class test taking tips that you can use to be even more successful when you are taking your test.

All that we ask is that you email us your feedback about your study guide. To get your **FREE Test Taking Tips DVD**, email freedvd@studyguideteam.com with "FREE DVD" in the subject line and the following information in the body of the email:

- The title of your study guide.
- Your product rating on a scale of 1-5, with 5 being the highest rating.
- Your feedback about the study guide. What did you think of it?
- Your full name and shipping address to send your free DVD.

Introduction to the Series 7 Exam

Function of the Test

The Series 7 exam is administered by the Financial Industry Regulatory Authority (FINRA) [previously the National Association of Securities Dealers (NASD)]. General Securities Representative Qualification Examination (GS) is designed to test the proficiency of entry-level representatives to work as general securities representatives. The exam assesses whether the candidate has the skills required to work as a Registered Representative (RR).

Successfully passing the Series 7 exam gives candidates the license to trade, allowing them to solicit, buy, and/or sell all securities products, including corporate securities, municipal fund securities, government securities, options, direct participation programs, investment company products, and variable contracts in the United States and the U.S. securities markets. There is no prerequisite exam for the Series 7, but a candidate must be connected to and sponsored by a financial company that is a FINRA member. Over 40,000 people take the Series 7 exam every year; two-thirds of them receive a passing score.

Test Administration

The Series 7 exam is offered by appointment via one of two vendors: Pearson VUE Professional Centers (www.pearsonvue.com/finra/) or Prometric Exam Centers (www.prometric.com/finra/). Both have testing center locations throughout the United States and internationally. The Series 7 exam can be retaken any number of times. However, for the first three retests, candidates must wait thirty days after each try, and every additional attempt after that requires a six-month waiting period. In accordance with the Americans with Disabilities Act (ADA), FINRA provides modified testing and assistance for people with disabilities and/or learning impairments that significantly limit a major life function, such as learning, speaking, hearing, and vision. To make a test arrangement request, candidates must complete and submit the FINRA Special Accommodations Eligibility Questionnaire and Special Accommodations Verification Request Form. Candidates may propose the type of testing space they would like. However, FINRA determines the final verdict for each situation based on the submitted documentation. Candidates with temporary disabilities – such as pregnancy, sprains, and fractures – are not eligible for test accommodations under the ADA.

Test Format

The Series 7 Exam contains 135 multiple choice questions with four answer choices; there are 125 scored questions and ten pretest questions that are not included in the final score but are used by FINRA to help design future test improvements. The allotted time to finish the test is three hours and 45 minutes. There is no penalty for guessing; therefore, candidates should strive to answer all questions if possible.

Series 7 questions are comprised of the functions and rule knowledge related to the four main job functions of a Series 7 representative: (F1) seeks business for the broker-dealer from customers and potential customers; (F2) opens account after obtaining and evaluating customers' financial profile and investment objectives; (F3) provides customers with information about investments, makes suitable recommendations, transfers assets and maintains appropriate records; (F4) obtains and verifies customers' purchases and sales instructions and agreements; processes, completes and confirms transactions. The following table lists the number of test questions on the Series 7 by major job function.

Major Job Functions	Percentage of Test Questions	Number of Questions
F1: Seeks Business for the Broker-Dealer from Customers and Potential Customers	7%	9
F2: Opens Accounts After Obtaining and Evaluating Customers' Financial Profile and Investment Objectives	9%	11
F3: Provides Customers with Information About Investments, Makes Suitable Recommendations, Transfers Assets and Maintains Appropriate Records	73%	91
F4: Obtains and Verifies Customers' Purchases and Sales Instructions and Agreements; Processes, Completes and Confirms Transactions	11%	14
TOTAL	**100%**	125

Some questions on the Series 7 Exam may involve pictorial exhibits such as diagrams, graphical representations, or numeric indexes. In these cases, the directions will reference them accordingly. Some test questions require calculations. The test administrator will distribute electronic calculators and whiteboards/dry erase markers for candidate use during the test. These must be returned to the test center administrator at the end of the test session. Only calculators supplied by the test center may be used during the test. Applicants are not allowed to have any items to be used for reference purposes during the test.

Scoring

A score of 72 percent is required to pass the Series 7 Exam. Two-thirds of candidates taking the test receive a passing score. Series 7 Examinations may vary slightly in difficulty, since no two versions are alike. These slight discrepancies are taken into account by statistically comparing a candidate's exam to a standard version of the test. This is designed to put all the exams on the same level.

Candidates receive the test score report the same day of the exam. In addition to the score summary, every applicant gets an outline detailing achievement in the various exam sections. The score report lists whether the candidate passed or failed, the complete comparative score, and a score synopsis, implying how well the applicant would perform the job duties according to the skills tested.

Recent/Future Developments

Beginning in October 2018, candidates must pass both the Securities Industry Essentials (SIE) exam and an updated Series 7 exam to obtain their General Securities Representative registration. The SIE exam is a general knowledge corequisite to the Series 7 exam.

Seeking Business for Broker-Dealers

Customer Contact

Standards of Public Communication

All public communication must be approved by a supervisory member of the firm before it is distributed or filed with FINRA, whichever is first.

Accurate records of all public communications must be kept, including the date and content of the communication. The records must be in a FINRA-approved format.

Certain public communications must be filed with FINRA at least 10 business days prior to their use or publication. This includes information related to certain investment company products, such as exchange traded funds or mutual funds, communications about security features, and certain bonds that feature a volatility statistic.

All communication must follow certain general guidelines, such as using clear and accurate information, avoiding misleading investors, and being sure to include differences between products when those products are compared in sales literature or other communication.

Any products that claim to be or are exempt from certain taxes, such as state or federal taxes, must state explicitly from which taxes the product is and is not exempt from.

Research reports are not to be approved or checked before publication by any member of the firm's investment banking department or any department which sells securities – debt, equity, or derivative – in order to avoid conflicts of interest.

No salesperson or employee of a FINRA member firm may make an outbound telephone call to any residence before 8 a.m. or after 9 p.m., unless a prior business relationship has been established with that person.

They also may not call any individuals who have stated they do not want to receive outbound telephone calls from that specific number or are on the National Do-Not-Call List (National DNC). To be exempt from the National DNC restriction, there must be a business relationship, a personal relationship, or prior written consent.

Telemarketing salespeople and their firms must have established practices for maintaining a do-not-call list, training employees about the regulations of this list, and a process for adding individuals to the list.

Telemarketing salespeople of FINRA member firms must not conceal identification information, such as the number they are calling from, in any way. Firms must get permission before leaving most automated messages.

Types of Communications

The Financial Industry Regulatory Authority, FINRA, categorizes communications into three separate types: retail, institutional, and correspondence. Retail communications include both written and electronic communications that are shared with more than 25 retail investors within a 30-day period.

Retail investors are any investors that are not institutional investors. Retail communications require approval from a qualified registered principal prior to their filing or use. Some retail communications must be filed with FINRA within ten business days of use, while others are excluded from filing requirements. To be sure that all communications are treated appropriately, firms should consult applicable rules of FINRA, the Securities and Exchange Commission (SEC), the Municipal Securities Rulemaking Board (MSRB), and the Securities Investor Protection Corporation (SIPC).

Institutional communications consist of written and electronic communications that are not internal to the firm and are provided to institutional investors. Examples of institutional investors are savings and loan associations, banks, insurance companies, and registered investment companies and advisors. Individuals or entities with assets of at least $50 million, government entities and subdivisions, employee benefit plans and qualified plans that have at least 100 participants, registered persons and FINRA member firms, and any individual acting on behalf of an institutional investor are also included as institutional investors. Institutional communications are restricted to institutional investors only. Written procedures for the review of institutional communications by a qualified registered principal should be created to meet any applicable standards. These procedures and their supervised application must be documented and provided to FINRA upon request.

Correspondence consists of both written and electronic communications that are distributed to 25 or fewer retail investors in a 30-day period. All correspondence must adhere to supervisory procedures that are established with consideration given to the individual member's business, structure, size, and customers. Procedures should encompass the review by a registered principal of all incoming and outgoing correspondence as well as internal communications.

Group Forum Requirements

Seminars, lectures, interviews, participation in public forums, and other unscripted public speaking activities are considered public appearances and defined as a category of communications called "communications with the public." This broader category does not include certain group forums like interactive electronic forums and social media status updates. These are treated as retail communications instead of public appearances.

Public appearances must meet the usual standards applied to communications with the public in that they must be fair and balanced, have a reasonable basis, and not present any false or misleading information. Certain disclosures must also be made including the associated person's financial interest in the recommended securities and any material conflicts of interest held by the associated person or member. Public appearances are excluded from the rule that requires pre-use approval for written communications. However, any written information generated to accompany such public appearances, such as slides, handouts, or scripts, is considered retail communications or correspondence, depending on the size of the intended audience, and it must follow applicable rules.

Product Specific Advertisement and Disclosures

Investment Company Products and Variable Contracts

FINRA Rule 2330 is a key rule governing the solicitation and sale of variable annuity products. A key feature is that the salesperson must "reasonably believe that the customer has been informed of the various features of this type of annuity, such as a surrender charge, potential tax penalties, various fees and costs, and market risk."

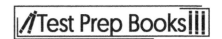

In addition, a registered representative selling a variable annuity must "make reasonable efforts to determine the customer's age, annual income, investment experience, investment objectives, investment time horizon, existing assets, and risk tolerance."

Finally, the registered representative must have a reasonable basis or belief that the customer would actually benefit from the features of a variable annuity.

Principals of firms must review all applications for variable annuities within seven days before they are sent to the insurance company that will actually issue the annuity.

In general, advertisements concerning mutual funds must be careful not to mislead investors by either having false or untrue statements or having misleading statements or statements that could be construed as misleading in certain contexts.

Two common areas where misleading statements could occur are: (1) in regards to the performance of a said mutual fund product and (2) in regards to the characteristics or attributes of the mutual fund or the company managing or offering the mutual fund.

Most mutual fund products must include a statement that advises the investor to "consider the investment objectives, risks, charges, and expenses" of the mutual fund. The statement must also let the investor know what the prospectus contains, where to find the prospectus, and that the prospectus should be read very carefully before investing in the mutual fund.

Options Related Communications

Retail and institutional communications about options must be approved by a designated Registered Options Principal. Correspondence does not need to be approved by this individual.

In general, no communication can occur between a member firm and a retail or institutional investor before the investor receives the current Options Disclosure Document (ODD). Any communication that takes place before this document is delivered must be very general in nature and cannot contain performance statistics or other more specific material related to particular options.

Municipal Securities

In general, all professional and product advertisements concerning municipal securities must contain information that is not knowingly or willfully false.

Advertisements may contain information with respect to a yield or a price that is outdated or has changed, as long as the date is provided as to when the yield or price information was accurate.

All municipal products must include a basic disclosure containing the following information:

- All investors should consider the details of the security, such as its risks and attributes and whether those are appropriate for them.
- The investor can find more information in the official publications from the issuer.
- The advertisement must identify where and how the investor can obtain the official statement from the issuer, whether online or through another means.
- All investors should consider and diligently read the official statement before they think about investing.

Products that refer to, by name, any issuer or government entity that sponsors the issuance of municipal securities must include additional disclosures. These disclosures include the following information:

- A source where the investor can find an official statement
- A warning that the investor should consider if this security is beneficial to him or her based on his or her state of residence if the security is issued as part of a qualified tuition program

If the security has the characteristics of a money market fund, some language must be included explaining that the security is not insured or guaranteed by the FDIC in the same manner as a checking account at a chartered bank.

Performance data must include disclosures relating to the following:

- Past performance is not necessarily representative of future performance.
- Fees, sale loads, and total operating expense ratio

Performance and other disclosures must be located in a particular part of the advertisement. For example, the disclosures about the performance data must be presented in close proximity to the actual performance data.

Research Reports

As with other rules, research analysts shall be completely and totally separate from a firm's investment banking department. They may neither be supervised by nor be influenced in any way by a member of investment banking. They also cannot solicit or contribute in solicitation of investment banking business. Research analysts may not be paid or compensated based on the results of investment banking transactions.

Research reports may be submitted to the subject company only as needed to verify factual information before publication. Certain opinion information, such as the summary, rating, and price target, must be omitted, and the document must be reviewed by the legal or compliance department before being sent to the company.

Research analysts must be annually reviewed by an independent panel that reports to the board or senior executives of the firm (which should not contain any members from the investment banking department). There are additional restrictions on ownership and the purchase of securities that the analyst covers or has been involved in managing in the past.

Conflicts of interest of the analyst, such as family ownership, interest in a security of his or her firm, or related entities interest in a security, must be disclosed.

Price targets and ratings in research reports must contain information about past ratings and price targets, along with the underlying security's stock price over that timeframe.

Government Securities

All retail communications and correspondence concerning collateralized mortgage obligations (CMOs) must explicitly state that it is a CMO. Additionally, the communication may not compare the CMO to other investments, and it cannot imply that any government agency guarantees the security in the event of default.

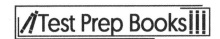

Statistics, such as average life, yield, rates of return, and other information critical to making an investment decision, must also be disclosed.

Before the sale of a CMO to any investor other than an institutional investor, a FINRA member must offer educational material to the investor that discusses the characteristics and risks of the CMO, such as prepayment risk and credit risk, costs associated with executing the purchase and sale of the CMO, and the liquidity of the security.

The structure of the CMO should be explained by the FINRA member so that the investor is aware of how the overall structure works and where his or her investment fits in with the other loans and items inside the CMO. The basics of mortgage loans and securitization should also be explained so it is clear the investor is not buying a loan or debt security, but rather a bundle or derivative of those. Lastly, the firm or its employee should provide the investor with some basic questions to ask before investing in a CMO, as well as a guide to some of the advanced language used, such as collateralized and tranche.

The items noted above must be given equal prominence in the advertisement. Data, such as the coupon rate, yield, specific tranche, final maturity date, and underlying collateral, must be disclosed and presented in equal size type as each other and the rest of the disclosures.

It is optional to include other product features, such as ratings, income payment structure, and minimum denominations, and to do so is up to the discretion or preference of the selling institution.

The institution may also add its name, memberships, address, and telephone number.

The following oral disclaimer must precede any radio or television advertisement in lieu of the information about yield, maturity, and other details listed here previously:

"The following is an advertisement for Collateralized Mortgage Obligations. Contact your representative for information on CMOs and how they react to different market conditions."

Radio or television advertisements must contain the following oral disclosure statement in lieu of the performance disclosure listed previously that refers to changes in payments, yield, and average life of the investment:

"The yield and average life reflect prepayment assumptions that may or may not be met. Changes in payments may significantly affect yield and average life."

Describing Investment Products and Services

Bringing New Issues to Market

An underwriter conducts due diligence when they offer potential investors the chance to ask the issuing company about their financial health and what they intend to do with the capital they raise. Typically, due diligence involves attorneys who ensure all the appropriate steps are taken in the event an issuance falls through. Due diligence is required for merger and acquisition (M&A) activity, privatization of a company, and issuance of shares or debt. The process involves the auditing of financial information, legal documents, information systems, and management.

A registration statement is a statement a company must file with the SEC before it proceeds with offering shares to the public.

A preliminary prospectus, which is subject to change, is called a "red herring" prospectus. It is shorter in length than a final prospectus but contains all the important facts about the issuer and the issue except for final prices and dates. The red in the "red herring" refers to the red lettering on the cover of the preliminary prospectus to indicate it is not the final version. The final prospectus is a legal document that must have all material information about the issuer and new securities being issued. The following are included in the final prospectus:

- The final offering price
- The underwriter's spread
- The delivery date

An underwriting agreement between the investment bank (or syndicate of banks) and the issuing company contains the transaction details. This includes any agreements to purchase shares and the price at which shares will be sold. This document reduces the chances for conflict and clearly outlines each party's role in the transaction. With this agreement, the issuer guarantees:

- To comply with all laws and the Securities Act of 1933, and to make all the required SEC filings
- That the registration statement and prospectus contain accurate and complete information
- The disclosure of any legal action currently being undertaken with the company
- That the proceeds from the issuance will be used as they were originally intended
- Compliance with all securities laws
- That the shares will be listed on the agreed-upon stock exchange
- The indemnification of the underwriters for liability arising out of omissions, for which the issuer is responsible

A selling group agreement describes the terms of the relationships among the syndicate underwriters. It states the commission to be received by each party and when the relationships terminate (usually within thirty days of the syndicate forming). This agreement identifies:

- The issuer, title, and estimated amount of the securities to be issued
- The scheduled offering date and the closing date
- The names of each syndicate underwriting member
- All broker dealers who will assist in the sale and placement of securities
- The contact manager's information
- Instructions on how to obtain preliminary and final information on the offering

Blue sky laws are set by states to protect investors from fraud and they require the registration of brokerage houses. Most of the laws are based on the Uniform Securities Act of 1956. Some states no longer have these types of laws and instead require that filings be registered through the National Association of Securities Dealer's Central Registration Depository system. The laws usually provide private causes of action (i.e., the right to sue) for private investors who have lost money due to securities fraud. Blue sky laws were originally enacted in Kansas in 1911.

Regulatory Requirements for Initial Public Offerings

The Securities Act of 1933 requires the registration of securities before they are sold to the public, and it was the first major federal legislation to regulate the offer and sale of securities. It ensures the public will receive all necessary financial information in the offering prospectus for securities being sold. It confirms there is no fraud or misrepresentation by any of the parties involved (the syndicate or the issuing corporation). Due diligence is required to ensure the prospectus contains complete and accurate information. Regardless of whether an offering is registered with the SEC, this law makes it illegal to commit fraud in conjunction with offering securities to the public. A defrauded investor can sue the issuer, the broker, or the underwriter if any of these parties was negligent in allowing fraud to be committed.

Transactions performed by individuals with access to special, non-public information for a company are defined as insider trading activities. Since there are inherent risks associated with these types of transactions, they're subject to SEC regulations. According to the SEC, insider trading violations occur when confidential information is used to perform illegal trades that are "in breach of a fiduciary duty or other relationship of trust and confidence." An example of this would be when friends or business associates trade securities after being "tipped" with information from an officer.

Securities and Exchange Commission (SEC)

The SEC was formed in 1934 by Franklin D. Roosevelt after the stock market crash. It was meant to restore public confidence in U.S. markets and regulate the securities industry. It's an agency of the U.S. Federal Government and is today responsible for protecting investors, maintaining fair, orderly, and efficient markets, and facilitating capital formation. All broker-dealers must register with the SEC to conduct transactions and are subject to many rules and regulations. The SEC has the authority to file civil and criminal lawsuits against anyone who violates SEC rules.

Financial Industry Regulatory Authority (FINRA)

FINRA is a self-regulatory organization (SRO) accountable to the SEC. It develops and implements rules and regulations specifically for brokerage firms and their employees and associates involved with securities trading and investments. FINRA also has the authority to settle disputes between customers from the general public and banking firms. All firms trading securities must be registered with FINRA.

Municipal Securities Rulemaking Board (MSRB)

The MSRB is an SRO overseen by the SEC that develops rules for banks and securities firms to follow when they're involved with underwriting, selling, purchasing, or recommending municipal securities. Its goal is to promote fair trading and to prevent fraudulent or manipulative practices. The MSRB sets the standards of conduct for all broker-dealers, as well as the standards for banks, financial institutions, and municipal advisors. However, it's not authorized to enforce violations of its rules.

Chicago Board Options Exchange (CBOE)

The CBOE is an SRO and the largest options exchange in the United States. It was established by The Chicago Board of Trade in 1973 and offers options on the S&P 500 Index, S&P 100 Index, Dow Jones Industrial Average, NASDAQ-100 Index, and several others. The CBOE creates the rules for all options exchanges and has the authority to enforce them. CBOE options contracts are all cleared by the Options Clearing Corporation (OCC). The CBOE also calculates the CBOE Volatility Index (VIX) and shares its findings with the appropriate parties.

Primary Financing for Municipal Securities

In a competitive municipal bond sale, bonds are advertised. The advertisement includes the terms of the sale and the particular issue. The bonds are sold to the bidder with the lowest interest rate and therefore the highest price. In a negotiated sale, the bonds are structured to meet the demands of both the investors and the issuer. An underwriter is selected to buy the bonds being sold. This type of sale will have the underwriter seek indications of interest. Negotiated sales occur when the issuer has poor credit, the issue is large, the terms of the deal are exotic, the company does not have a strong earnings history, or when the market is volatile.

In a public offering, all the SEC requirements must be fulfilled. The investment bankers and the investors agree on the offering price. Sales to 35 or more people are typically deemed to be public offerings. In a private placement, the securities are sold directly to the investor, typically a large institution like an insurance company. These types of deals are not required to be registered with the SEC. An advance refunding occurs when new bonds are issued in place of callable bonds prior to the existing bonds' call date because the rate of interest is lower on the new bonds. The proceeds from the issue are invested in treasury bonds.

Syndicate Formation and Operational Procedures

Syndicates are formed under a syndicate letter or agreement among underwriters. There are two types of syndicates, divided and undivided. In a divided syndicate, there is no liability for the syndicate for unsold bonds after the issuance. In an undivided syndicate, the member firm still has liability at the same percent rate as the original commitment. The syndicate is formed through a proposal process conducted by the issuer. The issuer may choose to have a negotiated sale process when the offering is going to have complex terms.

Orders for bonds are filled by priority per the underwriting agreement. The order period is normally the day after the syndicate wins the bid and is set by the syndicate manager. The allocation sequence includes pre-sale, when customers commit before the syndicate wins the bid, group net sale proceeds are placed in the syndicate bank account; designation, which specifies which member of the syndicate receives credit for the order; and the member, when syndicate members can purchase the issue as their own investment. The "takedown" is what is earned by the syndicate for their own sales. An outline of the structure is below:

Gross Profit = Syndicate Manager Fee

+ Additional Takedown

+ Selling Concession

A syndicate bid is a bid to stabilize the price after the IPO, but prior to the secondary offering of shares. This makes the shares easier to place with investors. There are regulations and rules around syndicate bids. According to the SEC, the bid can't be above the initial offering price of the shares. SEC Rule 10b-7 does not allow syndicates to adjust stabilizing bids to reflect market prices. Some recent studies have shown these bids are anticompetitive and hinder the supply and demand forces that traditionally determine the price of an asset. Sometimes this is referred to as "pegging" (although pegging in the secondary market is illegal).

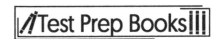

A penalty fee discourages the resale of securities that require a syndicate bid to stabilize the price of the offering. This ensures that shares will be allocated to investors, rather than speculators looking to capitalize on short-term fluctuations in the price of a newly issued security (also known as "flipping" the security). The penalty is assessed to the broker who sold the shares but then offers them back to the underwriter. Sometimes the penalty can be passed on from the broker to their client (this would be the case if the client misled the broker and had planned on flipping the issue). Typically, it involves the broker returning some or all the fees back to the underwriter.

The underwriter pays a reallowance fee to a brokerage or securities firm that is not an actual part of the syndicate of investment banks but still markets and sells shares in the offering. The reallowance is usually calculated as a percent of the underwriting spread. This gives the brokerage firm the incentive to sell shares to its own clients. The selling syndicate may be willing to reduce their percent of the underwriting spread in the form of a reallowance for large issues for which there may not be sufficient investor demand. For example, if the spread on a stock that is priced at $100 is $10, the reallowance may be $3 depending on how hard it is to place that issue.

Pricing Practices and Components of Underwriters' Spread

Debt and equity are sold, issued, and traded in capital markets. Corporations and governments use capital markets to borrow money, raise capital, and finance everything from operations, to forming new companies, to mortgages and loans. The U.S. capital markets are mostly regulated by the Securities and Exchange Commission (SEC), but other entities like the Consumer Finance Protection Bureau, the Federal Reserve, and the U.S. Treasury have some level of oversight. Modern capital markets trade on electronic platforms. Capital markets are usually associated with long-term sources of capital as opposed to money markets, where short-term and overnight financing occurs. Capital markets are also different from traditional bank lending (though sometimes traditional banks sell loans to be repackaged and sold in capital markets). Traditional banks are more heavily regulated and require greater capitalization than corporations in the capital markets.

As of 2013, there were approximately $283 trillion in stocks, bonds, and bank assets globally. This is compared to $75 trillion in world Gross Domestic Product (GDP).

An investment bank is a corporation that advises companies when they begin to operate in capital markets. The basic activities of an investment bank include:

- Raising equity capital for a corporation. Sometimes this is an Initial Public Offering (IPO).
- Raising capital through debt issuance.
- Launching new financial products and instruments (derivatives, credit default swaps, new forms of securitization, etc.).
- Proprietary trading of the firm's own capital, including speculation, arbitrage, and other complex trading strategies.

Investment banks typically have a front office, middle office, and back office. The front office handles mergers and acquisitions, private equity, and research, which they sell as a product to investors to provide investment recommendations. The middle office handles compliance and capital flows. The back office confirms and settles trades.

Some critics believe investment banks have a conflict of interest, as they can use their investment opinions and research to acquire clients. They also have the means to manipulate markets. In recent years, some companies that are traditionally associated with investment banking have shifted their strategy to wealth management and broker-dealer activities. During the most recent financial crisis, investment banks shifted their structure to a more traditional commercial banking structure.

An underwriting syndicate is a group of investment banks that come together to underwrite an issuance of equity or debt. There is typically one investment bank that takes on the lead underwriter role and gets a larger portion of the underwriting spread (the difference between the amount the underwriter pays an issuing company and the amount the investment bank receives when those shares are offered). The purpose of syndicating is that it spreads the risk of not being able to sell an issue in its entirety across the syndicate banks. Typical underwriters include Goldman Sachs, Morgan Stanley, Citigroup, and Wells Fargo, among others.

An underwriting commitment—also called a firm commitment—is when the underwriter guarantees the purchase all of the securities being offered in a sale (in case all of the shares can't be sold in an offering, though even when an offering is fully subscribed, investment banks will retain shares in their own portfolio). This type of agreement assures they will collect their underwriting fee right away. This puts the investment bank's own capital at risk if the entire offering can't be sold. Sometimes the investment bank only makes a "best efforts" commitment to sell all the securities. In this situation, they would try to sell all the shares but would not have to buy the unsold shares with their own capital.

Underwriter compensation is the underwriter's profit margin (as mentioned earlier, it is the difference between the amount paid by the underwriting group and the price the securities that are offered sell for). The amount is expressed in points per unit of sale. This increases the incentive for the underwriter to sell the offering at the highest possible price. The components of the spread are:

- The manager's fee
- The underwriter's fee
- The broker-dealer fee (i.e., the concession)

If there is a two-point spread (meaning two percentage points, 2%) the manager would get 0.25%, the selling group 1.00%, and the underwriting syndicate 0.75%. Factors that determine this spread include:

- The types of the securities in the offering
- The size of the issue
- The quality of the securities being issued
- The expected demand for the securities (the spread will be smaller for bigger companies who have a long history of offering shares and debt; for new issues that may be harder to market and place with investors, the spread will likely be higher as there is more perceived risk.)
- The type of underwriting agreement
- The quality of the issuer's business

Prospectus Requirements

An offering document must disclose all necessary information to potential investors. The document must contain all of the basic information about the company. This includes location, type of business, contact information, and any type of jurisdictional information. The document must disclose offering price, number of shares being issued, the form of the securities being offered, how escrow is handled, and how the proceeds will be used (to fund operations, to develop new products, to purchase new equipment, etc.). The offering document must also discuss management's experience, all risks involved with the investment, and the type of industry. The financial position of the company should be included as well.

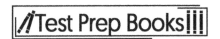

A prospectus is similar to an offering document, but is issued with mutual funds, stocks, and bonds. The prospectus is provided to potential investors by brokerages, underwriters, and investment bankers. The prospectus includes the financial status of the company, financial statements, information on executive compensation, pending litigation against the company, and profiles of the managers, the CEO, and the board of directors. The prospectus must be filed with the Securities and Exchange Commission. A preliminary prospectus is typically issued before a final prospectus, which may be amended. A mutual fund prospectus contains information on the fund's risks, investment strategy, performance, investment types, fund manager profiles, fees, and expenses.

A red herring prospectus is a preliminary prospectus. It is issued when a public offering of securities is made. It must be filed with the SEC. A red herring clearly states that the offering information is subject to change. Investments cannot be made based on information solely found in the red herring. Investors may only make an indication of interest. The red herring contains information on underwriter fees, purpose of the proceeds, a description of how securities will be marketed and offered, three years of financial statements, the underwriting agreement, a legal opinion, and copies of the articles of incorporation.

Registration Statement and Offering Material

A registration statement typically includes a prospectus, a complex legal document that includes a proposed business plan of the enterprise, financial information, the company's history, its business objectives, its operations, the backgrounds of its board of directors and management, and any pending litigation against the company.

Once a corporation files a registration statement, there is a waiting or "quiet period." This is typically 20 days long, during which time only limited information may be released to the public so as not to influence the value of the stock offering. The first day after the waiting period is over is the effective date. This is the date when an offering that is registered with the SEC may commence. During the pre-filing period, the time between when a corporation agrees to offer shares and files their registration filing, the company is prohibited from making any oral or written offers to sell securities. This ensures all potential investors will get their information from the prospectus and will have equal access to information on the company and the filing.

An indication of interest is when an investor shows interest in shares that are still awaiting clearance by the SEC. These investors should receive a prospectus from the broker who will sell them the securities. This is not a commitment to buy securities. For large sale, new issuance (which is slightly different than a pre-IPO indication), the indication will contain:

- The security name
- Whether the participant wishes to buy or sell securities
- The number of shares the investor is considering buying
- An indication of the price they may be willing to pay for the securities

Indications of interest can happen on electronic trading platforms. These indications can happen in dark pools, so there is less of a chance investors will take advantage when large orders of interest are in the pipeline.

Official Statements

For municipal bonds, an official statement is the equivalent of a bond prospectus. The statement describes the official terms of the offering. The statement includes the interest rate, the manner of principal payments, the minimum denomination, the redemption terms, the sources of funds for payment, guarantees, the consequences of default, covenants, the trust agreement, and any legal matters. A preliminary statement is usually made available as well. Along with an official statement comes a notice of sale, which advertises the offering to the public.

Qualified Institutional Buyer

The Securities Act Rule 144A was put in place to increase the liquidity in the restricted security market. The rule allows for easier trading of restricted securities by qualified institutional buyers (buyers with at least $100 million in assets). This rule induced foreign companies to sell restricted securities in the U.S. capital markets as well. It essentially provides a safe harbor from the registration requirements of the Securities Act of 1933. Since 1990, the National Association of Securities Dealers Automated Quotation (NASDAQ) offers a compliance review process that grants access to securities falling under this exemption. This rule should not be confused with Rule 144, which permits public (as opposed to private) unregistered sales.

Regulation A Offerings

Regulation A allows small public offerings of less than $5 million (total over a 12-month period) to be exempt from filing with the SEC. An offering statement still needs to be filed. Audited financial statements are not required to complete this type of offering. There is also less liability against the board of directors and company management if there is fraudulent activity. The issuer still must provide investors with a document that has similar contents to a prospectus. Regulation A also means there are no Exchange Reporting Act requirements applicable and enforceable until the company has more than $10 million in assets or more than 500 shareholders.

This regulation is intended to make access to capital markets for small and medium-sized companies easier. It also allows nonaccredited investors to participate in the offering (the costs of SEC registration are minor for much larger companies that issue stock on a regular basis but are much more of a burden for smaller and growing companies that could potentially use that capital elsewhere). This regulation is found under Title 17 of the Code of Federal Regulations.

Regulation D Offerings

Securities Act Regulation D – 4.2 and 4.6 determine whether a corporation can raise an unlimited amount of money. A company falls under this rule if it:

- Can't solicit or advertise to the public
- May sell shares to an unlimited number of accredited investors
- Does not violate anti-fraud prohibitions
- Is available to provide information to investors
- Has audited financial statements

If these criteria are met, a company will fall under the exemption of registration.

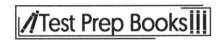

Intrastate Offerings

Intrastate stock offerings occur when an offering is limited to only one state in the United States. This type of issuance does not fall under the jurisdiction of the SEC but does fall under the regulators of the state of the issuance. To be exempt, the offering must only be sold to the residences of that state, the issuer must do significant business in that state (80% of gross revenues), and the issuer must be registered in that state. The company must also disclose any limitations on the resale of the securities. Many companies choose this type of issuance as it is less expensive than registering with the SEC.

Private Placement and Resale Regulation

Securities Act Rule 144 sets standards for selling restricted or controlled securities. The rule provides an exemption depending on how many securities are held, the amount that can be sold at one time, and how the securities are traded or sold to an investor. These sales involve control persons, which are usually considered to be the board of directors and C-suite level management (CEO, CFO, etc.).

A reporting company is the company responsible for reporting requirements to the SEC. If the company that issued the securities is the reporting company, the securities must be held for at least six months (the holding period, which is the required amount of time an investor must hold the securities). Other requirements for restricted securities sales are that current public information about the issuer must be available, no more than 1% of outstanding stock can be sold per quarter by an affiliate, and if an affiliate sells more than 5,000 shares or $50,000 in market value, they must file that sale with the SEC.

Nonregistered Foreign Securities

Securities Act Regulation S is another filing exemption that allows for certain offerings to be exempt from registration. The two criteria for this exemption are that it must be an offshore offering and no selling efforts are directed to U.S. investors. It was adopted in 1990 as a safe harbor from the registration requirements of the securities act for offshore sales of securities. Unfortunately, this regulation brought about fraud and was used to issue domestic securities, so the regulation has had several amendments. Microcap securities were often the securities used to commit fraud under this act (simply because little information around these types of securities is available for investors).

The new amendments to the law include these changes:

- Equities placed offshore by domestic issuers will be classified as restricted securities under Rule 144, so resales without registration will be restricted.
- The holding period for restricted securities is now specified.
- The distribution compliance was lengthened from 40 days to one year.
- Certification, legending, and other requirements will be imposed.
- Any hedging of the securities will comply with Rule 144 and any other applicable laws.

Prohibited Foreign Securities

Certain foreign securities are prohibited from being sold to U.S. investors under the Regulation S registration exemption. These include transactions that seem to comply with the rules of Regulation S but are in fact meant to evade registration under the Securities Act of 1933, specifically Section 5 of that Act. Offers and sales of securities issued by entities required to be registered such as open-end investment companies, unit investment trusts, or closed-end investment companies that are required to be registered are not eligible for registration exemption under Regulation S.

Practice Questions

1. Which of the following is important to NOT include in an advertisement concerning a collateralized mortgage obligation(CMO)?
    a. The yield
    b. A government guarantee
    c. Information about the risks of the investment
    d. The tranches already in existence and the specific tranche that is being solicited in the advertisement

2. Broker-dealers must apply which of the following standards to all investments that they sell to clients?
    a. Fiduciary
    b. Growth
    c. Value
    d. Suitability

3. Reports from a firm's research department must be made independent of any influence from which of the following departments?
    a. Human Resources
    b. Investment Banking Department
    c. Compliance Department
    d. Board of Directors

4. Which of the following is true concerning disclosures and review of public communications?
    a. Records must be kept in a SEC-approved format.
    b. Certain public communications must be filed at least 15 business days before their publication.
    c. Public communication does not have to be approved by a supervisory member of the firm.
    d. Records must include the date and content of the communication.

5. What is the ODD?
    a. Option Deposit Designation
    b. Options Disclosure Document
    c. Opportunity Disclosure Declaration
    d. Options Declaration Document

6. When can a municipal security advertisement contain information related to an outdated yield or price?
    a. When the date is provided as to when the yield or price was accurate
    b. When the outdated information was not knowingly included
    c. When it is not included in the official statement
    d. When the security acknowledges certain risks

7. If a security has the characteristics of a money market fund, language must be included that explains that the security is not insured or guaranteed by what agency?
   a. FINRA
   b. SEC
   c. FDIC
   d. CBOE

8. Disclosures related to performance data must include which of the following?
   a. Past performance is indicative of future performance
   b. Sales Ratio
   c. Fees
   d. Operating Cycle

9. What information about a customer must a registered representative determine before selling a variable annuity?
   a. Weekly income
   b. Investment time horizon
   c. Tax bracket
   d. Level of education

10. Which of the following information should be included with a mutual fund product?
    I. What the prospectus contains
    II. Where to find the prospectus
    III. How to interpret the prospectus
    IV. What to consider with regards to the mutual fund

   a. I, II, III, and IV
   b. I and II
   c. III and IV
   d. I, II, and IV

11. Which of the following is an optional product feature to include in a CMO advertisement?
   a. Final maturity date
   b. Income payment structure
   c. Coupon rate
   d. Underlying collateral

12. Which of the following is true about research analysts?
   a. Conflicts of interest include family ownership of subject company securities.
   b. Research analysts must be reviewed quarterly.
   c. Review is completed by the board of directors.
   d. Conflicts of interest must be noted in a research analyst's file.

13. A mutual fund prospectus will contain information on which of the following?
   a. Fund risk and performance
   b. Analyst opinions
   c. Economic analysis
   d. Shareholder names

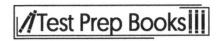

14. What part of investment banks confirm and settle trades?
    a. The front office
    b. The middle office
    c. The back office
    d. The research division

15. A registration statement does NOT include what information?
    a. Information on a company's board of directors
    b. Financial information and company history
    c. A background of each of the company's employees
    d. Information on any pending litigation

16. Which of the following is true concerning intrastate offerings?
    a. They are regulated by the SEC.
    b. The issuer must earn at least 85% of their gross revenues in that state.
    c. The offering must be sold to the residences of less than three states.
    d. This type of issuance is less expensive.

17. Which of the following is used by the underwriting syndicate to stabilize the price of a new issue?
    a. Reallowance
    b. Advance refunding
    c. Syndicate bid
    d. Penalty bid

18. A company issues $2 million in stock in January and another $2 million in May. Is this company exempt from filing the offering with the SEC?
    a. Yes, a company that issues stock in $2 million increments is exempt.
    b. No, all stock offerings must be filed with the SEC.
    c. Yes, a company is exempt if the offering totals less than $5 million over a one-year period.
    d. No, only debt does not need to be registered with the SEC.

19. Under Regulation A, what is the maximum amount of stock a company can issue over a 12-month period without having to register the shares with the SEC?
    a. $2 million
    b. $5 million
    c. $10 million
    d. $50 million

20. What are the components of the underwriting spread?
    a. Manager fees, the syndicate bid, and SEC fees
    b. Underwriter fees, the syndicate bid, and investment banking fees
    c. Manager fees, broker dealer fees, and stock exchange fees
    d. Manager, underwriter, and broker dealer fees

21. What does the underwriting commitment ensure?
    a. A new issue will be accurately priced.
    b. That all securities being offered will be purchased.
    c. The par value of the offering will be $1 per share.
    d. A syndicate will be formed.

22. What are the basic functions of an investment bank?
    a. Raising capital for companies and regulating stock exchanges
    b. Issuing debt and equity for companies, as well as trading their own capital
    c. Trading the capital of its clients and advising the Federal Reserve
    d. Taking customer deposits and providing loans to customers

23. If the gross profit is one point on a municipal bond's par value at offering (assuming $1,000 par), what is the additional takedown on 100 bonds, assuming the manager fee is $200, and the selling concession is $150?
    a. $350
    b. $3,500
    c. $650
    d. $100

24. In a negotiated municipal bond sale, how is the deal structured?
    a. To meet demands of investors and the issuer
    b. At the lowest rate the issuer can receive
    c. To match the municipalities tax revenue
    d. To withstand the worst possible economic downturn

25. When does a syndicate bid occur?
    a. Prior to the IPO
    b. After the secondary offering
    c. Once the shares are publicly offered
    d. After the IPO, but before the secondary offering

26. What is the purpose of a penalty fee?
    a. It discourages the immediate resale of an IPO for short-term gains.
    b. It penalizes the issuer when its stock price drops.
    c. It is a fine imposed by the SEC.
    d. It discourages a company from paying dividends.

27. What is an indication of interest?
    a. When an investment bank shows interest in representing a company in an IPO
    b. When the SEC displays interest in having a company issue shares
    c. When a company indicates they will be issuing a dividend
    d. When an investor shows interest in a company's stock before the company has received clearance from the SEC

28. What are Blue Sky Laws?
    a. State securities laws
    b. SEC regulations that apply to foreign investments
    c. Laws governing American Depositary Receipts and their custodians
    a. Credits that investors may receive for supporting clean energy projects, such as wind and solar

29. Which of these individuals is considered to have a control relationship with Company X?
    a. A wife of the CEO of Company X
    b. The chairman of the board of Company X
    c. A low-level HR recruiter working at Company X for more than five years
    d. A retail investor owning 1 percent of Company X's common stock

Answer Explanations

1. B: CMO advertisements are explicitly forbidden from implying, or otherwise mentioning, that the government guarantees the security in any way. The rest of the options are elements that must be provided in a CMO advertisement to assist the investor with making an educated decision about whether to invest.

2. D: Suitability is a standard that applies to all investment products sold to retail investors. The seller has an obligation to document how and why he or she feels the investment is suitable for the investor. The fiduciary standard is a much higher standard that only a few advisors and trustees will adopt. This standard requires the advisor to put the best interest of the client above his or her own and includes legal ramifications if he or she does not. The other two options are not standards but rather investment styles or strategies.

3. B: Research reports, the individuals doing the research, their compensation, and all other aspects of a firm's research should be completely and totally separate from the firm's investment banking department. This is to avoid conflicts of interest that could result from a firm providing favorable research in exchange for investment banking opportunities. The compliance department and board of directors oversee all compliance and operations at a company but are not expressly forbidden from interacting with research reports by regulators, although it would be unusual for them to do so.

4. D: Accurate records of all public communications including the date and content of the communication must be kept in a FINRA-approved format. Certain public communications must be filed with FINRA at least 10 business days prior to their use. All public communication must be approved by a supervisory member of the firm.

5. B: The ODD is the Options Disclosure Document which must be received by investors before any other communication can take place.

6. A: An advertisement may include information related to a yield or price that is outdated or has changed if the advertisement also contains the date when the yield or price was accurate.

7. C: If a security has the characteristics of a money market fund, language must be included that explains that the security is not insured or guaranteed by the FDIC like a checking account at a chartered bank would be. The SEC, FINRA, and the CBOE are not relevant to this situation.

8. C: Performance data must include disclosures related to fees, sales loads, and total operating expense ratio. There also must be a disclosure to explain that past performance does not always represent future performance.

9. B: Registered representatives selling variable annuities must assess a customer's age, annual income, investment experience, investment objectives, investment time horizon, existing assets, and risk tolerance.

10. D: Most mutual fund products include a statement that advises the investor to evaluate investment objectives, risks, charges, and expenses for the product. Also included in the statement is what the prospectus contains and where to find the prospectus.

11. B: An advertisement for a CMO must include coupon rate, yield, specific tranche, final maturity date, and underlying collateral. Other product features including ratings, income payment structure, and minimum denominations are optional.

12. A: Conflicts of interest for a research analyst include family ownership, interest in a security of his or her firm, and related entities interest in a security. Any conflict of interest must be disclosed, not just noted in the analyst's file. Research analysts are reviewed annually by an independent panel that reports to the board of directors or a senior executive.

13. A: A mutual fund prospectus contains information on the risks of the fund and its historical performance against a benchmark and peer funds. The prospectus does not contain an analyst's opinions; these are found in research reports issued by investment banks. Economic analysis may be distributed by the fund but will not be found in its prospectus. There is no disclosure of investors or shareholders in the fund prospectus.

14. C: The front office handles mergers and acquisitions. The middle office handles compliance. The research division offers investment opinions on stocks.

15. C: There is information about the company's management and board of directors, but not about each employee at the company. All the other answers are legally required parts of a registration statement.

16. D: Intrastate offerings are less expensive than registering with the SEC. They are not regulated by the SEC but by the regulators of the state of issuance. The issuer must do significant business in that state which is equal to at least 80% of their gross revenues. The offering must be limited to the residences of the state of issuance.

17. C: A syndicate bid is used to stabilize the price of an issue after the IPO. The reallowance is a fee the underwriter pays to brokers that are not part of the syndicate to incentivize them to sell shares. Advanced refunding occurs when new bonds are issued in place of callable bonds before the existing bonds' call date. A penalty bid prevents speculators from flipping shares.

18. C: The increments of issuance are irrelevant; it is the total amount that is issued in a year that determines whether or not registration with the SEC is required. All stock offerings do not require registration if they are less than $5 million in aggregate over a one-year period. The type of security is not a factor in determining whether or not an offering is exempt.

19. B: Under Regulation A, the maximum amount of stock a company can issue over a 12-month period without having to register the shares with the SEC is $5 million.

20. D: A syndicate bid is not part of the fee structure, as well as SEC fees and stock exchange fees.

21. B: The commitment assures all shares will be purchased, or with "best efforts" to sell all of the securities but is not a guarantee of the syndicate to purchase any unsold securities. The commitment has nothing to do with deal pricing or the par value. The commitment is set up after the syndicate has been formed.

22. B: Investment banks raise capital and will often invest their own proprietary funds in capital markets. Investment banks are regulated by government agencies; they do not regulate on their own. They do not advise the Federal Reserve. Traditional commercial banks take deposits and provide loans to their customers.

23. C: The gross profit equation is as follows:

Gross Profit ($1,000) = Manager Fee ($200) + Selling Concession ($150) + Takedown

$$\$1{,}000 = \$200 + \$150 + Takedown$$

$$\$1{,}000 = \$350 + Takedown$$

$$Takedown = \$650$$

24. A: These deals are set up to meet the needs of the investor and the issuer. The lowest rate is not necessarily the best deal for the investor. Tax revenue may be considered but is not part of the actual structuring of the deal. Economic downturns are also not part of the deal structure.

25. D: A syndicate bid occurs after the IPO but before the secondary offering.

26. A: It prevents short-term speculators from flipping their shares to make a quick profit. An issuer is not at fault when their stock drops upon being issued (assuming the company completed due diligence, and it has nothing to do with poor management of the company). The SEC does not impose penalty bids. There is no device for discouraging a company from paying dividends.

27. D: This is when a potential investor shows interest before a company has issued its shares. Choices *A* and *B* have no formal term. Choice *C* could be considered a corporate action or corporate resolution.

28. A: Blue Sky Laws are state-specific securities laws that need to be followed by investors and firms operating in that state. Most of the securities laws discussed in this guide are federal laws that apply regardless of what state a firm resides in or operates out of.

29. B: Control relationships stem from individuals, such as C-suite level management, board of directors, and other individuals who have a large amount of control and influence over publicly traded corporations. Control relationships must be disclosed in public filings and during an IPO, usually in the prospectus. Retail investors do not usually have control relationships and can hold their shares in their broker's name to avoid publicity.

Opening Customer Accounts

Informing Customers About Accounts

Types of Accounts

To best serve financial customers, brokers can set up different account types:

- Cash Account: A standard brokerage account in which the customer makes cash deposits for trading purposes. Under Regulation T, a cash deposit must be made within two days of purchasing a security. Funds cannot be borrowed from the broker using this type of account.
- Margin Account: An account created when a broker lends money to a customer and uses cash and securities as collateral for the loan. The margin covers some or all of the credit risk for a transaction.
- Option Account: A higher risk trading account where the customer is allowed to hold options.
- Retirement Account: An account set up specifically to earn a retirement income.
- Day Trading Account: An account designed for only trading securities within the same day.

Some customers need special services such as operational support, cash management, and securities lending. In these cases, the broker sets up a prime brokerage account, which is used mostly by hedge funds as a clearing facility and to net transactions. These brokers profit from the "spreads" earned on each transaction with these funds.

Other account types and procedures include:

- Delivery Versus Payment (DVP): A settlement procedure where the buyer's payment for securities is due at the time of delivery. It's also known as delivery against payment (DAP), delivery against cash (DAC), and cash on delivery. The purpose of this transaction is to mitigate settlement risk since both sides of the transaction are executed simultaneously.
- Receive Versus Payment (RVP): A settlement procedure where the buyer's payment for securities is due at the time of receipt. It's also called receive against payment (RAP).
- Advisory Account: An account for customers working with a financial advisor (to be better informed about investment decisions) but still wanting to retain all rights to authorize purchases. The fee structure for these accounts is asset based, not commission based. This eliminates the broker's incentive to turn a portfolio over or "churn" an account to receive the highest fees.

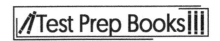

- Fee-Based Account: An account where the financial advisor receives a commission based on a percentage of the customer's assets.
- Discretionary Account: Also known as a "managed account," this is created when brokers are given the authority to manage transactions without the customer's consent. This account requires both parties to sign a discretionary disclosure document. Typically, the customer sets up specific parameters (asset class, transaction type, security type, etc.) around what can be traded.

Account Registration Types

Brokers are able to register several types of accounts (including joint accounts and business accounts) to assign control to appropriate parties. These accounts can include stocks, bonds, options, mutual funds, exchange traded funds, and IPOs. The broker may work with individuals and businesses to provide brokerage services and must obtain specific information to set up the accounts. These accounts include:

- Joint Tenants with Rights of Survivorship (JTWROS) Account: An account where authorized individuals have equal authority over the account and retain control even when one of the joint tenants dies.
- Joint Tenants in Common (JTIC) Account: An account where authorized individuals do not retain control over the account if the joint tenant dies but may receive a portion of the assets as outlined in the deceased's will.
- Community Property: Only married couples can maintain a community property brokerage account, which is a type of JTWROS account. Each person has equal rights to the income and appreciation of assets in the account.
- Business Account: These accounts are designed specifically for sole proprietors, business partnerships, and corporations. In a sole proprietorship, there's no distinction between the owner and the business. In a partnership, two or more individuals form a joint venture. In a corporation, a group of people or managers are authorized to act as a single entity.
- Nonprofits and Unincorporated Businesses: Accounts designed specifically for organizations comprised of volunteers.
- Marital Accounts: These accounts are set up to ensure that marital or community property and trust accounts are managed by a trustee.
- Custodial Account: A trust account managed on behalf of a minor (under 18 to 21 years of age depending on the state). These can be Uniform Gifts to Minors Act (UGMA) or Uniform Transfers to Minors Act (UTMA) accounts. UGMAs often fall under the UTMA category since they allow the transfer of all asset types, including real estate, art collections, securities, cash, and intangible assets.
- Numbered Accounts: This is when an accountholder's name is assigned a number or code word to protect their identity.

- Transfer on Death (TOD) Account: This is when an accountholder identifies which assets will be transferred to various parties upon their death without the probate process.
- Estate Account: This account is held in the name of the estate of someone who's deceased and is managed by a representative.

Requirements for Opening Accounts

To open a new account, the broker must obtain several pieces of identifying information from the customer. This includes contact information and details about other parties authorized to trade on the account. In addition, the broker will request details about the customer's income, net worth, and banking relationships.

Brokers typically ask new customers for the following information: full legal name, date and place of birth, address, all phone numbers in use, Social Security number, occupation, current employer, and citizenship status. It's also important for the broker to know if the customer is an employee of another brokerage firm or has experience trading on their own. This may prevent the broker from working with a particular customer or creating a conflict of interest.

Retirement Plans and Other Tax Advantaged Accounts

An individual retirement account (IRA) is an investment vehicle provided by most employers and corporations that provide investments with significant tax advantages. Most IRAs are managed by global investment managers and mutual funds. Investments from traditional stocks and bonds, to hedge funds to private equity, to alternative investments can be found in an IRA. In a traditional IRA, all contributions are invested before any taxes are applied. If funds are not withdrawn until retirement (or under some special circumstances), they will be taxed at the ordinary income rate. However, funds can incur taxes if withdrawn prematurely. A Roth IRA is a variation of a traditional IRA, but the tax break occurs when the money is withdrawn, not invested. The IRS has a set schedule with restrictions on the total dollar amount that can be invested in an annual basis. A Simplified Employee Pension IRA (SEP IRA) is an investment instrument used by small businesses to provide tax-free investing for its owner and employees. These funds are taxed at the ordinary rate when withdrawn if the beneficiary has reached the age of 59 1/2. Employees can contribute up to 25 percent of their wages into the SEP IRA. A SIMPLE IRA is similar to a 401(k) or 403(b) plan many employers offer. They can be funded with pretax dollars but are still subject to social security, Medicare, and unemployment taxes. Early withdrawals are taxed at 25 percent.

In 2015, the IRS introduced new rules on the rolling over of an IRA. This occurs when the beneficiary takes actual possession of the plan assets. Under the new rules, only one IRA can be rolled (per beneficiary) per 12-month period. There is no limit to how many times an IRA can be moved from trustee to trustee, and rollovers from traditional to Roth IRAs are unlimited. Rollovers must be completed within 60 days to avoid incurring taxes.

There are various strategies and different tools that investors should be aware of when investing in an IRA. IRS tax Form 5329 should be filed for any contributions over the restricted amount for a given year. Without this document being completed, penalties can be assessed years later when withdrawals are made. Investors should always take advantage of the trustee-to-trustee rollover when possible, since more than one direct rollover in a year will be penalized at a 6 percent rate.

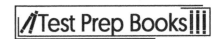

There are strategies for spousal beneficiaries as well. If a spouse is under 59 1/2 years old, one strategy is to set up an inherited IRA. Setting up the account this way makes it exempt from the 10 percent penalty for early withdrawal. A spousal rollover is the better choice if the spouse is over 59 1/2, since these funds can be rolled over after that age anyway.

For Roth IRAs, funds cannot be withdrawn for five years, or a tax penalty generally must be paid. The amount of the penalty depends on when the withdrawal is made, whether the amount was simply from contributions or from earnings on contributions, and what the purpose of the funds withdrawn is for. Funds can usually be used to make a down payment on a first home or to pay for education without a penalty.

IRAs often have required minimum distributions, typically on an annual basis. These distributions begin on April 1 after the beneficiary has reached 70 1/2 years of age. This is called a lifetime distribution. They are not required for a Roth IRA. There is a 50 percent penalty on the dollar amount that was required to be withdrawn (in addition to taxes and fees paid on funds that are withdrawn). The rules are designed to distribute the funds over the life expectancy of the beneficiary, as well as to incent the beneficiary to leave the funds as an inheritance. Required withdrawals are ineligible for being rolled over into another IRA.

IRAs allow a wide range of investments. Real estate, stocks, bonds, annuities, and mutual funds are all permissible investments in an IRA. There are some prohibited investments. For instance, life insurance can't be used in an IRA, nor can derivatives with undefined or unlimited risks be used. This includes uncovered writing of options contracts and other speculation using derivatives of options. Antiques and any other collectible items can't be used in an IRA. Real estate is a permissible investment but only if the beneficiary doesn't receive income directly from the property (so Real Estate Investment Trusts, or REITs, and other shares of real estate are permissible).

A Coverdell Education Savings Account is a tax-advantaged account that covers future education expenses, similar to a 529 savings plan. Currently, this education savings account has restrictions based on the contributor's income. Detailed and current information can always be obtained from www.irs.gov concerning these parameters. The maximum contribution per year, per child, up to age eighteen, is $2,000. There are no restrictions on how a Coverdell account can invest. The funds must be used by the time the beneficiary turns thirty or transferred to another beneficiary under age thirty, or there are penalties assessed to the account.

The 529 savings plan is probably the most well-known savings plan. These plans provide tax advantages. They can be used to match financial aid and education grants. 529 plans can be either prepaid or a savings plans. A benefit of the prepaid plan is that it shields the investor from the effects of inflation, but it does have stricter requirements on what it covers. Savings plans succeed based on how the market and the underlying securities in the plan perform. They are similar to IRAs, and contributions to the plans can't exceed the actual cost of the education they fund. These plans offer the flexibility to change the asset allocation, usually based on the risk the beneficiary can take given his/her age. Withdrawals can be made with the payment of a tax penalty. A 529 plan cannot be used to pay a student loan. Plans can be transferred and rolled over into another family member's plan. In 2011, computers became qualified expenses under 529 plans. 529 plans offer tax deductions at the state (but not federal) level. The donor maintains complete control, not the beneficiary, and can even make withdrawals from the fund. 529 assets can be reclaimed by the donor if not used in their entirety. While planning for college education, it is important to consider the potential impacts of anticipating the 529 plan to complement financial aid, as the funds in a 529 plan may reduce the eligibility for financial aid and potential tax credits. Per the Tax Cuts and Jobs Act, 529 plans can now be used to pay up to $10,000 a year towards K-12 tuition expenses.

A health savings account is designed to help prepare owners for rising healthcare costs and through assisting with out-of-pocket healthcare costs. Offered by employers, HSAs allow employees to make tax-free contributions. Funds accumulate and rollover, even if they are not used. Funds can be used to pay for any qualified medical expenses for the employee, his/her spouse, and claimed dependents. This product has evolved from consumer-driven healthcare. Part-time and full-time employees, families, and individuals can be treated differently in these types of plans. Employers may also contribute more to plans of employees receiving less compensation than those of highly paid employees. Contribution limits are currently $3,450 for individuals and $6,900 for families in 2018. Health savings plans can be self-directed and can invest in a variety of assets, including alternative assets and real estate. While funds do accumulate, they cannot be rolled over into a traditional retirement account, such as a 401(k) or Individual Retirement Account (IRA).

Employer-Sponsored Plans and ERISA

An employee-sponsored retirement plan provides employees of a company with a low-cost and tax-efficient way of saving earnings on a regular basis. Plans usually take the form of a 401(k) or an IRA. Non-profit employers provide 403(b) plans. All of these plans have mostly replaced employee pension plans that were often inflexible and only allowed employees to purchase company stock — not invest in a diverse pool of assets. The Employment Retirement Security Income Act sets minimum standards for pension plans. The rule requires full disclosure of financial statements and status of the plan to investors and beneficiaries. The act also sets standards for plan administrators and fund managers.

ERISA is enforced by the Department of Labor, the Internal Revenue Service, and the Pension Benefit Guarantee Corporation. ERISA requires employers to vest benefits after a specific number of years. There are also certain funding requirements that must be met. The Pension Benefit Guarantee Corporation ensures beneficiaries who have paid into a plan will receive benefits even if their company's plan is terminated. There are two types of pension plans: defined benefit and defined contribution. Defined benefit plans provide retirees benefits based on years of service, salary, and other variables. Defined contribution plans provide benefits based on how the portfolio of investments performs.

A 401(k) is a tax-qualified defined contribution plan. Under these plans, most employers match contributions at some level and at a pre-tax rate, meaning funds are contributed before income taxes. This gives the beneficiary the incentive to contribute to the account. In 2018, the maximum amount an individual could contribute was $18,500 per year. Nonprofits have 403(b) plans, and the government has 457(b) plans that are similar to how a 401(k) is structured. Required minimum distributions are required for 401(k)'s (unless it's a Roth 401(k) account). Under certain circumstances, a 401(k) can be "forced out," meaning if a fund is not above a minimum amount, typically $1,000, the account can be closed.

In a profit-sharing plan, the employer decides how much is paid into a plan and when those payments are made. The amount each employee receives is based on salary and tenure with the company. The amount employees receive also depends on the company's financial performance, typically as measured by its net income and profit margin. This aligns the incentives of both employees and management of the company. A money purchase plan is a similar type of defined contribution plan. The amounts paid into the plan are fixed, though. Regardless of how profitable a company is, the same amount must be contributed each year. At the end of an employee's employment, the amount he or she is entitled can then be rolled into an annuity.

Some companies have employee stock options or stock purchase plans. Employees can sometimes purchase stock at a discount through these plans. These plans also align the incentives and management. In public companies, management often receives stock options that are only profitable if certain benchmarks are met or if the stock price of the company reaches a certain level, much like how a call option works. In a deferred compensation plan, an employee's income is simply paid out at a later date. Pension plans, retirement plans, and stock options can be in the form of deferred compensation. These plans can be both qualifying and non-qualifying. Under a non-qualifying plan, companies choose who can get the deferred benefits. They are generally more flexible than qualified plans. These plans are called "golden handcuffs" because the benefits are used to encourage employees to remain employed with their current employer. Some characteristics of non-qualifying plans include:

- The employer chooses the vesting schedule and rate.
- Contractors can be included.
- Under non-qualified rules, contributions are not tax-deductible.
- Earnings are taxed as earned (not when they are actually paid).

Account Registration Changes and Internal Transfers

The broker may have registered the account as individual, joint, or custodial. Customers can change the registration of the original account at any time but must follow a specific process to make the necessary changes. This process varies by firm but typically involves completing an account registration change form and obtaining the notarized signatures of all parties. In some cases, an entirely new account must be opened. The broker's firm has strict policies and guidelines to authorize account registration changes, so the broker must use appropriate forms.

Customers may want to transfer funds between their own accounts at some point and will want their broker to coordinate the transfer. The broker will provide a report and confirmation of all transactions completed. Customers can also authorize the following:

- Transfer on Death (TOD): This authorizes the transfer of securities from the former owner to a beneficiary without the probate process. It requires beneficiaries to register assets under their own account by sending a copy of the death certificate and an application for re-registration. The broker may ask for additional materials or documentation before authorizing the request.

- Divorce Transfer: This is when an account is split between the divorced parties according to agreed-upon terms. It may require providing a certified copy of the Divorce Decree or Legal Separation Order signed by the judge. The broker can provide details about specific documentation needed to coordinate this type of transfer.

Customer Information and Documentation

Customer Screening

Brokers must identify the risks of working with certain customers, such as corporate insiders, foreign residents, and broker-dealer employees. This is accomplished through formal programs and customer interviews, allowing the broker to determine who is a valuable customer and who does not serve their best interests. This screening process can include:

- Customer Identification Program (CIP): A result of the Patriot Act, this requires financial institutions to identify and assess anyone wanting to engage in financial activities. The program began in 2003 and is used primarily to verify a customer's identity.
- Know Your Customer (KYC) Forms: This set of documents provides brokers with information on place of residence and citizenship to determine whether the customer is a foreign resident. The forms also assess the customer's assets, knowledge, and willingness to assume the risk of trading securities.
- Identifying Corporate Insiders: Identifying anyone with access to material and non-public knowledge about a corporation, including directors and officers of the company as well as those owning over 10% of the voting shares. These individuals are subject to an additional set of restrictions on all securities transactions.
- Identifying Employees of a Broker-Dealer: Working with broker-dealer employees and competitors is risky. Brokers must identify these prospective customers and receive consent from their employer to proceed.
- Identifying Employees of Self-Regulatory Organizations (SROs): Working with employees of SROs is also risky, and they are subject to certain restrictions. To proceed, the broker must receive consent from the prospective customer's employer.

Information Security and Privacy Regulations

Broker-dealers must follow specific privacy regulations (set forth by the SEC in Regulation S-P) to protect customers from identity theft, fraud, and unauthorized access to privileged information. Financial institutions are prohibited from disclosing nonpublic, customer information to third parties unaffiliated with the customer unless the customer has agreed, in writing, to share this information. Institutions must also provide a current notice of privacy policies and practices that outlines how they protect their customers' information.

Under this act, the SEC has the authority to establish appropriate standards for financial institutions to protect customer information. Brokers and dealers are subject to these rules and requirements of the Gramm-Leach-Bliley Act.

They must also take steps to protect confidential information, such as proprietary, personal customer, and transaction data. Encrypting email interactions, using password-protected laptops and software programs, and using appropriate measures to safeguard information are a few ways to increase information security.

Account Authorizations

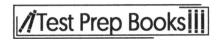

"Authorizing" an account means setting it up so that certain individuals are granted specific rights, privileges, and controls. Account authorization must be completed according to a specific set of guidelines. Brokers can authorize accounts in several ways:

- Power of Attorney (POA): Authorizing an individual to represent someone for all legal, private, and business matters. For investments, this means someone oversees an individual's investments and financial affairs when they're unable to do so.
- Corporate Resolution: A corporation functions as a unit and all actions are voted on by a board of directors. When applicable, most resolutions are filed with the Securities and Exchange Commission (SEC).
- Trading Authorization: The customer grants various levels of power to the broker (or other party), allowing them to trade securities on their behalf and with their consent.
- Discretionary Account: When the broker is authorized to trade securities without the customer's consent. This requires both parties to sign a discretionary disclosure document.

Customer Investment Profile

Customer Essential Facts

The Know Your Customer rule requires member firms to exercise due diligence to obtain essential facts about a customer at the time an account is opened. These facts allow firms to better handle and service the customer and their account. These facts include any special instructions about how the account is to be handled as well as issues such as account authority and customer citizenship. Any facts that affect the application of laws and regulations are considered essential. These facts must be obtained regardless of whether any recommendations have been made, and they must be maintained along with the customer's investment profile and other information.

Financial Factors

One key responsibility of an investment advisor or broker is to have a complete understanding of their customer's financial profile so that they can recommend suitable investments for them. This includes ascertaining information relating to the customer's security holdings, other assets, liabilities, annual income, expenses, net worth, liquid net worth, and federal tax rate.

Chicago Board Options Exchange (CBOE) Rule 9.14 states the rules for communications to customers regarding their current financial status. The rule requires that all communications about a customer's investments be sent to the customer unless they've provided written instructions in the prior year that such communications can be sent to another party. The rule ensures that there's proper documentation regarding who can be given information about the customer's financial status.

FINRA Rule 2111 addresses determining the suitability of an investment for a customer. The rule states that the advisor must take reasonable steps to do due diligence when deciding the best investments for their customer. Advisors are required to collect information on: the customer's age; what comprises their total investment portfolio (e.g., 401(k), pension fund, mutual fund, etc.); their net income and any debt; their tax bracket; their retirement goals; and how liquid their investments need to be. For example, customers who are closer to retirement need income, so bonds are a more suitable investment. For customers who manage their own businesses, more liquid investments such as money market funds may be needed to pay their employees. Another example would be investors who plan to leave investments to their children and may want an allocation in equities with the potential for price appreciation. The rule also discusses how recommended strategies should be implemented around customer profiles.

FINRA Rule 2360 covers options. The section on due diligence is the most relevant for suitability considerations. The advisor is required to obtain the customer's: objectives, employment status, income, net worth, liquidity, age, marital status, educational needs (of the account owner or their dependents), and experience with investments. Even when used carefully and properly, options are inherently risky instruments. They have more volatility than most investments, and there are such risks (e.g., credit and counterparty risk) that even if an investment is profitable it may not be paid off.

Investors with high risk tolerance (those who are willing to allow their investments to decline more in anticipation that they will rebound) are typically best suited for options trading, even when it's for hedging or insurance purposes on a balanced portfolio in which they're invested. The rule is very specific about where the customer information is retained and how it's verified (customers must be specifically approved to execute options trades on an exchange). An account agreement must be signed by the customer before any trading in their account can commence, and the customer must fully understand the rules in the agreement.

This rule also has specific guidelines for trading uncovered short options contracts. For these transactions, the investor bears the risk of buying the security in the open market. For example, if the investor is selling call options on a stock with an exercise price of $10, and the price of the security goes to $100 for each share in the contract, the investor now has to pay $100 per share and sell it at $10 (so the potential for large losses is present). To execute such trades, advisors must evaluate their customer's stability because a customer must have the liquidity and net worth to pay for such large losses.

Investment Objectives

The Municipal Securities Rulemaking Board (MSRB) Rule G-19 covers the suitability of investment recommendations, and its guidelines are similar to FINRA Rule 2111 regarding due diligence. The rule states that investment concepts (e.g., risk vs. return, potential returns of different investment classes, inflationary effects, and taxability) should all be used with the customer's finance profile to determine the best investments.

FINRA Rule 2114 is specific to over-the-counter (OTC) securities and covers due diligence on the investment as opposed to the customer. The rule specifies that the issuer's current financial statements must be reviewed before the advisor can make an investment recommendation (this isn't a requirement for securities traded on an exchange). The requirements are slightly more stringent for foreign issuers. OTC securities are inherently riskier than securities traded on an exchange such as the NYSE or NASDAQ, so advisors need to be especially diligent when investing in an OTC security for a customer. FINRA Rule 2330 covers deferred variable annuities. Most investors assume that annuities have limited risk, which isn't always the case. Therefore, investors must be informed about specific aspects of these securities. These annuities have a surrender period, which is a stated period of time when the investor can withdraw funds without a penalty. The customer must be made fully aware of what this means, and that these investments aren't highly liquid because of the surrender periods. However, the benefits of these securities must be outlined as well. It's incumbent upon the advisor to understand their customer's needs when investing in these securities to maximize their investment while, at the same time, meeting any flexibility requirements. To make an appropriate recommendation, the advisor may need to take other factors into account, such as: home ownership, employee stock options, life and disability insurance, creditworthiness, liquidity needs, household income, and the existence of a retirement plan.

There are two primary factors an advisor should consider when making an investment for a customer. One is the willingness of a customer to take risks, while the other is the customer's ability to take risks. The ability to take risks is easier to gauge than the willingness to do so. Only investors with high, stable incomes, significant net worth and savings, and significant investment experience have the ability to take risks. For example, a retired couple with $3 million in savings doesn't have the capital to handle large swings in the value of their investments, whereas a person in their thirties who earns an average of $300,000 a year with a $5 million portfolio can sustain the ups and downs of more volatile investments.

An individual's willingness to take risks is more difficult to measure. Just because a customer says they're willing to take a risk, doesn't actually mean they're willing to do so. Only through conversations with customers can their true willingness to take risks be known and, as the market evolves, that investor's appetite for ups and downs can be better understood. Investment horizon is a key factor in determining the right strategy. An investor in their early twenties could potentially invest entirely in equities if they don't need the funds until they retire. However, if that same investor is saving money for a down payment on a house they want to buy in five years, they may want to invest in short- to medium-term bonds to ensure they have the funds for the down payment. If the market has one or two down years, it can erode the value of the investor's portfolio enough to prevent them from doing so. For a retired couple, there's a greater need for vehicles such as money market funds and bonds.

Investment Strategies

Tax advantages are often part of an investment strategy. Municipal bonds, partnerships, UITs, and annuities are all investments that have tax advantages for investors. The best way to avoid taxation is to invest in Roth IRAs or a 401(k) plan. These vehicles allow contributions to be made on a pre-tax basis, which means if someone contributes $1,000 per month to a 401(k) that money is contributed before income taxes are paid. For 2018, a person can contribute up to $18,500 per year to a 401(k) and put up to $5,500 in a personal IRA. Municipal bonds are often exempt from taxes at the state and federal levels.

An advisor may also need to discuss options for portfolio and account diversification, liquidity, speculation, trading profits, and long-term versus short-term risks based on the customer's goals, financial standing, and needs.

Verification of Investor Accreditation

Offerings of securities must adhere to certain regulations regarding investors and their accreditation and sophistication. Depending on the issue, securities may be offered only to accredited investors or non-accredited investors who are sophisticated. Generally, accredited investors include entities such as banks, partnerships, corporations, nonprofit organizations, and trusts that meet certain criteria. An accredited investor can also be a natural person who satisfies earned income or net worth requirements. The investor's earned income must be more than $200,000 (or $300,000 when combined with a spouse's income) in the each of the two years prior to the current year. The net worth requirement states that the investor have a net worth greater than $1 million, either alone or with a spouse. For this calculation, the value of the primary residence is not included.

Sophisticated investors are those who possess enough knowledge and experience in the financial and business fields to ascertain the advantages and risks of potential investments. It is the responsibility of the issuer to take reasonable steps to verify that any prospective investors meet the necessary criteria for investment.

Opening Accounts

Account Opening and Maintenance

At the time a new account is opened, basic customer account information is collected. This information must be sent to the customer to be verified within 30 days of the account's opening. Firms must also independently verify the identity of the customer by matching provided information with government-issued identification or through the use of a database service intended for such verifications.

Customer account information must also be verified and updated (as needed) every 36 months. Customers can also report to the member firm any errors or inaccuracies on their customer account statements. Depending on the type of account, customers may also receive disclosure statements or risk disclosure documents for review and approval. Some accounts will require the customer to return signed agreements before accounts can become active. Customers must also be given contact information for SIPC so that a SIPC brochure can be obtained.

Physical Receipt, Delivery, and Safeguarding of Accounts

The broker is responsible for protecting the customer's assets and must take appropriate steps to safeguard all physical assets the customer owns and furnishes to them. This includes checks, cash deposits, and cash equivalents.

When taking customer assets into their possession, the broker must set up a safe or a locked drawer and store them appropriately. They must also take necessary security measures (e.g., changing lock combinations, changing locks, periodically changing access codes) to reduce the risk of theft. Anyone with access to a safe, lockbox, or another security device must be authorized by the broker. The broker assumes the liability associated with possessing a customer's assets when they enter into the customer agreement.

Refusing or Restricting Account Activity

There are several situations where account activity can be restricted or refused.

A mutual fund, or open-end investment company, must define the role certain activities play in the investment portfolio and whether they intend to perform certain activities. Failure to list these in the prospectus prohibits the investment company from participating in:

- Buying stocks and bonds on margin
- Short sales
- Participating in joint investment accounts
- Distributing securities without an underwriter

Money market funds are <u>not insured</u> by the FDIC (Federal Deposit Insurance Corporation**)**. Therefore, the SEC mandates that the prospectus states that the federal government doesn't guarantee the money, and there's no guarantee that the funds will maintain a net asset value of a dollar. In addition, money market funds must be mainly invested only in short-term securities with the average maturity not exceeding 90 days. No securities in the portfolio can have a maturity of more than 13 months.

Customers are prohibited from selling securities before the shares are paid for in full. Attempting to sell securities before full payment is made may put the account on a 90-day trading restriction.

Practice Questions

1. Which of the following is NOT a financial factor that an investment advisor should include in their customer's investment profile?
   a. Other assets
   b. Net worth
   c. Political party
   d. Federal tax rate

2. What is it called when an investment advisor takes reasonable steps to make appropriate recommendations to a customer?
   a. Due diligence
   b. Research
   c. Fiduciary responsibility
   d. Suitability analysis

3. Which of the following is an investment concept that should be applied to a customer's financial profile to determine the best investment for a customer?
   a. Turnover ratio
   b. Total investment portfolio
   c. Current financial status
   d. Risk vs. return

4. Diana and Greg are a newly retired couple. Which of the following would be the most appropriate investment vehicle for them?
   a. Stocks
   b. Options
   c. Roth IRAs
   d. Money market funds

5. How much money is an employee allowed to contribute to their 401(k) on a pre-tax basis?
   a. $6,000
   b. $15,000
   c. $19,000
   d. $10,000

6. Which of the following investments have tax advantages for an investor?
   a. Treasury bonds
   b. Partnerships
   c. Options
   d. Convertible stock

7. What is a stated period of time when an investor can withdraw funds without penalty?
   a. Deferred charge
   b. Potential return
   c. Investment lag
   d. Surrender period

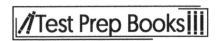

8. Which of the following is an example of a corporate resolution?
   a. A declaration of a special dividend resulting from an asset sale outside of the regular course of business
   b. An email to the accounts receivable department about outstanding balances
   c. A regularly scheduled quarterly report
   d. An agenda for a quarterly board of directors meeting

9. What type of brokerage account would need to be opened for a customer who wants to invest long-term without using debt?
   a. Margin Account
   b. Option Account
   c. Cash Account
   d. Day Trading Account

10. What does the acronym RAP stand for?
   a. Reverse Away Payment
   b. Recapture Account Pension
   c. Receive Against Payment
   d. Remit Against Payor

11. John and Sarah are a married couple. They wish to open an account with a broker that allows them to both have authority over the account. They also would like to be able to continue to have control over the account if the other spouse dies. What type of account should the broker recommend?
   a. Joint Tenants in Common (JTIC) Account
   b. Marital Account
   c. Transfer on Death (TOD) Account
   d. Joint Tenants with Rights of Survivorship (JTWROS) Account

12. A customer is considered a corporate insider if they own more than what percentage of the voting shares of a company?
   a. 15%
   b. 10%
   c. 5%
   d. 8%

13. Which of the following is true of a money market fund?
   a. Money market funds must mainly be invested in short-term securities with a maturity not exceeding 120 days.
   b. Money market funds are not insured by the Federal Deposit Insurance Corporation (FDIC).
   c. Money market funds cannot have a maturity of more than 12 months.
   d. Money market funds are guaranteed to maintain a net asset value of a dollar.

14. Which of the following is a way to increase information security?
   a. Using password-protected laptops
   b. Encrypting the company website
   c. Sharing software programs between employees
   d. Allowing employees to take files home with them

15. When are taxes incurred on a traditional IRA?
   a. Never
   b. When the initial investment occurs
   c. When the money is withdrawn
   d. Annually, when the beneficiary pays income tax

16. Which of the following is a non-profit retirement plan?
   a. 529
   b. 457(b)
   c. 401(k)
   d. 403(b)

17. A tax penalty is incurred on Roth IRA investments if funds are withdrawn within how many years?
   a. 5 years
   b. Never
   c. 10 years
   d. 7 years

18. Which of the following represents the penalty on IRA-required withdrawals that are not taken?
   a. 50% of the funds that were not withdrawn
   b. 25%
   c. 39.6%
   d. 20%

19. Which of the following investments is not permissible in an IRA?
   a. Stocks
   b. Bonds
   c. Real Estate
   d. Uncovered options

20. Which of the following is an advantage of a Roth IRA when compared to other types of IRAs?
   a. Contributions to the plan are tax-deductible.
   b. RMDs are not required at the age of 70 and a half when the original owner is alive.
   c. Funds are taxed as ordinary income when withdrawn in retirement.
   d. There is no provision for catch-up contributions.

21. Which one of the following statements is true regarding non-qualified plans?
   a. The plans are governed by ERISA.
   b. Companies cannot offer these plans to independent contractors.
   c. These are referred to as "golden handcuffs."
   d. Offering these plans is extremely commonplace.

22. Which of the following statements is true regarding IRA rollovers?
   a. An individual is allotted two tax-free rollovers of an IRA during a single calendar year.
   b. An individual has 90 days in which to roll over an IRA to another IRA.
   c. An individual can use a rollover to simply move his or her IRA funds between financial institutions.
   d. An individual is prohibited from rolling over his or her required minimum distributions (RMDs) at the age of 70 and a half.

23. Which of the following statements is true regarding employer-sponsored retirement plans?
   a. Creditors can access money in the plans to satisfy the repayment of debts.
   b. Employers automatically deduct employees' contributions to the plans from their paychecks.
   c. Employers are required to match their employees' contributions at 100 percent.
   d. Employees pay taxes on investment earnings inside of the plans.

24. How much can employees contribute from their wages to a Simplified Employee Pension IRA (SEP IRA)?
   a. 10% of wages
   b. 20% of wages
   c. 25% of wages
   d. 15% of wages

25. Which of the following is one of the entities that enforces the Employment Retirement Security Income Act (ERISA)?
   a. Department of Labor
   b. Federal Deposit Insurance Corporation (FDIC)
   c. Securities and Exchange Commission (SEC)
   d. Department of the Treasury

26. How does a Coverdell account differ from a 529 plan?
   a. They can only invest in bonds.
   b. They are taxable accounts during investment growth.
   c. They are nontransferable.
   d. They have an annual contribution limit.

27. What item became eligible to be paid for by 529 plan funds in 2011?
   a. Student health care
   b. College expenses
   c. Computers
   d. Tuition and books

28. What are health savings accounts a product of?
   a. Government
   b. Healthcare legislation
   c. Medicare
   d. Consumer-driven healthcare

29. By what age must Coverdell account funds be used or transferred to avoid penalties?
   a. 30
   b. 27
   c. 25
   d. 32

30. Which of the following is NOT true of 529 plans?
   a. Funds in a 529 plan do not reduce the eligibility for financial aid.
   b. 529 plans can be prepaid.
   c. 529 plans allow for changes in asset allocation.
   d. The donor maintains control of the fund.

31. What is the contribution limit for Health Savings Accounts (HSAs) for individuals?
   a. $6,750
   b. $3,500
   c. $5,000
   d. $7,000

32. What is a perceived drawback to Health Savings Accounts (HSAs)?
   a. HSAs only benefit older people who must see the doctor regularly.
   b. High income individuals often lose benefits.
   c. Individuals with high deductible plans may forgo doctor visits due to high costs.
   d. HSAs can invest in a variety of assets.

Answer Explanations

1. C: A customer's political party is not a financial factor that an investment advisor should include in a customer's investment profile. The customer's security holdings, other assets, liabilities, annual income, expenses, net worth, liquid net worth, and federal tax rate are all pieces of information relevant to an investment profile.

2. A: Investment advisors must do due diligence before advising customers on what the most suitable investments are for that customer. Reasonable steps must be taken, including collecting information about that customer, to ensure that recommendations are applicable and appropriate.

3. D: Investment concepts include risk vs. return, potential returns of different investment classes, inflationary effects, and taxability. These should be used in correlation with a customer's profile to determine the best investment for that customer.

4. D: The most appropriate investment choices for retired couples are money market funds and bonds. Options and stocks have more variable swings in the value of investments which is usually not appropriate for a retired couple living on a fixed income. Roth IRAs would not be an appropriate investment because Diana and Greg are already retired.

5. C: For 2019, a person can contribute up to $19,000 per year to a 401(k) on a pre-tax basis without any income tax being paid on that money.

6. B: Municipal bonds, partnerships, UITs, and annuities all have tax advantages that can be used as part of an investment strategy for investors.

7. D: A surrender period is a stated period of time when the investor can withdraw funds without incurring a penalty. The other options are not the correct term for the definition.

8. A: Corporate resolutions are used to announce and declare stock splits, dividends, management changes, and other significant corporate events. The other events in the options listed are either regularly scheduled or not significant enough to be considered a corporate resolution.

9. C: A cash account is a common type of brokerage account with the customer making cash deposits to be used in trades. A margin account is used for when a customer borrows money from the broker. An option account is an account in which the customer can hold options. A day trading account is used to trade securities in the same day.

10. C: RAP is an acronym for Receive Against Payment which signifies that a buyer's payment for securities must be paid at the time of receipt. It is also known as receive versus payment (RVP). The other three choices do not represent actual acronyms.

11. D: John and Sarah would need to open a Joint Tenants with Rights of Survivorships (JTWROS) Account to meet their specifications. The Joint Tenants in Common (JTIC) Account would not allow them to retain control of the account in the event of a joint tenant death. A Marital Account allows for marital property and trust accounts to be controlled by a trustee. A Transfer on Death (TOD) Account helps with the transfer of assets upon the accountholder's death.

12. B: A customer that owns over 10% of a company's voting shares is considered a corporate insider. Directors and officers of corporation as well those that are privy to material and non-public knowledge about a corporation are also considered corporate insiders.

13. B: Money market funds are not insured by the FDIC. Also, there is no guarantee that that they will maintain a net asset value of a dollar. They must mainly be invested in short term securities with an average maturity not longer than 90 days rather than 120 days. The maturity cannot be more than 13 months instead of 12 months.

14. A: Using password-protected laptops would be one possible measure that would help protect confidential information. Encrypting the company website would not be helpful, but encrypting email interactions would increase information security. Software programs should be password-protected to help protect data. Allowing employees to take files home with them would not increase information security.

15. C: Taxation occurs when the money is withdrawn. People invest already taxed income into Roth IRAs. No IRAs require annual taxation.

16. D: Non-profit organizations have 403(b)s as retirement plans; 457(b)s are government-sponsored plans; and 401(k)s are found in the private sector.

17. A: A tax penalty is incurred on Roth IRA investments if funds are withdrawn within five years of being invested.

18. A: The penalty on IRA-required withdrawals that are not taken is equal to 50 percent of the funds that were not withdrawn but should have been.

19. D: Investing in uncovered options is not permissible in an IRA because they are considered highly speculative investments. Traditional investments such as stocks, bonds, and real estate are all permissible IRA investments.

20. B: An advantage of a Roth IRA is that required minimum distributions (RMDs) are not required at the age of 70 and a half, when the original owner is alive. The other options listed are not advantages of Roth IRAs.

21. C: Non-qualified plans are referred to as "golden handcuffs." These plans are not governed by ERISA. Companies can offer these plans to independent contractors. Finally, offering these plans is not very common.

22. D: When performing an IRA rollover, an individual is prohibited from rolling over his or her RMDs at the age of 70 and a half. An individual is only allowed one tax-free rollover of an IRA during a single calendar year. An individual has 60 days in which to roll over an IRA to another IRA. Finally, an individual should use a transfer to simply move his or her IRA funds between financial institutions.

23. B: Employers automatically deduct employees' contributions to employer-sponsored retirement plans from their paychecks. Creditors cannot access money in these plans to satisfy the repayment of debts. Employers are not required to match their employees' contributions at 100 percent. Finally, employees do not pay taxes on investment earnings inside of the plans.

24. C: Employees can contribute 25% of their wages to a Simplified Employee Pension IRA (SEP IRA).

25. A: ERISA is enforced by the Department of Labor, the Internal Revenue Service, and the Pension Benefit Guarantee Corporation. These agencies are in charge of ensuring that minimum standards of the act are being met.

26. D: Coverdell accounts are restricted to an annual contribution limit. They can invest in any security type, not just bonds. They are tax-exempt vehicles during investment growth. They are transferable accounts, as long as the next beneficiary is under thirty years of age.

27. C: Computers became eligible to be purchased with these funds in 2011. Student health care is not a qualified 529 plan expense. 529 plans have always covered college, tuition, and book expenses.

28. D: These accounts have evolved from consumer-driven healthcare.

29. A: Funds in a Coverdell account must be utilized by the time the beneficiary turns thirty, or they can be transferred to another beneficiary who is under age thirty. If not, penalties will be charged to the account.

30. A: Funds in a 529 plan may reduce the eligibility for financial aid and potential tax credit. 529 plans can be either prepaid or a savings plan and also allow for changes in asset allocation. The donor maintains control of the fund including being able to make withdrawals from the fund.

31. B: The contribution limit for Health Savings Accounts (HSAs) for individuals is $3,500. For families, the contribution limit is $7,000.

32. C: One of the issues that can arise with HSAs is that individuals with high deductible plans may forgo doctor visits or filling medication they need due to high costs. Other perceived drawbacks include the idea that HSAs only benefit young, healthy people and that low-income individuals can lose benefits. The fact that HSAs can invest in a variety of assets would not be considered a drawback.

Providing Customers with Investment Information

Investment Strategies, Risks, and Data

Customer-Specific Factors

FINRA Rule 2111 addresses the suitability of investment recommendations to customers. This rule requires that a recommended investment or strategy be provided to a customer only after the broker-dealer has established that the recommendation is suitable for the customer based on their individual investment profile and factors specific to that customer. Broker-dealers must exercise due diligence to obtain customer-specific factors to compile into an investment profile. Factors to consider include the following:

- Risk tolerance: This represents the amount and types of risk the customer is comfortable with taking regarding their assets.
- Investment time horizon: This refers to the timeline for when the customer would like to get a return on their investment or achieve other financial goals.
- Investment objectives: These are the outcomes that the customer wishes to achieve through their portfolio.
- Liquidity needs: This refers to the portion of investments that need to be readily available to convert into cash—without suffering a major loss in value—to meet possible monetary demands a customer might have.

Any additional information the customer discloses must be added to the investment profile, especially as it pertains to specific recommendations. The broker-dealer must also have a reasonable basis to think that the customer is able to evaluate investment risks regarding certain transactions and strategies independently.

The suitability rule does not have a strict documentation component. Individual firms and brokers must use their best judgment on when to provide explicit documentation regarding suitability. Documentation of what customer-specific factors led to a recommendation may be appropriate with more complex securities and strategies.

Portfolio Analysis

Portfolio analysis is the breaking down of the components of an investment portfolio or account to determine how well the current mix of securities benefits the customer. Advisors should use portfolio analysis to assist in security selection. By examining the current account elements, the advisor can make recommendations based on concepts such as diversification, asset allocation, concentration, volatility, and tax ramifications.

Diversification addresses the variety of investments in a current portfolio. Different asset classes and sectors have different rewards and risks. By investing in the appropriate mix of market opportunities, the portfolio can have a greater chance of achieving higher rewards with lower risk of loss. Diversification can occur within different classes of securities, among various sectors of the economy, and across geographical areas.

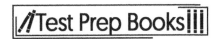

Asset allocation principles are similar to diversification in that the aim is to maximize rewards while minimizing risks. The strategy used in asset allocation involves adjusting a portfolio's investments among different asset categories including stocks, bonds, cash, cash alternatives, and real estate. The percentage of investments in each category should be adjusted so that there is a mix of assets that have a low correlation with each other.

Concentration in a portfolio is the opposite of diversification. Portfolio concentration is when there are fewer investments in a portfolio and a large percentage of investments from the same company or the same industry sector. Concentration is sometimes used by more experienced and less risk-averse investors to try to earn higher rewards not offered by a more diversified (and less risky) strategy.

Volatility refers to the fluctuations of a particular security or market index. A security or index is considered volatile if it has a trend toward drastic highs and lows. As a statistical measure, volatility is computed using the standard deviation or variance of returns. Typically, a volatile security is also a risky security.

When analyzing the different components of a portfolio, potential tax ramifications should also be considered since different investment options have different tax consequences. Whether securities are in tax-sheltered accounts, taxable accounts, or have tax-exempt status will affect the after-tax return of the portfolio.

Portfolio Theory

The basis of modern portfolio theory is that investors are compensated for the risk they take (i.e., the volatility of their investment or portfolio) with higher returns. The chart below is a graphical representation of the capital asset pricing model (CAPM). The vertical axis represents the return an investor can expect to earn given the amount of volatility (risk) they're willing to accept (the horizontal axis). To apply asset classes to the chart, to the left under "Risk" would be the safest asset class. Short-term treasury bonds, highly rated money market funds, and other safe, short-term securities would be expected to earn the risk-free rate. If an investor wants to earn a higher return, they should move further out on the efficient frontier, but this requires the willingness to take on more volatility. Securities such as equities, options, and commodities will be on the far end of the curve.

This can be seen in the CAPM graphic below:

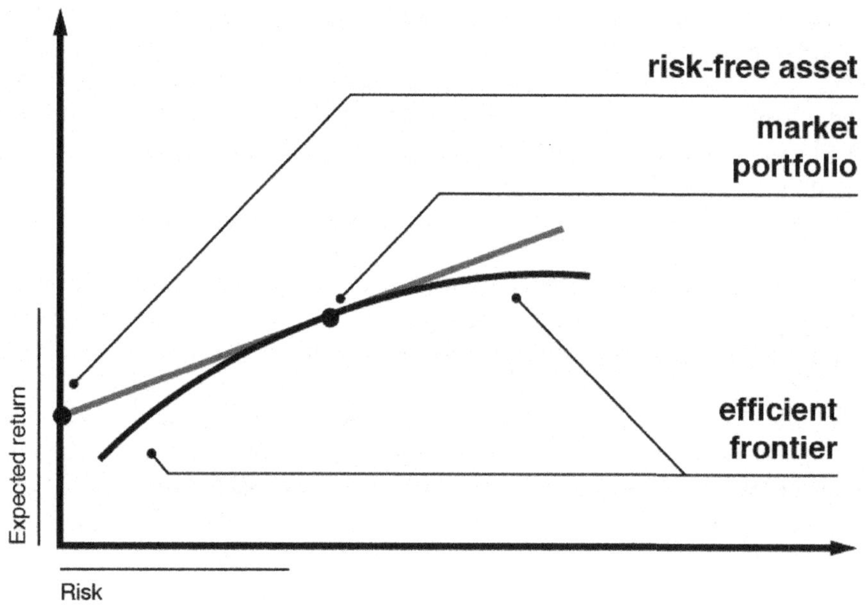

Most customers invest hoping to outperform some type of broad market index. The S&P 500 and NASDAQ are examples of indices that many fund managers will benchmark themselves against. Fund managers want to achieve excess return (also known as Alpha) so that their customers know they're earning a greater return than if they simply invested in the index itself. For example, if the S&P 500 returns 5% in 2016 and a fund manager whose benchmark in the S&P 500 returns 8%, they've generated an Alpha of 3%. However, investors often look at the return on a net basis. If the index returns 5% and the fund returns 5.5%, but the fund fees are 1.5% per year (meaning the net return of the fund is 4%), then the investor would have been better off buying the index. Beta is another concept that's the foundation of the CAPM. Beta is the relationship or correlation between a stock and the broader market index. A stock with a Beta of 2 means that, when the market rises by 5%, the stock rises 10% (theoretically, though, the relationship between a stock and its index changes over time). A stock with a Beta of 0 will be uncorrelated with the broader market, and a stock with a negative Beta will be inversely correlated with the market.

Annual Reports and Notices

When customers have shares or interests in a corporation, it's the broker's responsibility to notify their customer about all corporate actions that might affect the value of their stocks. This includes activities such as: splitting stock, issuing new stock, establishing shareholder voting, and repurchasing stock. The broker can furnish a corporation's annual report and other reports, as well as provide copies of all notices of corporate action at any time. It's the broker's responsibility to communicate major changes in a timely manner, which they can do via regular mail or email correspondence, depending on the nature of the information.

Fundamental Analysis of Financial Statements

The four primary statements companies provide on an annual and quarterly basis are: an income statement, a balance sheet, a cash flow statement, and a statement of retained earnings. Companies typically provide schedules on debt maturities, stock issuance, lease schedules, earnings estimates, cash reserves, and other schedules to help investors and analysts evaluate the financial status of the company. The income statement shows the revenues and expenses of the company over a period of time and calculates a net profit or net income number (net of expenses, interest, taxes, etc.). Usually, this statement is reported using the accrual method, which means a line item like revenue represents money that's been billed but hasn't been received.

The income statement provides significant information for investors, but it also includes additional footnotes and disclosures about accounting methods, depreciation, intercompany transactions, purchases and sales of securities, and other information that investors must read when taking into account the reported information. The cash flow statement is reported with the income statement and represents cash flows from investing, operating, and financing activities. The statement represents operating results and changes in the balance sheet. Healthy companies typically generate their cash flow from operating activities, which represent the cash flow from day-to-day business activities and the company's core business. The cash flow and the amount of cash on the company's balance sheet are good indicators of how solvent the company is. Adjustments to the income statement are used along with the cash flow statement to help investors value a company's stock price.

Balance Sheet

Two key concepts in accounting and how the balance sheet is constructed are the LIFO and FIFO accounting methods. FIFO stands for "first in first out." This means the cost related to the first items purchased as inventory are expensed first on the income statement. In other words, rising costs indicate that the company is slightly more profitable than they are in reality (particularly if the company is selling that inventory at current market rates). In periods of declining prices, their profitability is understated. Depreciation can also affect the appearance a company's financial position. Depreciation is how companies allocate costs to the use of specific assets (e.g., a fleet of cars, property, computers, construction equipment, etc.).

The key variable is how long a period of time companies depreciate assets over. A more aggressive company may depreciate a fleet of trucks over a twenty-year period, where in reality heavily used trucks may only last half of that time before needing to be replaced. Depreciation is recognized as an expense on the income statement during the period in which it's expected to be used. It isn't an actual cash flow and is usually added back when adjusting financial statements to determine the financial health of a company. The matching principle is used to determine in what period to expense depreciation. Depreciation is run through the income statement once that particular asset has started to be used. The other key decision when calculating depreciation is the assumed salvage or resale value of that particular asset. If the asset can be sold at 20% of its cost, then the company only needs to depreciate 80% of its value. The straight-line method of depreciation expense is calculated as:

$$\text{Depreciation Expense} = (\text{Cost of Asset} - \text{Salvage Value}) \div \text{Useful Life (Years)}$$

The units of production method of depreciation is calculated as:

Depreciation Expense = [(Cost of Asset – Salvage Value) ÷ Estimated Production] x Actual Production

Income Statement

The primary purpose of the income statement is for investors to understand how effective the company is at producing a profit. There are a number of metrics used across the investment industry to gauge earnings strength. Earnings Before Interest and Taxes (EBIT), a widely used measure, is the difference between operating revenue and operating expenses. It represents the total dollar amount a company has earned before paying interest on any outstanding debt and/or taxes owed. Typically, the calculation for EBIT is Revenue less Cost of Goods Sold, Overhead and Administrative Costs, Depreciation and Amortization, and Other Expenses (then non-operating income is added back). Earnings Before Tax (EBT) is a similar measure to EBIT, but it deducts interest expense. EBT is most useful when comparing companies that face different state taxes. Neither measure is a GAAP calculation, but they're still widely used in the industry for analysis and reporting. Net Profit is equal to Gross Profit less Overhead less Interest. This is all of the money left over after a company has paid off all expenses. Two formulas that best represent Net Profit are:

Net Profit = Operating Profit – Taxes – Interest

Net Profit = Net Sales – COGS – Operating Expense – Taxes – Interest

Financial Health Measurements

There are a number of ways to measure the financial health of a company. One of the best measures is a company's liquidity. This is the ability of a company to pay its bills or liquidate inventory. Working capital is the difference between a company's current assets and current liabilities. A working capital ratio (or current ratio) is current assets divided by current liabilities. A ratio of less than one indicates negative working capital. A ratio greater than 2.0 means the company isn't investing in new assets. A ratio between 1.2 and 2.0 is usually considered sufficient. A quick ratio is another liquidity ratio. It backs inventory out of the numerator of the current ratio. If a company's inventory isn't highly liquid (e.g., they sell computers that only the government buys vs. home PCs), a quick ratio is a better indicator of short-term liquidity. Some investors like to gauge the chances that a company will go bankrupt. The bond ratio and the debt-to-equity ratio are calculated to gauge a company's risk of bankruptcy. A bond ratio is the ratio of a company's outstanding debt to its total capitalization. The ratio is usually calculated by taking the total interest and principal due after one year (which eliminates the short-term liabilities of the company) and dividing it by that same amount plus equity. Most investors look for a ratio of 33% with anything higher meaning a company has excessive leverage. The debt-to-equity ratio is the ratio of a company's entire debt to its outstanding equity. The ratio may be calculated using either book or market values.

Investors also look at how efficiently companies generate cash and manage their assets. Inventory turnover indicates how quickly a company can turn their inventory over, and its formula is calculated as either Net Sales or Cost of Goods Sold over Average Assets. Typically, companies want to turn over inventory as quickly as possible to reduce holding costs, increase net income, and allow the company to adapt to changes in customer preferences. It's important to note that the ratio is only comparable across companies in the same industry. Simple cash flow analysis can also help investors determine how efficiently a company's assets are being used. Strong revenue can just be an indication of good marketing, but cash flow is a true indicator of how productive a company's assets are.

Companies usually want cash flow from their operations since it's generated by the assets they own (e.g., property, equipment, software, etc.). Ultimately, investors want to know how profitable a company is. Net Profit is calculated as Net Profit over Sales. This indicates how effectively a company turns revenue into actual earnings and, ultimately, into cash flow. It's also an indicator of how well the company manages its pricing strategies and costs. The metric must be used carefully when applied across companies. A company with high volumes (e.g., office supply stores, grocery stores, etc.) will have lower margins than a company that has higher profit margins but doesn't depend on high sales volumes (such as luxury car or boat dealers).

Many financial metrics and ratios are geared toward equity investors, but there are metrics that are more meaningful to bond investors, banks, and lenders. The net asset value per bond is total assets less current liabilities (which are the net assets available to meet the claims of bond holders) divided by the dollar amount of long-term outstanding debt. The metric is most meaningful to bond investors since they have the first claim to company assets in the event of liquidation. Bond investors are also interested in the interest coverage ratio. This tells them how much of a cushion there is in the company's ability to service their debt. The ratio is expressed as EBIT/Interest Expense. EBIT is used because the earnings' number includes earnings before interest is paid. A ratio of 2.0 indicates a company is currently generating enough income to cover its interest payments twice over. A ratio of less than 1.0 means the company doesn't earn enough to service its debt. The ratio is also called the "times interest earned ratio." Equity investors are interested when the ratio is less than 1.0 since the company must service its debt with cash (which is essentially the claim of equity investors). Variations sometimes include principal in the calculation. Another ratio of importance to bond holders is the book value per share. In the event of liquidation, this indicates a company's worth. The ratio is equity less preferred equity divided by shares outstanding.

Investors also want to see financial metrics on a per share basis. The most common measure is earnings per share (EPS). The standard calculation is earnings less preferred dividends divided by the average number of shares outstanding. There's also a diluted EPS metric. This accounts for the "dilutive effects" of stock option grants and the convertibility of bonds in the capital structure. The inverse of EPS is a company's P/E ratio, which indicates how much an investor is paying for each dollar of earnings of a stock. Technical analysts analyze P/E ratios to determine if a stock is over- or under-valued compared to similar companies.

Investors also want to know how consistently a company is paying out its earnings. The ratio is the dollar amount of dividends divided by earnings. Typically, the number is annualized. Investors look for companies that pay a stable dividend and have enough of an earnings cushion to pay the dividend going forward. A company that consistently pays a 10% dividend will be more attractive to an investor than a company that pays a 2% dividend one quarter and a 25% dividend the next. The dividend yield is another metric for comparing companies. This is the dollar amount of the dividend (per share) divided by the stock's price. Two companies with the same stock price of $10 per share might have different current yields. This can indicate that one company is confident in its ability to sustain earnings while the other is not. It also can simply mean the company with the lower yield sees more profitable investment opportunities and wants to invest that capital to increase share value.

A metric that is specific to equity investors is return on equity (ROE). This is the rate of return investors receive for their ownership in company stock. It's a measure of how well a company manages its investments to grow its earnings. A healthy ROE is typically between 15% and 20%. The DuPont identity is a breakdown of ROE into its components. It is Net Income/Sales x Sales/Assets x Assets/Equity.

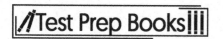

Investment Recommendations

Equity Securities

Types of Stock

Authorized stock is the total number of shares a company is permitted to sell on the open market. The amount is typically found on the company's balance sheet and listed in its articles of incorporation. A company usually doesn't issue all of its authorized stock to trade publicly since some shares may be used for employee stock purchase programs or retained by management to maintain a controlling interest in the company.

Issued stock and outstanding stock are the total amount of capital invested by shareholders and owners. The difference between them is that issued stock is the total number of shares ever issued, while outstanding stock is only the shares currently being traded on the open market (and excludes any shares repurchased or retired by the company).

The key reason investors are often interested in the number of authorized shares is to know what risk their own shares have of being diluted. For example, if a company has 1,000,000 authorized shares and 950,000 outstanding shares, the company can issue the remaining 50,000 shares with minimal dilution. However, if 500,000 shares are issued and the company decides to issue all of the remaining 500,000 authorized shares, the existing shareholders will have their shares diluted by half.

Treasury stocks are shares that have been repurchased by the company (i.e., shares issued but not outstanding). Treasury stock has no voting rights, doesn't receive dividends, and is excluded from any financial ratios involving common stock. The primary reasons to have Treasury stock are to:

- Allow for the conversion of convertible securities (e.g., convertible bonds or warrants) to stock.
- Stabilize the market upon new share issuance.
- Alter the debt-to-equity ratio of the company by selling debt to repurchase shares (i.e., to increase the company's leverage).
- Fend off an acquisition.
- Avoid paying taxable dividends (i.e., decreasing outstanding stock should increase its market value as it increases the per share value).

The par value of a stock is set by the company issuing the shares. The amount simply assigns an accounting value to report on the balance sheet. The stated value is the dollar amount assigned; however, it does not fluctuate like the market value of a stock and is credited to the capital stock of the company. The stated value offers shareholders some protection in the event of a total loss of stock value (e.g., if a stock is delisted).

Limited liability means an owner is only liable for their initial investment. For example, if a company loses all of its equity value and still has debts due, the limited liability owners aren't required to repay the debt.

A stock certificate is a physical certificate stating the number of shares owned by an investor, the par or stated value of the stock, the class of stock (e.g., common, preferred, convertible, etc.), and the share voting rights. Historically, these were used when investors wanted to show their right to a dividend. Today, many companies use a holding statement in place of a stock certificate.

An escrow receipt guarantees that an underlying security is held by a bank or exchange for any option or derivative being traded on that security. This ensures that, when the contract expires or is exercised, the physical asset can be delivered or sold.

Endorsements are when ownership is transferred to another party or when the owner of an asset signs the negotiable contract or instrument. A transfer agent is typically a commercial bank that is a client of the corporation (or in some cases is the corporation itself) and that maintains records of all equity and bond holders. The transfer agent cancels and issues new certificates and resolves issues with certificates. A registrar coordinates with the transfer agent to keep track of stock and bond ownership. The registrar also ensures that only the authorized amount of stock is in circulation at any time. For debts, the registrar ensures that the issuance is a corporation's genuine obligation.

Transfer procedures are the steps governed by the Securities and Exchange Commission (SEC) that determine how stock shares are transferred from one owner to another.

Corporate Capital Structure Hierarchy

High Asset Protection/Coverage

Yield Potential		
Low	Bank loans	Debt
High	High-yield debt	
Medium	Convertible bonds	
Medium	Preferred equity	Equity
Low (if any)	Common equity	
No	Rights & warrants	

Minimal Asset Protection/Coverage

Investors should have a basic understanding of the risks associated with traded securities and how such securities fit into the company's capital structure. Companies typically pay off the revolving debt to banks before making payments on any principal or interest. Some companies issue commercial paper that can mature a few days after (but no longer than 270 days after) the date of issuance. This is considered the least risky part of a company's capital structure and, therefore, pays the lowest interest rate to investors. It should be noted that even though short-term debt markets are considered highly liquid and a minimal credit risk, some short-term money market funds "broke the buck" (i.e., the value of those funds declined significantly) during the 2007-2008 U.S. financial crisis for holding commercial paper.

The next part of the capital structure in the risk hierarchy is senior debt, followed by mezzanine debt and then residual debt. Some companies, such as banks providing mortgage and auto loans, package that debt and sell it. In most cases, this debt doesn't have the guarantee of the company that made the loans, so it's only as strong as the underlying collateral and the willingness of the borrowers to make payments.

Next in the risk structure is preferred equity followed by common equity, which is typically the riskiest security in a company's capital structure.

Common Stock

The primary risk that an investor must understand is that common stock only has a claim to the residual value of a company. This means the value of the common stock is what's left over after all credit facilities, short-term debt, long-term debt, loans, and other senior obligations of the company are paid off (which occurs if a company is liquidated).

Dividends are the portion of a company's earnings paid out to stockholders. Typically, dividends are paid on a quarterly basis and determined by the company's board of directors. Some companies increase their dividends at the same rate as the growth of earnings. Investors often value securities based on how consistently they pay dividends and maintain stability in the company's retained earnings. Though dividends are typically paid in cash, some companies pay dividends in the form of stock shares (often at a discount to the stock's market value). For non-traded Real Estate Investment Trusts, this is referred to as a Dividend Reinvestment Plan (DRIP). Dividends are calculated using the dividend yield formula, which involves dividing the annual dividend by the current stock price.

The cash or cash equivalents line item on the balance sheet shows any paper currency, bank balances, or highly liquid securities (usually money market funds, which are often broken out as a series of line items).

Common Stockholder Rights

The rights of shareholders are specified in the company's charter and bylaws. Generally, these rights include:

- The right to inspect the financial records, systems, and bookkeeping of a corporation
- The right to evaluate the assets of a corporation
- The right to sue managers and officers of the corporation due to mismanagement
- The rights to transfer and sell their shares
- The right to recover the residual value of a company in the event of liquidation
- The right to receive an equal share of dividends (i.e., pro rata dividends)
- The right to vote on all issues affecting the corporation
- The right to purchase additional shares before the general public (see "preemptive right" below)

A preemptive right is the right granted to some shareholders to purchase new shares before the general public. This typically occurs after an initial public offering when a second round of shares is issued. The preemptive right ensures that the company's original investors maintain their ownership percentage of the company.

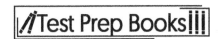

Most corporations allow one vote per share of stock owned when voting for or against management and the board of directors. This ensures that whoever controls more than 50% of the shares also maintains control of the board to represent their interests.

Proxy voting occurs when someone delegates their voting power to another party. Sometimes "proxies" are used to create a voting bloc to give a group that has common interests more influence when voting. In a proxy fight, another company may try to persuade the shareholders of the company they want to acquire to sign over their proxy rights because they think management hasn't performed well.

As noted above, dividends can be in the form of cash or stock. Some companies have a dividend requirement, which means the company has to achieve a certain dollar level of earnings or earnings per share to pay a dividend (usually for preferred share classes). The dividend payout ratio is the percentage of earnings paid out as a dividend. More mature companies typically have higher payout ratios since they have less room for growth and investment. Younger companies usually have a lower ratio since they have more investment opportunity and the chance for a greater rate of return.

Stock Spin-Offs/Transfers

A spin-off occurs when a corporation divests itself of a subsidiary which then becomes a separate company. A "leveraged buyout" is an example of a spin-off. This is when one company acquires another with a sizable loan, and the assets of the company being acquired are pledged as collateral. Stockholders of the corporation being acquired receive shares from the divestiture on a pro rata basis.

A stock transfer is when the ownership of shares is transferred to another party.

Stock Splits/Consolidation

A stock split occurs when a company increases the number of outstanding shares. This should not affect the shareholders' dollar amount of equity or the market value at the time of the split. It simply means that the share price will decline relative to the number of new shares issued. For example, a company has 100 outstanding shares and the price per share is $1.00. If the company issues 100 new shares, the price would drop to $0.50 per share. If an investor previously owned 10 shares (totaling $10 in value), they would now own 20 shares (still totaling $10, but at $0.50 per share x 20 shares = $10). Stock splits (also known as "stock consolidation") make shares more affordable to a broader investor base. In a reverse stock split, the opposite occurs. If the same company does a reverse split, there would be 50 outstanding shares at $2 per share.

Penny Stocks

Penny stocks are a type of share traded over the counter (as opposed to being traded on an exchange). Typically, they are considered high-risk investments since these companies often have volatile revenues and earnings as well as liquidity issues (particularly when the company is in distress). Many brokerages require a written letter of consent from their investor before buying these shares. Penny stocks usually trade at less than $1 per share, though sometimes they can trade as high as $10 per share.

Preferred Stock

Cumulative preferred stock accumulates dividends in arrears. If a company doesn't have sufficient earnings to pay a dividend, common shareholders simply miss out. Once the company has the earnings to pay a dividend, all the dividends in arrears for preferred shareholders must be paid in full before any common stock dividends can be paid. Non-cumulative preferred stock is just like common stock. Missed dividends don't accrue and won't be paid even if there are earnings to do so.

Participating preferred stock is used when special measures are needed to attract new investors. These shares receive dividends and give stockholders the right to receive additional dividends along with common stock shareholders. This is a common form of financing used by private equity and venture capital corporations. Non-participating preferred stock only pays stipulated dividends.

Convertible preferred stock grants the shareholder the right to convert their shares into a specific number of shares within a specified future time period. However, there are provisions that allow the issuer to force conversion of the shares. Convertible preferred stock is typically issued so the issuer can have more favorable terms than a traditional common stock issuance. These types of shares often carry a rating like traditional bonds.

Callable preferred stock shares give the issuer the right to call the shares back at a specified price over a specified time (as stated in the prospectus for the shares). This type of financing is advantageous to the issuing company if finance conditions become more favorable (i.e., interest rates are lower). The risk to the owner of the shares is that they will only be able to reinvest at a lower dividend or interest rate.

A sinking fund accrues a balance that's used to redeem bonds or preferred stock. This means the company must retire a specified amount of debt on an annual basis. This has advantages and disadvantages to the original bondholder. It does create liquidity for the bonds, but it also means funds will be invested at a lower interest rate.

Adjustable rate stock pays a dividend that's adjusted on a quarterly basis. The adjustment is typically tied to the change in Treasury rates or some other index rate. The price of these securities is typically more stable as it does not need to adjust to compensate investors for the rate of return they require given changes in interest rates.

Preferred stockholders typically receive priority treatment when it comes to the payment of dividends and the distribution of assets upon company liquidation. This means preferred stockholders must be paid dividends prior to common stockholders and have a better claim on company assets than do common stock holders in the event of dissolution. However, preferred stock ordinarily does not come with voting rights.

Rights and Warrants

A rights offering allows existing stockholders to buy newly issued shares at a discount, before the general public can buy them. These transactions typically involve an investment bank having the right to buy any offered shares if the existing investors don't purchase all available shares in the rights offering.

Warrants are contracts attached to the ownership of a bond or preferred stock. They grant the holder the right to purchase additional stock over a specified time and at a set price (the "exercise price"). This creates an incentive for the warrant holder should the market price rise above the set price. Basically, warrants are a "sweetener" when debt is issued by a company. The company wants to issue debt at a lower interest rate than the market dictates (given the company's risk profile), so the warrant compensates the investor for buying the debt at the lower rate.

Warrants are tradeable securities and can be separated from the instrument to which they're attached. Typically, they're traded on over-the-counter markets. A warrant experiences "time decay" as it gets closer to its expiration date. Some examples of warrants include: basket warrants that mirror the performance of an industry; index warrants whose value is determined by the performance of an index; detachable warrants; and naked warrants. Warrants sometimes have an anti-dilution provision, which allows existing shareholders to purchase new shares on a pro rata basis. A convertible bond's value equals the bond's straight value plus the value of the warrant.

Electronic Exchanges and Auction Markets

Electronic exchanges are exchanges that bring buyers and sellers together through an electronic trading platform. The NASDAQ is an example of an electronic exchange. The benefits of these exchanges include lower transaction costs, better liquidity, faster trade execution, increased competition, improved transparency, and smaller bid-ask spreads. Some of these exchanges use algorithms to improve trade execution. An auction market establishes a price through competitive bidding through brokers (who represent their respective clients and investors). Most auction markets have the following rules:

- The first bid has priority.
- The high bid and low offer "have the floor."
- A new auction begins when all bids at a certain price are exhausted.
- There are no secret transactions.
- Bids and offers must be audible.

Equity markets have specialists and market makers who assure liquidity and market stability for specific equities. To trade on an exchange auction market, companies must meet certain listing requirements. To trade on the New York Stock Exchange, a company must have $1.1 million public shares with a market value of at least $40 million. They must also have a pre-tax annual income of $10 million aggregate for the last three fiscal years. Most exchanges have trading curbs or circuit breakers. This means all trading is stopped when markets have a significant decline. The New York Stock Exchange sets these breakers on a quarterly basis. Depending on the size of the decline, trading may stop temporarily and resume that same day or stop for the day entirely.

Electronic communication networks (ECNs) are systems that display and match orders placed on exchanges and OTC markets. The SEC requires ECNs to register as broker-dealers. These networks eliminate the need for a third party to participate in each trade. These exchanges can be used for after hours and foreign exchange trading. They serve both institutional and retail investors.

Instinet is a prominent ECN, which traded 22% of the stocks on the NASDAQ (as of 2002). ECNs increase trading competition by lowering the transaction costs of participating investor firms, giving clients full access to their buy and sell volume, and matching buyers and sellers outside of normal trading hours. Some ECNs use autonomous agents that exchange not only values but offers and counter-offers as well.

The two fee structures of ECNs are the classic structure and the credit (or rebate) structure. The classic structure offers liquidity removers, while the credit structure attracts liquidity buyers.

Matching this trading is quote driven. Currency trading is more advantageous on an ECN because there is greater transparency, faster processing, better liquidity, and more availability in the marketplace. ECNs experienced a resurgence when they adopted Regulation NMS, which requires networks to show the best available price if one is available on another exchange or ECN that the investor could easily access.

Dark pool liquidity is the liquidity created by institutional orders not yet available to the public, generated in the form of block trades. Some investors feel dark pools create a conflict of interest for the owners of the securities. Dark pools help prevent downward surges in stock prices when investors wish to sell a large number of shares. The advantages of dark pools are that they reduce transaction costs for these investors and prevent large price movements in the publicly traded shares. The downside of dark pools is that they may not reflect the true value of a stock, as the broader market hasn't had a chance to reflect their expectations and participants may not get the best price.

Non-U.S. Market Securities

American Depositary Receipts (ADRs) are securities that allow U.S citizens to purchase shares of foreign companies in the U.S. market without having to make the purchase on a foreign stock exchange. They're denominated in U.S. dollars and help reduce the administrative costs normally incurred with international transactions. It should be noted that ADRs do not eliminate currency or economic risks associated with investments in foreign companies.

Tax Treatment of Equity Securities

Capital gains tax can be incurred by an investor when an asset (e.g., stock, bond, or piece of property) is sold. The tax occurs when the cost of the investment is less than the price received for the sale of that asset. Gains are taxed at long-term and short-term rates. Short-term capital gains are incurred when the asset is sold within 12 months of its original purchase. These gains are taxed at the ordinary income tax rate, which is a rate higher than the long-term tax rate. Essentially, this provides an incentive for investors to hold onto the security for longer periods of time. Long-term capital gains are taxed at a maximum rate of 20% for investors in the 28% tax bracket (10% for those in the 15% tax bracket). There are laws that allow for the deferment of capital gains tax. Strategies used to defer capital gains tax include structured sales, private annuity trusts, and installment sales.

A capital loss occurs when an investment is sold at a price less than its initial cost of investment. Capital gains and capital losses are netted to determine the appropriate tax rate.

A qualified dividend is a dividend that can be taxed at a lower rate than the long-term capital gains tax rate if it meets certain criteria. The three criteria are that the dividend has been:

- Paid after December 31, 2002
- Paid by a U.S. corporation, a corporation in U.S. possession, or a foreign stock tradable in U.S. markets
- Held for 60 days during the 121-day period after the ex-dividend date

Non-qualified dividends are those taxed at the ordinary rate.

There's no tax on a bond or a preferred share of stock converted to common stock if the option was part of the security's structure when purchased. If there is a tax, its tax base is equal to the rate prior to conversion. If a cash payment is required for the conversion, then the holding period and the tax basis of the acquired stock must be divided between the amount paid for the purchase and the amount of cash paid for the conversion.

Typical cost basis per share is determined by the purchase price per share plus any fees per share. The basis per share on convertible securities exchanged for common shares of stock usually are valued at the same basis as the convertible security. Cost basis per share on equity that is inherited is based on the market value on the date of death of the original owner. The cost basis for gifted securities depends on whether it is sold for a gain or a loss. With the former, the basis is equal to the gift giver's basis. If securities are sold for a loss, then the basis is the lesser of the original owner's basis or the market value on the date the gift was received. Average cost basis calculations take into account the total cost of an investment including purchases, dividends that are reinvested, returns of capital, and capital gains.

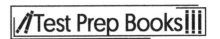

When selling shares, there are different methods to determine cost basis of the particular shares that are sold. Identified shares are those bought at a particular date for a particular price. Marking shares in this way allows the investor to possibly lower his or her tax liability. The FIFO (first in, first out) method assumes that the shares sold were the oldest shares, or those purchased the earliest. The LIFO (last in, first out) method in turn prices the shares sold at the price of the most recently purchased shares. The final way to determine cost basis is based on the use of identified shares to state specifically which shares are being sold and determining basis on the original purchase price of those specific shares.

A wash sale is the purchase and sale of securities in the same trade. Usually the term means one investor; however, two different parties can execute a wash sale to manipulate stock prices for their own benefit and gain (which is illegal). The Wash Sale Rule states that a loss can't be claimed on the sale of a stock if a replacement stock is bought within 30 days of the sale date. This law prevents investors from claiming the loss as a tax benefit and then immediately buying back the shares.

Packaged Products

Investment Companies, Exchange-Traded Funds, and Unit Investment Trusts

Offering investors diversification and professional management, mutual funds are very attractive to a wide range of investors. Through pooling funds, investors enjoy both safety and high-growth opportunities. Mutual funds are utilized by individual investors, individual retirement accounts, 401(k) accounts, and 403(b) accounts. Mutual funds are typically divided into three classifications: open-end funds, closed-end funds, and exchange-traded funds.

Types of Mutual Funds

Closed-end funds differ from open-end funds in that shares are publicly traded, and capital is raised through an initial public offering of the fund's shares. Most closed-end funds focus on a specific industry or sector. Closed-end funds have a finite number of shares issued at the fund establishment. Usually, after the IPO, the number of shares is constant and new shares cannot be issued. Where open-end funds usually have an NAV directly tied to their assets that is calculated on a daily basis, closed-end funds often trade at a discount or premium to their actual NAV. This usually depends on how well or poorly the assets of the fund are being managed. An exchanged-traded fund (ETF) is a basket of securities that is traded in exchanges and usually passively managed, like an index fund. ETFs can be made up of all of the stocks in an index, bonds, commodities, or currencies. ETFs typically trade at their NAV. ETFs have grown in popularity due to their low cost structure relative to mutual funds, which are managed against an index. ETFs are usually offered through broker dealers, who distribute shares through creation units, but some ETFs are available through mutual-fund companies or can even be purchased online. ETFs are liquid investments.

Just like open-end funds, closed-end funds can be small cap or large cap, and they can be growth or value oriented. They can focus on a certain sector, or they can be managed to beat an index like the S&P 500 or the New York Stock Exchange. Closed-end funds themselves do not pay taxes. Their taxation is the responsibility of the investor and shareholder. To maintain their tax-free status, closed-end funds must pass on to investors 90% of their income from dividends and interest payments. They also must pass on at least 98% of capitalized gains. Distributions must be linked back to their initial source.

Exchange traded funds (ETFs) are shares of mutual funds that trade on exchanges, like actual shares of stock. These typically trade in 50,000 share blocks. The advantages of ETFs are that they can be traded at any time during the trading day, bought on margin, sold short, and they have low expense ratios.

ETF shareholders are entitled to a percent of profits, such as earned interest or dividends paid. They will receive the residual value of the securities owned by the fund if a fund is liquidated. Shares of ETFs are highly liquid and easily traded in a similar way to equities. Some ETFs utilize gearing or leverage through the use of derivative securities. There are also inverse ETFs, so investors can profit from a basket of stocks in that ETF going down. ETFs provide diversification to investors, and their expense ratios are usually lower than a mutual fund. The SEC defines an ETF as a company that:

- Issues shares in exchange for the deposit of basket assets
- Identifies itself as an ETF in any sales literature
- Issues shares that are approved for listing on an exchange
- Discloses its daily net asset value publicly, as well as any premium or discount from the actual basket of underlying securities
- Is an index fund

Some ETFs use derivatives to enhance the return on the index they are modeled after or to protect their value when the market declines. ETFs can consist of large cap, small cap, growth, or value companies. They can replicate entire indices of just one sector of the market—i.e., energy, industrials, consumer staples, or technology. Some ETFs are actively managed, but this means the manager must disclose all holdings to investors. Inverse ETFs are designed to produce the inverse of an index. For example, the ETF may be the inverse of the S&P 500, so when the S&P returns 5% the ETF should see a decline of 5% in value. Basically, this is a product investors can use as a hedge if they anticipate a market downturn. ETFs are also permitted in Roth IRA accounts where short selling is not permitted, so investors who anticipate a bear market might invest in an inverse ETF.

ETFs are also tax-efficient vehicles with low transaction costs. Shareholders receive an annual report, similar to that provided to shareholders by management of individual companies at the year's end. When there is strong demand for an ETF, such as if it is a new and successful product or a stable bond fund during an equity market downturn, the share price may rise above the actual NAV. This creates a small arbitrage opportunity some larger investors try to take advantage of, usually by selling ETF shares short and buying the underlying securities until the prices align, and the NAV accurately reflects the value of the underlying securities.

Unit Investment Trusts (UITs)

Unit investment trusts are different from traditional funds, closed-end funds, and exchange-traded funds. They are fixed portfolios that are established for a specific duration of time. UITs are redeemable securities that the issuer will buy back at the NAV. Shares are issued with an IPO. UITs can be made up of bonds or stocks or both. Investors can make a decision based on the UIT's strategy, the sectors it invests in, its credit quality, or the its weighted duration (if rates rise, a UIT with a shorter duration will perform better than one with a long duration). UITs can be redeemed by having the originator repurchase the shares, assuming the issuer has enough cash and is liquid enough to purchase shares of the UIT.

UITs invest across all asset classes. Some trusts specifically employee a buy-and-hold strategy and have a stated termination date on which the fund will sell all holdings and pay out to all shareholders. Strategy trusts have a specific strategy, typically long or contrarian, based on the historical data the fund uses to select securities and on their outlook. Sector trusts invest in companies in one specific industry that are typically newer, less established companies.

A UIT's expenses and costs are listed in its prospectus. Fees include annual operating expenses, creation and inception fees, deferred sales charges, and initial sales charges. There are also administration fees.

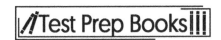

The initial sales charge is paid upon the purchase of the UIT. The deferred sales charge is paid monthly. The creation fee is paid from trust assets and covers the costs of developing a strategy, marketing the trust, and purchasing the securities.

Sales charges are made up of three components: the initial sales charge, the deferred sales charge, and the creation and development fee. The initial sales charge is usually a percentage of the dollar amount of the investment, 1.0% in most cases. The deferred sales charges are deducted in increments on a quarterly or monthly basis during the offering period. Finally, the creation and development fee are costs allocated to establish and build the fund. The UIT needs to create an objective, develop a strategy, pay marketing fees, pay administrative fees, pay salaries, and pay broker and trading fees to start the trust. These fees are charged at the end of the offering period.

Unit holders are subject to taxation on dividends, interest, and capital gains. UITs can be found in IRAs and receive the same tax benefits, so taxes on distributions are deferred until distributions are taken from the account. When shares are traded, the investor is responsible for reporting any gain or loss with his/her annual tax filing.

Structure of Investment Companies

An open-end investment company (OEIC) is a company or fund that has significant flexibility in the types of securities it can invest in and how large the fund can grow to be. Open-end mutual funds deliver diversity to their investors. They can be domestic or international. They can vary across economic sectors. The investments within a mutual fund may even provide an additional dimension of diversity with varying lifecycles. For example, for investors seeking short-term opportunities, the mutual-fund money market is a viable option. It typically comprises securities that are high in quality, yet it allows invested funds to remain accessible to the investor.

Shares for open-end funds are issued and redeemed by the investment company, but share issuance and redemption is initiated at the request of the investor. Investors buy and sell their shares based on the net asset value (NAV), which will be discussed later. Traditional mutual funds typically list restrictions on what they can invest in their prospectus, and they are limited to a certain dollar amount of assets they can manage. OEICs are listed on the London Stock Exchange. What is unique about the trading of these assets is there is no "spread" allocated to the broker or exchange. The buyer and seller receive the same amount for shares exchanged.

Fund Objectives

Investors usually select a fund based on the fund's goals and objectives relative to their risk profile, as well as their market outlook:

- A value fund invests in established companies that the fund manager feels are undervalued relative to where the market is pricing them.
- A growth fund invests in companies that are relatively young, have low earnings, and have significant growth potential in their industry.
- An income fund invests in securities that pay a consistent dividend.
- A balanced fund invests in both stocks and bonds.
- International funds invest in securities and sometimes currencies of other countries.

- Money market funds invest in the short-term-debt markets, including commercial paper, asset-backed commercial paper, short- term Treasuries, and municipal debt.

All funds attempt to generate excess returns over a defined benchmark, like the S&P 500 or the Dow Jones Industrial Average. Investors usually evaluate a manager's performance on a quarterly basis and consider both net and gross risk-adjusted returns. Net returns need to be considered to assure the performance of the fund is commensurate with fees being charged. Risk-adjusted returns are evaluated to assure the amount of volatility in a portfolio is in line with the benchmark and that the amount of excess returns is sufficient for the amount of risk in the portfolio. Mutual funds are rated by companies like Morningstar based on one-year, three-year, five-year, and ten-year performance. When investing in a mutual fund, investors should consider fund strategy, management experience, and prior performance prior to making an investment.

Mutual-Fund Characteristics

Mutual funds vary in their characteristics. Open-end funds report a net asset value (NAV). This is the total value of assets owned by the company less its liabilities. It is often reported on a per share basis to communicate to investors how much their investment has changed in value. This is the value at which the shares for open-end funds are bought and sold. Close-end funds are quite different. Their value is determined by supply and demand, combined with investor's expectations and the value of the counterpart investments in the portfolio.

Cost is another varying characteristic of mutual funds. Before investing in a mutual fund, the cost of the fund should be compared with other investments to ensure the financial benefits are greater than the required costs. In terms of cost, mutual funds are usually classified into two categories: load funds and no-load funds. A load fund requires investors pay a commission fee for every purchase. Load charges, also known as front-end charges, can quickly reduce gains. The average load charge is usually between 3% and 5% but can be greater than 8%. This cost supports the fund's sales team.

Here is an example of a load charge:

An investor decides to invest $100,000. The fund charges a sales load of 4.25%. The amount of the sales load is $\$100{,}000 \times .0425 = \$4250$. The sales load is subtracted from the initial investment of $100,000. The available investment is actually $95,750.

Unlike a load fund, no-load funds do not charge any commissions. No-load funds do not have a sales force. Therefore, investors choosing this option will purchase shares directly from the investment company. Load and no-load funds offer the same investment opportunities and the same potential for equivalent returns.

As an alternative to the basic load or no-load funds, some mutual funds charge a contingent deferred sales load, also known as a back-end fee. This charge is deferred until a withdrawal is made from the fund. This deferred fee can range from 1% to 5%.

Here is an example of a contingent deferred sales load:

An investor decides to withdraw $10,000. The contingent deferred sales load charge is 4%. This fee is deducted from the withdrawal. The amount of the fee is:

$$\$10{,}000 \times 0.04 = \$400$$

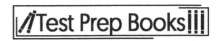

The amount the investor will receive is:

$$\$10{,}000 - \$400 = \$9{,}600$$

Funds also vary in the way they distribute capital gains. Most funds simply reinvest dividends in the same fund by purchasing more shares. Some simply distribute payments to shareholders to reinvest on their own. Funds also vary in their fee structures. Some funds charge up-front fees, and some have redemption fees when investors want to leave a fund. Most funds charge a management fee on a quarterly basis. The management fee is usually a percentage based on the fund's asset value, typically not more than 1.5%.

Additional fees may include a distribution fee, also known as a 12B-1 fee. It is an ongoing annual fee that is capped by the SEC at 1% of the assets' value. Investors should be sure to evaluate the net return of their investment to ensure fees being charged are commensurate with a fund's performance.

Mutual-Fund Sales Practices

There are certain practices for selling securities and shares of mutual funds. In selling mutual funds to investors, there are several sales techniques that can be employed; such as dollar-cost averaging, computing the sales charge, or breakpoints.

A systematic investment technique is achieved through dollar-cost averaging. With this technique, investors systematically purchase a set or fixed amount of a specified investment. This technique does not make adjustments for varying share prices. Rather, it incorporates the anticipated fluctuations and pursues returns based on the average of the share prices with consistent purchases over time.

Computing the sales charge is another sales technique. In this technique, a percentage of the public offering price (POP) is computed. The calculation for the sales charge is determined by subtracting the net asset value from the POP and dividing the determined difference by the POP.

For example: Assume a mutual fund has a POP of 25.08 and a net asset value of 23.06.

$$Sales\ charge = \frac{Public\ offering\ price - net\ asset\ value}{Public\ offering\ price}$$

$$Sales\ charge = \frac{25.08 - 23.06}{25.08}$$

$$Sales\ charge = \frac{2.02}{25.08} = .081\ or\ 8.1\%$$

In this example, the sales charge for the assumed mutual fund would be 8.1%.

In addition to dollar-cost averaging and computing the sales charge, breakpoints can be utilized to attract large investors. Breakpoints are discounts granted on the up-front fees on funds when investors purchase a certain dollar amount or amount of shares of a fund. The discount usually applies to Class A shares of a fund but, via a Letter of Intent or through Rights of Accumulation, an investor can receive the same discount. Rights of Accumulation basically allows an investor to aggregate shares (401k funds, pensions, related party shares) to receive the discount.

Late trading is the illegal selling of shares after the NAV has been calculated for shares of a fund. When there is bad news about securities in the fund, this practice gives the late trader the opportunity to dump shares before the market has moved, and the value is reflected by the NAV.

Mutual Fund Redemptions

Funds vary in the way they allow investors to redeem shares. The redemption price is the price at which the shares are sold on the market to receive the proceeds. Usually, this is equivalent to the fund's NAV. Some funds offer an exchange privilege option. This allows the investor to exchange shares of the same fund family without incurring a transaction fee. If an investor is in four different equity funds but wants to diversify into bonds, that investor can exchange shares in an equity fund for a bond fund in the same family. Some funds have contingent deferred sales charges, usually on Class B shares. Some funds are launched with these shares to give investors the incentive to hold shares for the long term. They only incur this charge if they decide to sell the shares within a specified time frame.

Taxation of Mutual Funds

Any shares of stocks or bonds held in taxable accounts are taxable at distribution, regardless of whether they are reinvested or distributed. The amounts should be reported on the investor's tax filing each year. Any capital gains the fund incurs through trading must be reported as well. Capital gains on shares held for longer than a year are taxed at the long-term rate, typically lower than the ordinary income-tax rate. Short-term gains are for securities held less than one year. They are taxed at the ordinary rate. If a fund has gains due to foreign-currency investing, they are required to make a distribution, which will be taxed at the ordinary rate.

Variable Life Insurance and Annuity Contracts.

Variable life insurance is a permanent life insurance with the added characteristic of reflecting the performance of a subinvestment. While this feature allows the policyholder the opportunity for higher returns, it also carries a greater risk, which is assumed by the policyholder. Variable life insurance does provide a minimum death benefit and maintains a fixed premium. Additionally, the policyholder can realize a greater death benefit when earnings on the subinvestment are performing well.

Variable Life Insurance and Annuity Contracts Characteristics

Variable life-insurance policies can also have unique modifications to a policy, such as an accidental death benefit or a cost-of-living protection. These examples of modifications are called "riders." Riders are modifications to a policy presented as an attachment to the actual policy.

While life insurance covers the death of the insured, his/her loss of income, contributions to the family, and perhaps even death, it does not offer a provision for usage during life. This is where annuities have responded to the need for additional income while living.

Annuities are contracts most often issued by life-insurance companies. They continue to provide an income as long as the annuity owner is alive. Annuities make either a fixed payment, like a coupon payment on a corporate or Treasury bond, or variable payments, based on the performance of an index of basket of securities. Because their payment is based on an index, a variable annuity is a riskier investment than a fixed annuity. An annuity with a minimum guarantee means payments are guaranteed for a specified number of years regardless of when the annuity holder passes away. Payments with minimum guarantees are typically smaller than with a regular annuity because they are less risky. If the annuity holder dies before the guarantee expires, the payments are made to an estate or beneficiary.

Annuity riders are options added to a typical annuity agreement. A cost-of-living-adjustment rider assures annuity payments will rise along with an inflation index. Lump-sum riders assure the full principal is paid if it has not been paid over the life of the annuity. The chart below shows the effects of reinvesting interest earned from annuities and other fixed-income securities.

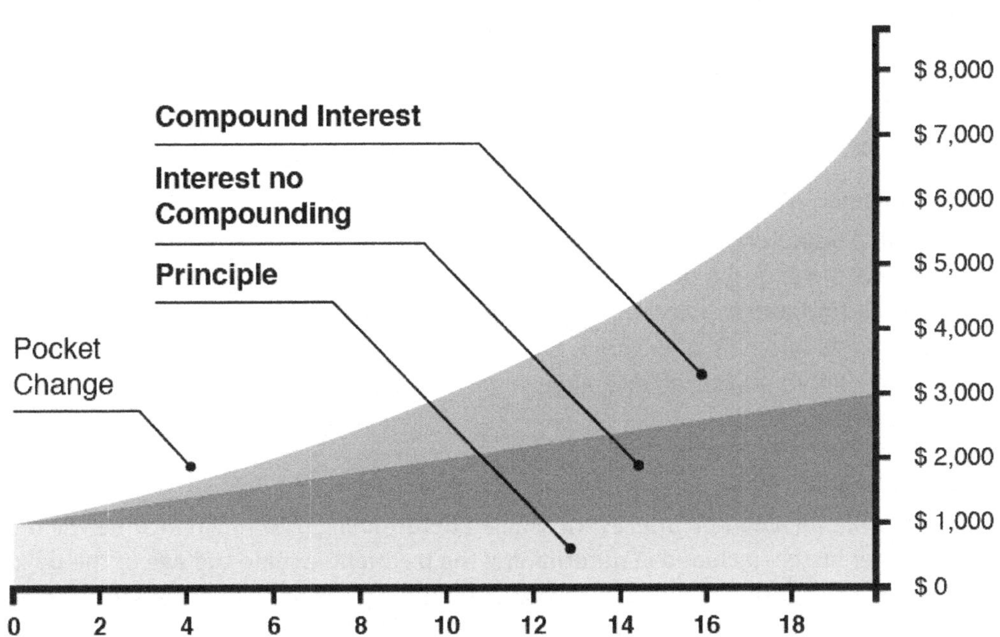

Separate Accounts

One of the key features of a variable annuity is that it is a separate account on the issuing insurance company's books. This feature keeps all interest, principal, dividends, income, gains, and losses separate from the company's general account. Separate accounts are required to have a prospectus when issued, just like when an IPO or a bond is issued. One of the key advantages of a separate account is that it can be constructed to meet the needs and risk profile of the investor.

Variable Annuity Contract Valuation

An annuity unit is a subset of an investor's total accumulated annuity. The unit entitles the investor to a specified amount of the insurer's larger investment portfolio. The unit could represent a fixed percentage (maybe one unit represents 0.01% of a $100 million portfolio, or $10,000). The surrender value of an annuity, not to be confused with its cash value, is the value paid to the policyholder in the event of voluntary termination before the maturity of the policy. The surrender value will be less than the actual cash value because early termination entails paying penalties and administration fees to terminate the policy. The investor is essentially paying a fee to have a liquid investment. Over time, the surrender fees are smaller. As the policy nears maturity, the cash value and the surrender value converge.

When valuing an annuity, the two phases of the contract need to be considered. The first phase is the accumulation phase, and the second phase is the annuitization phase. The accumulation phase is when the policyholder pays funds into an account. Those funds are invested by purchasing the accumulation units, and subsequent dividends and interest are reinvested. The value of the investment will vary depending on how the investments perform and how many units are acquired. The annuitization phase is when the investor draws funds based on the units they own. The amount paid out to the policyholder is determined by factors including the policyholder's age, sex, the layout option chosen, and the assumed interest rate.

Variable Annuity Purchases and Exchanges

An immediate annuity is an annuity that is purchased with a single lump-sum payment, as opposed to periodic payments in an accumulation phase. These are typically investments for retirees who don't want to outlive their investments. These annuities are terminated upon the death of the policyholder, so there is the chance the funds left in the estate will be smaller than had he/she purchased a regular variable annuity.

Most insurance companies reduce the fees associated with annuities as policyholders acquire more units; this happens at a predetermined Rights of Accumulation breakpoint. A "waiver of premium" is a rider clause that allows the policyholder to stop payments if they become ill. This allows the policyholder to benefit from the annuity even when they are unable to work. Tax-free variable-annuity exchanges are permissible under IRS Rule 1035. However, a regular annuity cannot be exchanged for a life-insurance annuity. Before making an exchange, investors should consider if any new fees may outweigh the tax benefit.

Annuitization

Insurance companies use an assumed interest rate when determining how much income will be paid to the policyholder. Other factors included in determining the payment include the age of the policyholder, spousal and other options chosen by the policyholder, and the type of annuity coverage received. The rate is calculated by determining how much the insurance company must earn to cover the company's costs and profit margin. The real rate of return on an annuity is determined when the policy is terminated, and a payout is made. The return is all of the income received, plus any appreciation in the value of the assets the variable-rate annuity is based on.

Variable Annuity Taxation

In the accumulation phase, no taxes are due on the earnings of the annuity. At withdrawal, all earnings are taxed as ordinary income. If funds are withdrawn from an annuity before the policyholder is age 59 ½ there is a 10% penalty tax imposed on earnings. There are exceptions to the penalty in cases of death or illness. Taxes are structured on a last in/first out (LIFO) basis. Earnings are taxed first as ordinary income, and any amount over that is taken from the principal and is nontaxable. Variable annuities allow policy loans that are loans the investor can receive without being taxed. Variable annuities also provide spousal continuation, so if the beneficiary dies his/her spouse can preserve tax-deferred growth. When a nonqualified annuity is annuitized, it will have an exclusion ratio calculated on payments to determine what amount will be excluded from income taxes.

Real Estate Investment Trusts (REITs)

Real estate investment trusts (REITs) are companies that own, manage, or finance income-producing (usually commercial) real estate.

Real Estate Investment Trust (REIT) Structure

REITs typically go through several rounds of financing as they purchase properties. Most REITs obtain some form of seed capital through initial investors, then issue shares through an IPO, and then obtain revolving lines of credit of bank loans to finance their operations. Shares are initially issued and typically cannot be traded until a specific time. Some REITs have a dividend reinvestment program (DRIP) that allows existing investors to purchase more shares at a discount, whereas new investors will be required to pay full price for shares. Shares of new REITs are often traded over the counter until they become available on exchanges. Some REITs calculate an NAV, which is normally calculated by valuing all of the properties or equity a REIT has in its portfolio—though some NAVs are calculated using the cash flow that comes from their properties. The NAV does not always equal the price of a REIT. If the price is higher than the NAV, it may reflect the investor's anticipation that management will create value as they acquire properties and improve cash flow and profitability. In other words, \$100 million in property represented by 10 million outstanding shares may have an NAV of \$10 per share ($\$100\ million \div 10\ million = \$10$), but investors may be willing to pay \$13 per share if they feel the managers of the REIT can enhance the property's value through better management. The chart below is a basic depiction as to how investors buy shares. Capital is used to buy properties, income is generated, and then profits are distributed to investors as dividends.

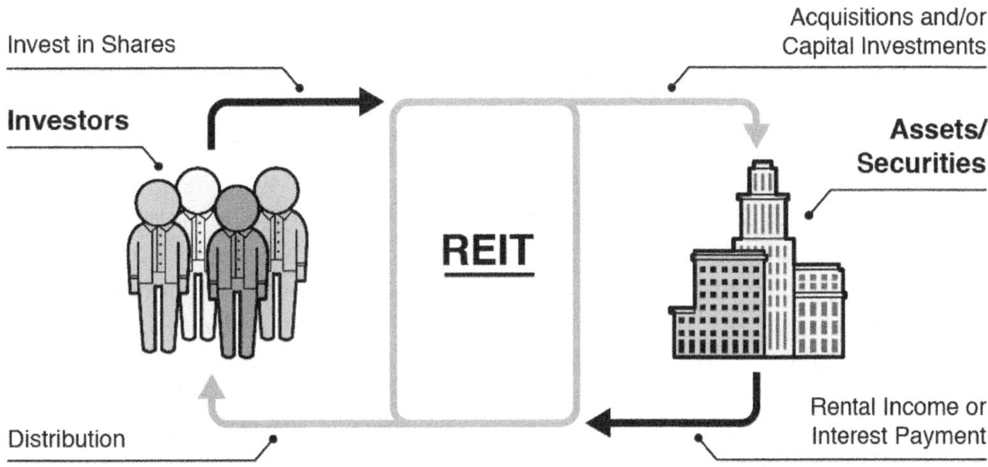

Real Estate Investment Trust (REIT) Types

REITs can vary by industry and strategy. Some are focused on one property type, such as office properties, hospitals, condominiums, or hotels. They can also be diversified. An equity REIT is a company that actually owns a property. These REITs also manage the property and find tenants. After expenses and management fees, the REIT pays out profits in the form of dividends to investors; to qualify as a REIT, they are required to pay out 90% of their income. Equity REITs also turn a profit by selling properties they own after they have appreciated.

Mortgage REITs invest in mortgage-backed securities, as well as commercial mortgage-backed securities, the financing behind properties. They are also required to distribute 90% of their income to qualify as a REIT. A hybrid REIT owns both actual properties and mortgage debt. REITs are often considered an alternative to investing in bonds because they consistently pay out income, as opposed to some stocks that pay no dividends. They also have appreciation potential, which fixed-income securities do not.

Real Estate Investment Trust (REIT) Taxation

REITs are often good investments due to their tax treatment. REITs follow the same taxation rules as UITs. This means REITs are taxed at the corporate level first, and then the investor is taxed by the IRS. REIT rental income is tax deductible, as this is a REIT's main income stream. All expenses related to rental income are tax deductible. Income that is currently earned is not taxed to the REIT under most circumstances. Basically, REITs are tax exempt as long as they pay out 90% of their income but taxed on any income retained on their balance sheet. The investor is taxed at the ordinary rate on received dividends. REITs may pay qualified dividends, which are taxed at the long-term capital-gains rate.

Direct Participation Programs (DPPs)

A direct participation program enables an investor to participate in a business venture's cash flow and taxation benefits.

Direct Participation Program Characteristics

These vehicles primarily invest in real estate, energy, futures and options, and equipment leasing. They are structured as limited partnerships or limited liability companies that allow profits to flow through to the investor on a pretax basis. There are no taxes at the corporate level with this type of investment. DPPs are usually not publicly traded instruments, so their value is not market driven and simply derived from the profits and cash flow they produce. Limited partnerships mean the partners have limited liability and no management authority. This means they are not responsible for any debts and have no liability if any legal action is taken against the company. The limited partners have a defined return they will receive outlined in the prospectus or partnership agreement.

Direct Participation Program (DPP) Types

There are risks that come with DPP investments. They rely upon the general manager to manage the investment, and these investments often consist of blind pools. This can potentially be compromising, as the investor may not have the transparency to evaluate the risks of the investment directly. DPPs are thinly traded, so there is significant liquidity risk. Real estate DPPs invest in raw land, the construction of new buildings (usually commercial properties), existing properties, and low-income and government-assisted housing. Land investments are mostly speculative investments to be sold at a later time. The land is not developed or rented, so it is a non-income-producing investment. These are highly risky investments as property values can go up or down, and there is no real strategy that can be changed to improve profitability.

Some DPPs buy existing properties, lease, and manage them much the same as a real estate investment trust would, but they are more likely to invest in more risky properties that don't have significant tenants or produce income yet. One of the more conservative DPP investments is in low-income properties. DPPs that invest in these properties are income-producing investments (through the rent their tenants pay), the investors receive tax credits that other DPPs are not eligible for, and they are backed by the US government. Equipment DPPs purchase equipment and lease it out to other companies. These DPPs have good cash flow and have the advantage of being able to write off the depreciation of the equipment they own.

There are four types of oil and gas DPPs: exploratory, developmental, income, and combination. Exploratory DPPs fund the search of unproven oil reserves. These are risky investments as there is potential that only small reserves will be found, or even none at all, which can result in the complete loss of investment. They do have the potential for significant returns if productive wells of oil and gas are found. Developmental DPPs drill close to where wells are known to have produced. Income-producing DPPs purchase wells that are developed and producing. Combination DPPs are diverse in that they invest in both producing and nonproducing wells.

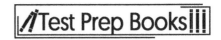

Direct Participation Program (DPP) Offerings

DPPs require potential limited partners to complete a subscription agreement. The general partner uses the criteria from this form to determine whether or not an investor is suitable to become a limited partner. The agreement is similar to what an investment advisor needs to consider when evaluating an investor's willingness and ability to take risk, so they can select the right investment for them. The agreement will include his/her net worth, income, a clear explanation of the risks of the partnership, and a power of attorney agreement that allows the general partner to make all investment decisions.

The more common DPPs include nontraded REITs, equipment leases, and energy companies. Like more traditional investments, due diligence and analysis should be completed by the potential investor. The investor needs to consider overall market conditions and whether or not there is a market for what the DPP will be investing in (DPPs often invest in new industries or niche markets). Financial statements (if available) should be analyzed, as well as where potential revenue growth will come from. Experience of the general partner should be considered as well.

Options

Listed Options

For investors seeking to add active investments to their portfolios, options serve as a unique tool to help reduce the risk of the investment. Given the potential of fluctuating stock prices, options can provide the investor a choice to buy or sell. Furthermore, options can also help investors increase their returns.

Options can be categorized into two forms: American and European. Both types of options have different parameters for how they are exercised. Primarily exclusive to the United States, American options are exercised or closed at any time prior to the date of expiration. Unlike American options, European options stipulate a shorter duration of time in which the option can be exercised. This window of opportunity is usually just prior to or on the expiration date.

An option that is sold on a registered exchange is called a listed option. Listed options include securities such as market indexes, common stocks, and exchange-traded options. These options have predetermined exercise prices and expiration dates. However, an options contract can be adjusted in special circumstances, such as when the underlying company experiences some type of reorganization.

Every listed option has the following characteristics: class, style, type, expiration date, symbol, strike price, multiplier, and contract size. The class identifies whether the option is a call or put option. The style of the option refers to whether the option is American or European. The type of the option identifies whether the option is an equity index or exchange-traded security. The symbol varies according to the company. The strike price varies as it is a specified price measured per share. Strike prices will be discussed in more detail later.

Another characteristic is the multiplier. Usually, the multiplier initially starts at 100. The multiplier is used to determine the amount of the underlying asset attached to some options contracts. This amount is called the contract size. Initially, the contract size is 100, meaning when one contract option is exercised, 100 shares will be bought or sold. As mentioned, when a company experiences a reorganization, some of these characteristics may experience an adjustment. These changes may affect some of the characteristics, such as the strike price, symbol, or even a multiplier. However, the expiration date typically remains unchanged. There are many reasons for adjustments to options. Some of these causes may include stock dividends, stock splits, or mergers.

The characteristics of options can be better understood by reading an options table. See exhibit 14-1A.

Assume the table references Jayne, Inc.

The symbol for Jayne, Inc. is JYNE.

The closing price of the stock as of July 24 was $10.

The expiration date is August 16.

JYNE 10 Stk	Expiration	Premium	Call Volume	Premium	Put Volume
5	*August*	9.80	22	.14	0
10	*August*	7.40	64	.96	42
15	*September*	3.60	154	2.40	250
20	*September*	.90	73	6.30	64

Options Table

Here's how to interpret the options table:

- The heading in the first column lists JYNE's closing price ($10) from the previous day; the numbers below it are the four exercise strike prices: $5, $10, $15, and $20.
- The second column lists the expiration month.
- The third and fifth columns list the respective premiums for calls and puts.
- The fourth and six columns list the volume or number of contracts. For example, the highest volume was realized at $15.

Option Characteristics and Types

Put and call options are types of derivative instruments whose value is dependent on a specific security, index, commodity, currency, or investment. A call option will increase in value when the price of the security to which it is tied increases in value. The amount of correlation (i.e., the amount the call option increases in value with the underlying asset) varies but can be as much as just a fraction of correlation to being completely correlated with the asset's value. A put option will increase in value when the underlying asset declines in value (or declines in value when the asset increases in value). These are assets that are a product of financial engineering and can be used for either hedging (when the investor owns the underlying asset and the derivative) or speculation (when the investor owns only the derivative instrument and not the actual underlying asset). Puts and calls have specific strike prices. The strike price is the price at which the option can be exercised by the investor. The exercise date is the time by which the option can be exercised, if it does, in fact, exceed the strike price.

For example, a stock that has a $20 price may have a call option with a strike price of $25 that expires in one month. If the stock price moves to $30 in two weeks, the investor can exercise the option and the stock will be "called" away from the seller (or "writer") of the contract at the strike price of $25. If the stock doesn't exceed the $25 stock price within that month, the option will expire as worthless.

An option class is all options tied to a particular stock or index. An option series is a subset of an option class that has the same strike price and expiration date.

Opening and Closing Transactions

Just like buying a stock or bond, an investor needs to open the transaction (and close it when wishing to sell the position, assuming it has not expired). A buy to open contract is when an investor buys a call option on a stock or index. A sell to open contract is when the investor sells the right to the buyer to call the stock from (or put the stock to) the investor. For this, the seller receives a premium for bearing the risk of the transaction. The inverse of each transaction would be a buy or sell to close, where investors would take the opposite of their opening positions. When investors close their positions, they will either earn a profit if they have bought calls and the stock rises above the strike price, or they have bought put options and the stock price declines below the strike price. The sellers or writers of the contracts profit when the options expire as worthless, with the profit being the premium they received upon entering into the contract. A loss will be the premium paid by the buyers of the options if the options expire worthless. The loss for the writers of the contract will be the difference between the securities price and the exercise price on the option contract under most scenarios. With European options, the closing transaction will only take place on the expiration date, assuming the option is not worthless (and is "in the money" or has exceeded the strike price of the contract). Option contracts can be closed simply by trading the actual contract to another party, which can be done through some brokers and exchanges.

Settlement Date, Exercise, Assignment

Settlement dates vary depending on the type of security. While stocks and exchange-traded funds settle three market days (a day public sales are held) after the trade date, options are settled only one market day after the trade date.

The trade date is the date when the buyer exercised the right to buy the underlying shares. Or, in a put contract, the trade date is when the buyer exercises the right to sell underlying shares. When the buyer has decided to exercise his or her right, the buyer must notify the writer of the option contract. This notification is called an exercise notice. The exercise notice is the broker's notification of the intended transaction. The broker then forwards the exercise notice to the seller. The forwarding process is completed through the OCC.

After buyers have executed their options, sellers or options writers are obligated to fulfill their terms of the contract and deliver the agreed-upon terms. This is known as the assignment. When the assignment is executed on a call option, the seller or writer is obligated to sell the specified quantity of the underlying security at the strike price. When the assignment is executed on a put option, the options writer is obligated to purchase the predetermined quantity of the underlying security at the strike price. To ensure compliance of these transactions, the OCC oversees the fair practices concerning the distribution of assignments.

Premium

An option premium is the price that an investor is willing to pay for the opportunity to buy an asset at a specified price within a specified time period. Some investors consider the equity of a company a call option, since the stockholder reserves the right to call the residual income away from a company. The premium is comprised of an intrinsic value and a time value. The intrinsic value is the value of the option were it to be exercised immediately. If the option is out of the money, that value will be zero; if the option is in the money, its intrinsic value is the difference between its price and the exercise price. The second part of the value is its time value. Although an option is out of the money, it still has some value because there is the possibility it will exceed the exercise price before the expiration date. An option that is in the money will have a premium value greater than its intrinsic value because there is the potential for the price to move even further past the strike price before expiration. As an equation, this means:

Option Premium = Time Value + Intrinsic Value

For a call option, this means *Value = Stock Price - Exercise Price*, and for a put option, the equation is: *Value = Exercise Price – Stock Price.*

Along with the strike price, asset price, and time to expiration, the volatility of the underlying asset will affect the premium of the option. The more volatile the asset, the more likely its price will exceed the strike price of the option contract. Quantitative analysts use various techniques and models to value options and calculate their premiums. The Black-Scholes model incorporates the asset value, the strike price, and the asset's volatility (among other variables) to calculate an option premium. Put-call parity is a more simplified model that traders and investors can use to determine if puts and calls are under- or overvalued than their relationship to each other. Put-call parity states that the call value less the put value should be equal to the difference between the forward value of the asset less the strike price of the contract discounted at the risk-free rate. When these relationships don't hold, investors can buy or sell options (or even the underlying asset) to take advantage of any mispricing.

Volume, Open Interest, Position Limits, Exercise Limits

Just like equities, there are published volumes on the number of options contracts traded on exchanges. Options traders usually evaluate options volume relative to the volume of the underlying security. When there is a spike in the volume of options and the underlying stock, it is a sign of a trend. Along with volume is open interest, the total number of open options contracts. With equities, there is a fixed number of shares. However, new options contracts can be created at any time as long as there's a buyer and seller. When options expire or have an offsetting contract opened, the open interest will decline. When investors open new positions, the open interest will rise. Of course, one side of the transaction may be opening a transaction while the other is closing a position, which would leave the total open interest number unaffected. Open interest is primarily used to evaluate the amount of liquidity in an options market to assure there is active trading. In options trading, a position limit is the maximum number of contracts an investor can hold on an underlying security. The Chicago Board Options Exchange usually establishes these limits based on the amount of liquidity in a stock and the number of shares outstanding. Limits prevent excess leverage in the market and promote price stability. Some experts believe that the excessive financial engineering in the collateralized debt obligations (CDO) and structured product markets helped create the financial crisis in 2008. This was the result of having too many derivatives being traded on a small number of underlying securities. An exercise limit is the maximum a person can exercise on one particular options class within a set timeframe. This prevents one investor from artificially influencing the prices of options.

Dividends

Options and derivatives must be adjusted when the underlying asset pays interest or dividends. When a bond makes an interest payment or a stock pays a dividend, it will affect the price of the asset and the value of the option. In the case of stocks, the stock price will fall by the amount of the dividend. The value of the option will increase as the option holder may receive the dividend or interest payment, depending on the date the option expires and if it is exercised. When a company pays a dividend on a consistent quarterly basis, the stock price should decline by the amount of the dividend on the ex-dividend date. Options reflect this information in the form of higher premiums for calls and lower premiums for puts when the dividend is high (which reduces the probability that a stock's price will exceed the strike price of the contract). The same applies to options on indices. Option traders and investors simply must account for stock dividends when valuing an option contract. If a company stops paying a dividend, the seller of the option may not have received enough of a premium for the risk he or she is taking. There is also the fact that the stock price will fall if the company fails to pay a dividend, since this may mean future financial difficulties for that company. Option investors must also account for the fact that if they own a stock at the time of the dividend payment, they receive the full dividend. This may give an investor the incentive to exercise an option early if the underlying asset will be paying a dividend. The investor needs to determine if the profit to be received from the exercise of the option, plus the amount of the dividend to be received, outweighs the potential upside of waiting for further price appreciation in the underlying asset.

Contract Adjustments for Corporate Actions

Adjusted options are options that account for corporate actions so that the options value is insulated from any effects of these actions. This means accounting for stock splits, mergers, acquisitions, special dividends, split offs, spinoffs, reverse splits, and extraordinary dividends. Changes can include a new trading symbol, a change in the strike price, a multiplier change, and a change in the contract size. As an example, a stock that is trading at $20 could have a reverse stock split and now trade at $40. If a call option is outstanding with a strike price of $25, it needs to be adjusted to reflect the change, otherwise the option would be $15 in the money, even though the stock saw no increase in value. In this case, the strike price would in all likelihood be changed to $50 (if all else held constant, the reverse split will result in shares priced at $50 per share). The OCC publishes regular bulletins around adjusted options contracts. All adjustments are approved by an OCC panel and are made on a case-by-case basis due to the infinite number of scenarios that can occur with adjusted options.

Minimum and Maintenance Margin Requirements

Investors who write options contracts are required to maintain margin accounts with their broker. The collateral in the account can be the cash of securities, but securities already have liens against them (posting securities pledged as collateral elsewhere is fraud). The Federal Reserve outlines margin requirements, but brokers can have requirements specific to their firms as well. According to the Fed's Regulation T, which governs the extension of credit by securities brokers and dealers in the United States, an investor must post at least 50 percent of the amount he or she borrows with cash collateral. No margin is required if the writer of an option contract owns the underlying security, since there is no risk that the investor won't have the capital to buy the security on the open market if the contract is exercised. Most brokers use software to calculate the minimum amount of margin required for their customers, so they do not commit more funds than necessary. According to the CBOE margin manual, LEAPS with expirations greater than nine months require margin of 75 percent of the market value of the position. Regular equity options require 20 percent, broad-based index options require 15 percent, and interest rate options require 10 percent. OTC options on puts and calls require 75 percent of the intrinsic value, plus the delta between its purchase price and its intrinsic value. In addition to the margin required at the start of a trade, the initial margin, there is also maintenance margin. This is the amount that must be maintained after a trade is entered into. If a stock that an investor has written a put option on increases in value, then no additional margin is required, since the position is profitable. However, if the stock decreases, and the buyer of the put is in the money, the broker will require the writer of the option to post additional margin by the amount the buyer of the position is in the money.

The Options Clearing Corporation (OCC)

The Options Clearing Corporation (OCC) is an equity derivatives clearinghouse that provides its services to 14 different exchanges. The OCC guarantees that contracts on each side of an options contract are fulfilled, which primarily means that the seller or writer of a contract received a premium, and that the buyer of the contract received the underlying security from the seller of the option exercised. The OCC holds about $100 billion in collateral each day and is regulated by both the Securities and Exchange Commission and the Commodity Futures Trading Commission. The OCC has its own board of directors and generates revenue on the fees it receives from settling options transactions. The OCC is rated by all three major bond rating agencies. The OCC settled options traded on exchanges only until 2011, when it began to settle over-the-counter options trades. The OCC has made changes to its settlement process in recent years. In 2013, expirations moved from Saturdays to Fridays. The OCC has both weekly and monthly expirations that can expire on a consistent and repeated process and is now aligned with global option market settlement schedules.

Assignment, American and European Style Exercise

When an option is "in the money" (ITM), it can be exercised, but the investor needs to decide when to exercise it. The assignment is when the investor makes the decision to exercise and notifies the broker. When the assignment occurs, the broker notifies the Options Clearing Corporation (OCC). The OCC then randomly selects another party at the exchange that has the opposite side of the position (a writer of the contract if the broker's client is the buyer). There are various opinions about the optimum time to exercise an American-style option. If an investor is long a call option that is in the money, some experts believe it's best to wait until the expiration date and only exercise the option if it's still in the money. In theory, this protects the investor from downside risk if the stock falls below the strike price. However, the investor could simply exercise the option and immediately sell the stock and receive the profit of the difference between the asset's price and the strike price. European options differ from American options in that after-hours trading does affect their settlement price. This means that a European option might actually be exercised "out of the money" when the investor thought the position was a profitable in the money position.

Long-Term Options (LEAPS)

Long-term equity anticipation securities (LEAPS) are simply options with expiration dates significantly further out than a typical option. Traditional options have maturities on a monthly basis going out 12 months. More liquid stocks may have more frequent options expirations, while companies traded more thinly may only have expirations every three months or so. LEAPS have maturities that go as far as two years or more. All LEAPS expire in January and are mostly traded on specific stocks that have significant trading volume. The expiration is always on the third Friday of January. Investors must pay a higher premium than on normal equity options, since they have significantly more time for the stock to exceed the listed strike price. In theory, an investor could simply roll into new options contracts as the regular contracts expire, but this does expose the investor to strike prices being adjusted as the security value moves in either direction.

Margin is required when purchasing LEAPS. 75 percent of the option's current value is required when there are more than nine months to the expiration of the contract. When selling or writing LEAPS (this is the party that agrees to deliver the underlying security at the exercise price), 100 percent of the contract value is required to be put down. LEAPS are taxed at the long-term capital gains rate of 20 percent. Just like regular options, LEAPS can be used for speculation or hedging, while strategies like straddles and butterflies can be used to take advantage of any anticipated movement in the price of a stock. LEAPS can be used in an IRA under certain circumstances.

Basic Strategies

Options strategies vary from the basic to the more complex. When investors own stocks and want to earn extra income, they may write call or put options on their shares by writing covered calls and puts.

Protective Put

Options can be used to hedge an investor's position. Essentially, the protective put can be used to protect the investor's unrealized gains. If the investor fears the market might decrease temporarily, they can buy put options to protect their portfolio investments. If the market instead rises, they will still see the appreciation in securities they held onto, but the rate of return will be reduced by the premiums they paid to buy the protective puts. Investors can even take advantage of markets that are trading sideways by simultaneously selling put and call options and collecting premiums as profit. Investors with large portfolios can hedge the risk of the entire portfolio using index options, assuming their portfolio is similar enough in structure to the index the options are tied to. International investors can also protect themselves from foreign currency value fluctuations in their international investments with options and derivatives.

Covered Call and Put Writing

When a party enters into an option contract and owns the underlying asset, the party is considered "covered." If the investor feels his or her stock will rise in value, put options can be written. This will increase the return on the investment by the amount of the premium the put buyer has paid. Investors can use the same strategy if they believe the value of a stock they own might rise, but not enough to exceed the strike price, in which case the security will be called away. Writing options is a risky strategy because their security can be called away. However, this is less risky than uncovered or "naked" option writing in which the writer will have to purchase the security on the open market, since this can lead to unlimited losses for the writer of the contract.

Yield-based options are valued using the difference between the exercise price and the value of the yield on the underlying debt instrument. A call position will increase when interest rates rise (which actually decreases the value of the underlying security).

A spread strategy is when an investor buys the same number of call and put options with varying maturities and strike prices. These strategies can be broken down further into horizontal, vertical, and diagonal spreads. In a vertical spread strategy, all of the options on the single security expire in the same month but have varying strike prices. In horizontal spreads, the expirations vary, but the strike prices are all the same. Diagonal spreads have varying expiration dates and strike prices. In each of these strategies, there is limited risk (the total loss is simply the sum of the premiums paid by the investor).

The butterfly spread is an even more advanced strategy. In a basic butterfly, an investor buys a call option at a certain strike price, writes two calls at a higher strike price, and buys a second call at an even higher strike price. This allows the investor to fund the two long positions with the premium earned from writing the two calls. There is the risk that if the stock has a significant price increase — and if the investor does not own the underlying shares, the investor will have to go onto the open market and buy the shares to cover the second position written. In a modified butterfly, the strategy becomes more complex, since calls and puts are both used. A modified butterfly has only one breakeven price.

Conversely, a regular butterfly has multiple breakeven points that can potentially be hit throughout the life of the trade. Below are various diagrams of some options strategies.

The graphic below is a long straddle showing strike prices at $35 for the put option and at $45 for the call option:

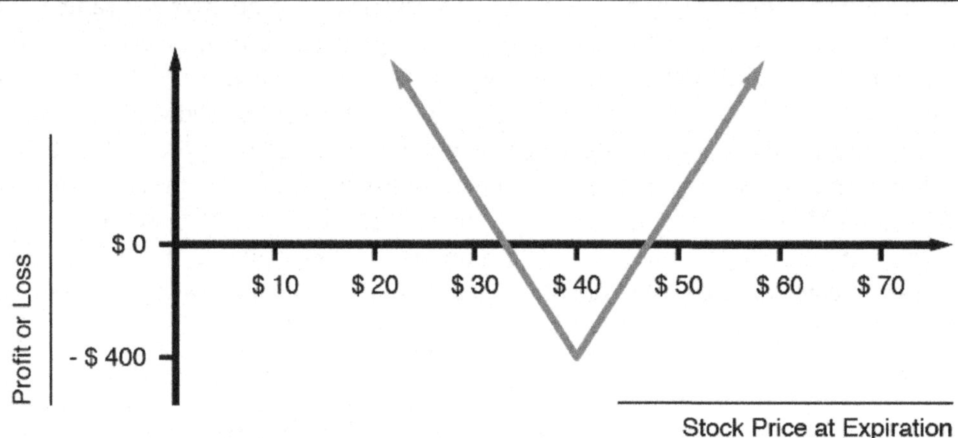

Below is the profit and loss for a bear put spread:

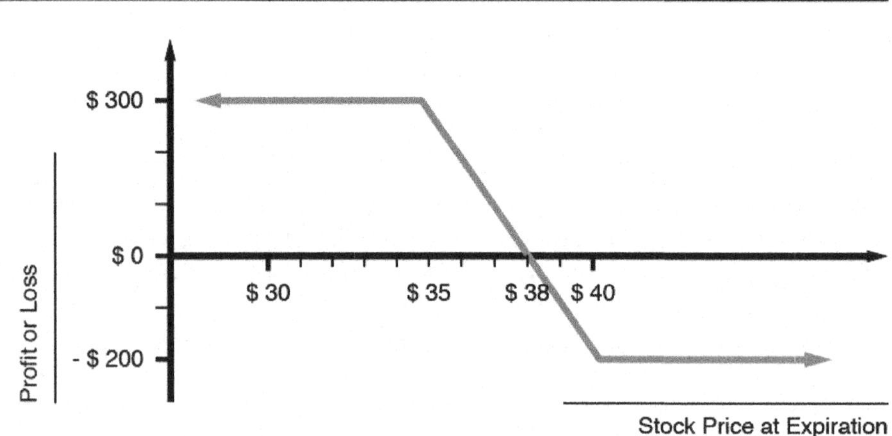

Below is a collar:

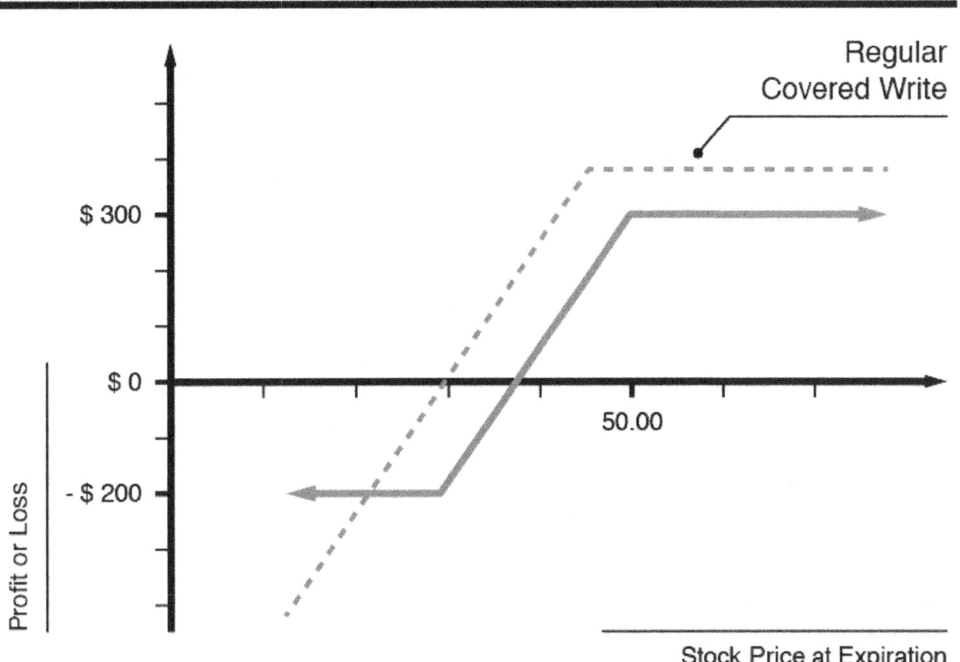

Below is a long butterfly:

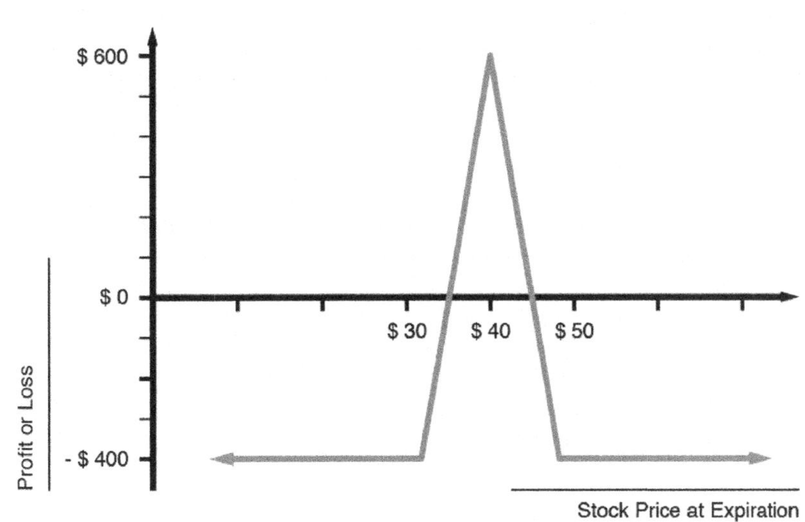

Advanced Strategies

Advanced strategies are employed by highly trained options traders. While high returns often await seasoned investors, novice investors should use caution, since risk can soar.

Long (debit) Spreads

A debit spread option trade occurs when two options with different prices are traded on the same underlying security. The option with the higher premium (the option that's closer to being in the money) is bought while the lower priced option is sold. The higher this spread is, the greater the cash flow the investor will receive. Debit spread strategies are best employed when implied volatility is low, and the investor believes actual volatility will be high. Volatility is positively correlated with option premiums despite whether they are puts or calls, since volatility increases the chances of strike prices being reached. When this volatility is low, debit spreads will be cheaper, and there is less likelihood that the written position will be exercised, and the security delivered. Implied volatility and actual volatility can change over time, though.

Short (credit) Spreads

The credit spread option is the inverse of the transaction. Here, investors receive net cash flow for entering into exposure for the position. In this strategy, the buyer pays an initial premium. The potential gain for the buyer exists if the credit spread between two specified benchmarks adjusts from their current levels in either direction. These potential spreads equal potential cash flows for the buyer.

Long Straddle/Combination

A long straddle using index options is a strategy that investors can use when they believe markets will become volatile. If there is an increase in volatility, this increases the probability of the strike price on one of the options being reached. In an index straddle, the investor buys both call and put options and is hedged in either direction. If American options are used, the investor will have more flexibility in deciding when to close his or her position but will need to pay more upfront in the form of higher premiums. If European options are used, the position can only be exercised on the day the options used expire. The position will be unprofitable if the index trades sideways and if neither of the strike prices is exceeded. The reverse of this strategy would be to take advantage of a lack of volatility by writing both put and call options. The position is significantly safer if the underlying securities are owned, since the writer of the position may have to go to the open market and purchase the securities or have securities put to them at a much higher price than their market value.

Straddle/Combination Writing

Writing calls and buying puts both have advantages and disadvantages. Buying a put allows the investor to maintain shares or sell them to someone. However, when buying a put, there's a risk of losing money, particularly when stock prices rise. On the other hand, writing a covered call allows money to go to the investor upfront. However, there are possible losses due to further price increases and/or possible share losses. In an effort to improve the investor's position, it is possible to do both: write calls and buy puts. This is a strategy known as a straddle or combination writing. This strategy combines both buying puts and writing calls at the same time, at the same exercise price, and at the same expiration date.

Here's an example:

An investor could write a covered call of $105 and buy a put at $105. This would secure the investor's profits without compromise.

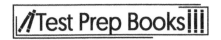

Uncovered (Naked) Call or Put Writing

As mentioned, uncovered or "naked" call or put writing exposes the investor to an extreme amount of risk. Experienced, risk-tolerant investors approach this strategy with caution. The term "naked" refers to the absence of an underlying instrument "backing" the options contract. Clearly, risk is imminent. However, this can prove to be rather profitable for the writer. Profitability can happen when the buyer is unable to exercise the option due to a lack of money.

Profit and Loss Calculations

It's important for options investors to understand the maximum potential gain and loss they can incur on a position, as well as the circumstances for them to break even on a trade. When an investor is long on a position, whether it is a put or a call, the maximum loss the investor can incur is the premium paid to enter into the position. This limits the downside to the investment. A stock may be priced at $20 and an investor pays $2 to buy a call option with a strike price of $25. If the investor enters into the contract and the stock price goes to zero, the investor has only lost $2. Conversely, if the same investor had bought the stock outright, he or she would have lost $20. However, if the stock is bought outright and it goes to $24, that is a 20 percent gain. However, if a call option is bought, the entire premium is lost because the stock did not reach the strike price.

The profit and loss dynamic changes for writing options. The maximum loss potential for writing an option while covered is the difference between the strike price and the price of the underlying asset when exercised. If an investor owns a stock that reaches $100 but can be called away for $80, that is $20 that would have been in the investor's return had he or she not written the contract. If the investor bought the stock at $40, this would mean the return of 250 percent will be reduced to 200 percent. If the investor doesn't own the stock, this means he or she must pay $100 for a stock that must be sold for $80 — immediately incurring a 20 percent loss. It's important for investors to understand that buying options has unlimited upside, but writing options has unlimited downside. It's also important for investors to realize the breakeven point is not the strike price of the contract. Instead, the breakeven point is only reached when the security has exceeded the strike price by enough for the investor to recoup the premium paid on the position.

Tax Treatment of Options

The taxation of options depends on a number of variables, but a gain is taxed when an option is exercised. There is a capital loss when a premium is lost on a long position. Short-term capital gains taxes are applicable to options. They are taxed at a marginal rate up to 39.6 percent. It is important to note that when a position is hedged, it does not count for holding period purposes. In other words, put options that turn out to be profitable on stocks held longer than a year will still be taxed at the short-term rate, if the put position was entered into less than a year ago. If an investor exercises a call option, he or she is considered to have bought the stock on the exercise date, not the date on which the long position was entered. If the security called is sold within one year of the exercise date, any gain or loss will be calculated at the short-term capital gains rate. All premiums are taxed at the short-term capital gains rate regardless of the exercise or expiration date of an options contract. Taxes get more complex the more complex the options strategy becomes.

Debt Securities

Corporate bonds can be traded on the secondary market after they are issued. In the primary market, prices are set by the underwriter, but in the secondary market, prices are purely influenced by the supply and demand of the investors trading the bonds. When investors buy bonds, they typically evaluate the yield of that security and other bonds with comparable risk profiles. When investors sell bonds, they consider how much the bond has appreciated (so price is more important when selling bonds).

A large part of the secondary bond market is the repurchase agreement (or repo) market. This is an agreement between the seller and buyer, where the seller agrees to repurchase the securities (usually government debt) at a set price and time. The repo market is used by both money market funds and the Federal Reserve when implementing monetary policy. Rates are negotiated directly by the seller and buyer.

Banks often use this market to raise temporary funds. Corporations issue commercial paper that can then be traded on the secondary market. Brokered CDs trade on the secondary market and typically pay a higher rate than a traditional CD. Brokered CDs are CDs bought in bulk by broker dealers and then sold to individual investors. Bankers acceptances can be found in money market funds. These are instruments issued by a company that are guaranteed by a commercial bank. They trade at a discount on the secondary market and are often used in international secondary markets.

Asset backed securities (ABSs) and collateralized debt obligations (CDOs) also trade on secondary markets. It should be noted that CDOs had significant liquidity issues during the most recent financial crisis and often had to be sold for pennies on the dollar.

Types of Debt Securities

Commercial paper is used by corporations, and sometimes municipalities, to fund operations on a short-term basis. Maturities typically range from overnight (often called the Repo market) to 270 days. The advantage to issuing commercial paper is that it doesn't require the cost of SEC registration if it matures within 270 days of being issued. Commercial paper is typically found in a money market fund. There is also Asset Backed commercial paper where corporations can fund inventory such as dealer floors for automobiles. This is also where mortgages might be warehoused before they can be packaged into Mortgage Backed Securities. Commercial paper doesn't pay a coupon but is simply issued at a discount that reflects current interest rates (usually LIBOR plus some type of spread given the risk of the issuer). There are restrictions, similar to bond covenants, around what the funds from commercial paper issuance may be used for. This usually means only using that capital for funding inventories but can't be used on fixed assets.

Brokered certificates of deposit (CDs) are bought in bulk by the brokerage firm and resold to its customers. These CDs typically pay a premium (usually 1%) as compared to CDs issued by traditional banks. They are tradeable instruments whereas regular CDs are not (which can result in a loss to the investor), and they don't require an investor to pay a commission upon purchase.

Eurodollar bonds pay principal and interest in Eurodollars (i.e., U.S. dollars held in banks outside of the U.S.). These bonds are not registered with the SEC, so there are typically lower costs and fewer regulatory issues. This means they can be sold with a lower interest rate than a comparable bond in the U.S.

Variable rate preferred shares are a preferred stock where the dividend varies with a specified index. This is typically the Treasury rate, and the dividend fluctuates based on a formula (i.e., the Treasury bill rate plus 1%).

Characteristics of Debt Securities

Debt securities represent a loan that must be repaid with interest to the investor by the corporation or entity that issued the loan. Debt securities have certain features and characteristics, including an issue date and price, a maturity date, a redemption price, an original maturity, a coupon rate, and coupon dates. Debt securities can have different structures depending on whether they are secured bonds (backed with collateral) or unsecured bonds. Within these categories are further subdivisions denoting the priority of debt repayment. For example, subordinated, or junior, bonds are those that are repaid after senior bonds.

Some of the benefits of debt securities are increased safety, higher repayment priority, and predictability. There is generally less risk with debt securities than equity securities because debt securities are generally repaid even when companies do not profit, whereas an equity security will decrease in value if a company loses money. Debt securities are also considered a higher priority for repayment in the event of a company's bankruptcy. Debt securities are more predictable because they pay a set interest rate and also generally fluctuate less in the market. The greatest risk of debt securities is that repayment of these investments depends on the corporation or entity having the ability to repay the debt. This is known as credit risk or default risk.

A call provision allows the issuer of a debt to repurchase the debt before its maturity date. Certain bonds are callable on a certain date or event, while others are callable at any time. Typically, at the time of the redemption, investors receive any accrued interest along with the return of the original investment. Callable bonds pay a higher interest rate than noncallable bonds. This higher rate can help compensate for the drawback of call provisions, which is reinvestment risk. Reinvestment risk means that the investor may not be able to find a similar investment with comparable rates to reinvest their debt security proceeds in.

Structured Products

Equity linked securities (ELKs) are debt that is tied to equity indices. The return of such a security depends on the actual performance of the index to which it is linked. These are often safer than traditional equities, as they guarantee the preservation of principal. They typically pay a percent of the actual index's return or have some type of cap on the return they can earn.

Exchange traded notes (ETNs) are an unsubordinated, unsecured debt instrument. Like ELKs, their performance is tied to an index, but there is no guarantee of principal protection and there is no coupon payment. ETNs are highly affected by the rating of the issuer. Holding company depositary receipts (HOLDRs) represent ownership in stock or American depositary receipts (ADRs), which are where Americans can buy shares of stock in foreign companies that are bought and reissued by an American financial institution. These ADRs trade on U.S. exchanges and all dividend payments are convert to U.S. dollars by the managing bank. A small fee is taken out of the dividend payment for the management of the ADR and the currency conversion process.

Non-U.S. Market Securities

Sovereign debt, debt issued by federal governments, and the corporate debt and equities of foreign companies all trade on the secondary market. More established global companies trade on the NASDAQ and the NYSE, but smaller and newer companies trade on the exchanges of their home countries. Investment managers, mutual funds, and ETFs often offer exposure to international companies.

Global indices track how baskets of these companies perform against U.S. indices, as well as those of other countries. Emerging markets are a large part of the secondary market for international investors.

These are markets that have a significant amount of high growth potential but also carry downside risks as they are in countries that are not highly regulated, have unstable economic growth, and volatile currencies. Russia and Brazil are considered emerging markets.

Types of Yields

There are a number of ways to calculate the yield on a Treasury bond. The Treasury coupon is the initial dollar rate paid on a bond. A bond that has a par value of $1,000 may have a stated coupon rate of 10%, which means the bond would pay $100 per year in interest. Treasury bonds typically pay interest on a semi-annual basis, so the bond would pay $50 every six months until its maturity. The coupon rate and the dollar interest are constant throughout the life of a regular Treasury bond so even if the bond's value declines to $900 (due to rising interest rates), the coupon rate stays at 10% and the bond's holder still receives $100 in annual interest. The current yield is the interest on the bond divided by the price. In the case above where the bond's value is $900, the bond's current yield would be 11.1%. If the bond's value increases to $1,000, the current yield and coupon would be equal at 10% each. The yield to maturity (YTM) is a more complex concept. This is the yield an investor can expect to earn if they hold the bond until it matures. This is the discount rate at which the present value of all interest payments equals the price of the bond. It assumes that all interest received is reinvested at the YTM (hence there are various assumptions that go into calculating a bond's YTM). Yield to call (YTC) is the reinvested interest rate an investor receives if they reinvest the interest payments until the bond's call date. The yield to worst (YTW) is the yield assuming the worst-case scenario for the bond, whether it matures or is called first. The discount yield is the yield on a Treasury bond sold at a discount (annualized).

Bond Ratings

The bonds of most major companies are rated by the major rating agencies, including Fitch, Standard & Poor's, and Moody's. Please note that these agencies are only rating the credit worthiness of the issuer and that particular bond issue. They're not making any buy or sell recommendations on the bonds. Also note that the rating agency is being paid a fee to rate them by that particular company. The agencies rate everything from corporate bonds and privately issued mortgage-backed securities to commercial paper, CMOs, and CDOs. Some critics feel these ratings don't accurately reflect the risk of the instruments that rated them highly before the financial crisis of 2007-2008.

Ratings agencies assign a rating to companies that are issued debt. There are three major rating agencies: Fitch, S&P, and Moody's. The ratings are intended to reflect the issuer's ability to make interest and principal payments on debt. Ratings agencies also rate government, municipal, and structured debt products. The ratings that the agencies publish are assumed to be independent because the agencies are not money managers or investment banks. This means there is no conflict of interest or incentive for them to assign securities a particular rating.

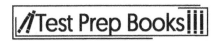

The table below shows the current ratings assigned by two of the major agencies and their meanings:

Moody's	S&P	Meaning
Investment Grade Bonds		
Aaa	AAA	Bonds of the highest quality that offer the lowest degree of investment risk. Issuers are considered to be extremely stable and dependable.
Aa1, Aa2, Aa3	AA+, AA, AA-	Bonds are of high quality by all standards but carry a slightly greater degree of long-term investment risk.
A1, A2, A3	A+, A, A-	Bonds with many positive investment qualities.
Baa1, Baa2, Baa3	BBB+, BBB, BBB-	Bonds of medium grade quality. Security currently appears sufficient but may be unreliable over the long-term.
Non-Investment Grade Bonds (Junk Bonds)		
Ba1, Ba2, Ba3	BB+, BB, BB-	Bonds with speculative fundamentals. The security of future payments is only moderate.
B1, B2, B3	B+, B, B-	Bonds that are not considered to be attractive investments. Little assurance of long-term payments.
Caa1, Caa2, Caa3	CCC+, CCC, CCC-	Bonds of poor quality. Issuers may be in default or are at risk of being in default.
CA	CC	Bonds of highly speculative features. Often in default.
C	C	Lowest rated class of bonds.
--	D	In default.

Taxable Debt Securities

The interest received on taxable debt (e.g., corporate bonds) is fully taxable whether it's interest from an individual bond or a distribution from a bond mutual fund. The capital gains on a taxable debt instrument are taxed at the ordinary rate if the bond is held for more than a year. The maximum rate is 15%. If the capital losses on bonds exceed the capital gains, the investor may deduct up to $3,000 of net capital losses from ordinary income. Capital losses exceeding $3,000 can be used in future years (i.e., carried forward).

Original issue discount (OID) bonds don't pay coupons and are issued at a discount from par value. If the bond is held until maturity, the investor has a built-in gain. The tax treatment for these bonds is very complex as the IRS assumes a certain amount of appreciation in the bond each year.

There are three potential tax liabilities with OID Bonds: the interest attributable to the original discount; the coupon payment; and the capital gain or loss. On the issuer's side, the issuing company expenses the interest payments and the amortization of the discount.

Corporate Bonds

Corporate Bond Characteristics

Corporate bonds are those issued by a corporation. Their basic features are:

- They are taxable securities.
- They have a set maturity (most corporate bonds pay the full principal at maturity, though some amortize like mortgage and asset-backed securities).

- They typically have a set par value of $1,000.
- They trade on major exchanges, but sometimes are traded over the counter.

A bond indenture is a formal agreement between the bond issuer and the investor. The key items in the bond indenture are:

- The form of the bond
- The total dollar amount of the particular bond issuance
- The property pledged behind the bond (though not all corporate bonds have property pledged)
- Any protective covenants. Covenants are acts that must be or cannot be performed by the issuer (e.g., working capital requirements, debt-equity ratio requirements, and restrictions on dividend payments)
- Redemption rights and call privileges

Corporate bonds accrue interest in the same manner as Treasury bonds except when a bond is "traded flat" (when the buyer doesn't have to pay the accrued interest to the seller). Usually this occurs when bonds are in default since there's no guarantee that the buyer will receive the entire interest payment that's due.

A callable bond or redeemable bond can be redeemed by the bond issuer before its stated maturity (i.e., the corporation has the right to call the bond away from the investor). Investors are usually compensated for this risk with a higher interest rate on a comparable bond, and a premium is paid to the investor when the call option is exercised. A bond is typically "called" when interest rates decline, and a company can find less expensive financing. A puttable bond grants the investor the right to "put" the bond back to the corporation that issued it and receive their principal. This typically occurs in a rising interest rate environment where an investor realizes they can receive a higher interest rate for investing that same principal. Investors in puttable bonds typically accept bonds at a lower yield than they otherwise would have gotten for the optionality. Some bonds have both call and put options embedded. A make whole call allows the issuer to call the bond if such a call gives the bondholder a lump sum equal to the present value of the coupons they'd have received if they'd held the bond until its scheduled maturity. This allows the issuer to reduce the amount of debt on its balance sheet.

Most bonds have an inverse relationship between their price and their yield. When the yield (i.e., interest rates) rises, prices fall. When interest rates fall, bond prices rise. Duration measures this relationship for small changes in prices and yields. Convexity (the second derivative of the price-yield relationship) is a more accurate measure of the relationship for larger changes in interest rates. For a bond with a duration of 4, each 1% rise in interest rates causes the bond to decline in value by 4% (or rise by 4% for each 1% decline in interest rates). The line marked duration in the graph below shows the price-yield relationship for Bond A and Bond B. Even when the bond price or yield moves, the relationship isn't reflected in the duration. This is where convexity is a better measure of the price-yield relationship.

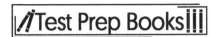

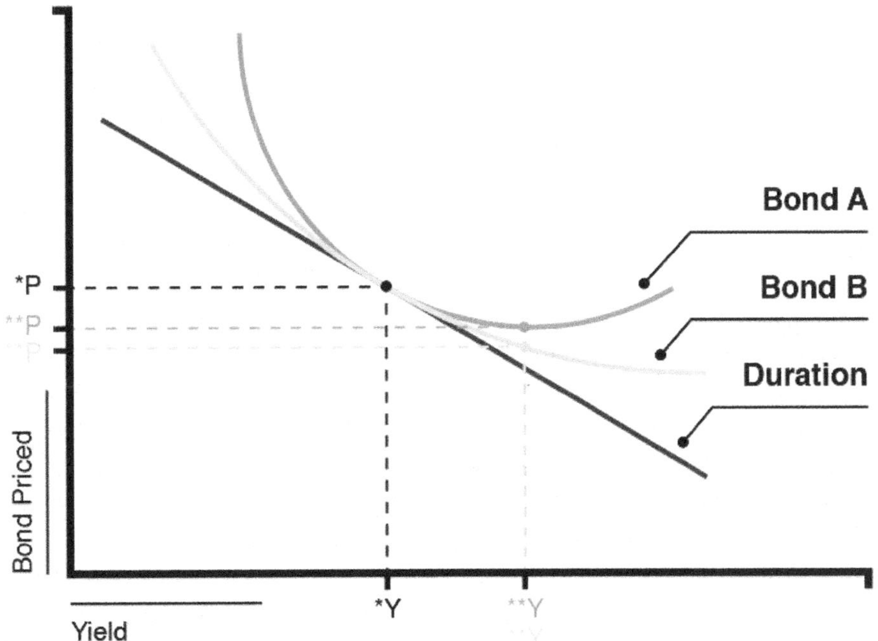

Corporate Bond Types

Mortgage bonds are backed by real estate that the issuer owns. In the event of a default, bondholders have a claim to that property. Equipment trust certificates (ETCs) are issued by transportation companies to finance new equipment. Debenture bonds are backed only by the general integrity of the issuer. The most profitable and stable companies with the highest bond ratings issue debenture bonds. Step coupon bonds or step-up bonds have an embedded call feature that pays one rate for one period and a higher rate after a specified date. Zero coupon bonds (or original issue discount bonds) pay no interest and are issued at a discount. These bonds have no reinvestment risk since there is no cash flow from them. The IRS taxes these bonds based on an accrued income calculation (this is called imputed interest). Though these instruments are taxable, there is no income received until they mature, so they are best invested in tax sheltered vehicles. However, these are typically the most volatile of fixed income securities. High-yield bonds or junk bonds are rated below Baa/BBB (see chart above) and are the riskiest bonds in a corporation's capital structure. Because of their risk level, they often have large price fluctuations and frequently trade like common stock. Companies with poor earnings records typically issue these types of bonds. Due to their risk, they often have the highest yields. Unfortunately, this high yield does not guarantee a high rate of return. Even though high-yield bonds have a high stated interest rate or are priced significantly below par value, they often default, don't yield as much as expected, or don't have 100% of their par value at maturity.

Convertible Corporate Bonds

Convertible bonds enable the bondholder to convert the bond into stock from the same company. These bonds sometimes have a variable interest rate (i.e., rather than a fixed coupon, the coupon rate fluctuates based on an index value). Variable rate bonds have more stable prices than fixed rate bonds. The conversion ratio determines the number of shares an investor receives upon the conversion of each bond. The ratio is the par value of the security divided by the conversion price, and there are conversion clauses that adjust the ratio to prevent shareholder dilution. With parity pricing, the price of the convertible bond is equal to the price of the underlying stock. When investors try to take advantage of pricing discrepancies between convertible bonds and the underlying stock, it is called arbitrage. Buying the undervalued asset and selling the overvalued asset until the prices align does, in theory, generate a profit for the arbitrageur. A forced conversion occurs when the issuer forces the bond holder to convert the bond to shares. This occurs when there's a significant decline in interest rates. The conversion ratio tells the investor how many shares they'll receive from converting each bond they own:

$$Conversion\ Ratio = \frac{Bond\ par\ value}{Conversion\ price}$$

Municipal Securities

Municipal Bond Characteristics

Municipal bonds are debt obligations issued by state or local governments. Municipal bonds are either general obligation (GO) bonds or revenue bonds. GO bonds are backed by the full faith and credit of the municipality and are paid with general revenue and borrowings. Revenue bonds are paid from the revenue tied to a specific project that the bonds have funded (e.g., tolls, stadiums, etc.). Municipal bonds are usually denominated in $5,000 increments. What makes them so attractive to investors is that they're often exempt from taxes on the federal and/or state level. Like corporate bonds, municipal bonds are often rated by the major rating agencies. Historically, they have very low default rates as they're backed by revenue from public utilities and governments with the power to tax. Municipal bond prices are determined by investor expectations of creditworthiness and marketability. Investors can use the following formula to calculate the tax-equivalent yield of a municipal bond:

$$Tax\ equivalent\ yield = \frac{Tax\ Exempt\ Yield}{(1 - Margin\ Tax\ Rate)}$$

An odd lot of bonds is $25,000 or less in municipal bonds for retail investors and $100,000 for institutional investors. For institutional investors, the dealer spread (i.e., the difference between the bid and ask price for a bond dealer) is rarely more than half a point (e.g., $50 on a $10,000 par value).

Some of the red flags for investing in general obligation bonds are:

- Declining property values
- An increasing tax burden relative to other regions
- General fund revenues falling below budgeted amounts
- Increased general fund deficits
- High unemployment and declining personal incomes

Some of the red flags for investing in revenue bonds are:

- Decreasing debt coverage

- Regular use of reserves for debt coverage
- Cost overruns on projects
- Frequent rate increases
- Management turnover

Municipal Bond Diversification

Investment advisors should diversify their customer's investments, and this should start at the highest level. The advisor should consider the right mix of money market funds, bonds, equities, and mutual funds, but diversification should happen at even lower levels. Investors who have high allocations of municipal bonds should diversify within municipals. Generally, municipal bond investors want bonds that have the highest tax equivalent yield and invest in municipal bonds that offer tax breaks based on the state they live in. However, they should try to invest in various states and municipalities, across different municipal bond types (revenue and general obligation), and in bonds with different ratings. Some municipalities have declared bankruptcy and experienced state-level financial crises, so it's important for investors to have geographic diversification.

General Obligation (GO) Bonds

Analyzing the debt of a general obligation (GO) municipal bond is different than analyzing a corporate bond. Some factors to consider include: the unemployment rate, demographic information, operational and management capabilities, the current debt profile, and the tax base. Investors can analyze the debt burden calculation to quantify a municipality's ability to pay debt. This is overall net debt divided by full valuation. Similar to a debt service coverage ratio, the ability of a municipality to make interest payments must be evaluated. Tax revenue must be evaluated on at least an annual basis to assure interest and principal can be paid. The demographics of the population must also be considered, as well as economic growth and activity of the municipality. The municipality's existing debt and when it will mature should also be considered.

Revenue bonds have different factors to evaluate. Though they're typically backed by the ability to pay the debt with general taxpayer money, their ability to generate revenue from the project they fund must be considered. Feasibility studies are created by economists and government officials to determine whether a project is really needed (i.e., if a bridge should be built, if a road should be paved) and if it can generate sufficient revenue to fund itself. Legal and operational factors, as well as environmental factors, must also be considered.

Revenue Bonds

Revenue bonds are tied to specific sources of revenue. Bondholders can't receive payment from the general taxpayer population for these bonds. Revenue can only come from the project pledged to repay the bonds and are from the actual operations of the financed project. If the project isn't profitable, a default may occur. Municipal bonds typically have strict bond covenants (negative and positive) to protect the issuer and the investor. Negative covenants prevent the issuer from certain actions (i.e., issuing additional debt, using funds from the finances project for something other than interest and principal payments), and positive covenants require certain actions by the issuer (i.e., having a sinking fund, requiring a set amount of cash reserves).

These bonds may also be subject to outside audits and financial reports. Investors can review credit ratings when assessing the credit risk of municipal bonds and be aware that credit ratings can change over time. Credit ratings are not a completely accurate source of investing advice or an indication that an investment is suitable. The Electronic Municipal Market Access (EMMA) website contains updated information regarding the issuer and municipal bond, as well as credit ratings information. It's also important to consider restrictions on the insurance of additional bonds and the flow of funds on a case-by-case basis.

Municipal Bond Types

Limited tax bonds are backed by the issuing entity but not by its full taxing power. Therefore, these bonds are riskier than bonds backed by the full taxing authority of a municipality. Tax anticipation notes are short-term obligations backed by expected taxes. These bonds even out cash flow and provide liquidity to balance out the irregularity of municipal and state income. Bond anticipation notes are issued in anticipation of the sale of long-term municipal bonds. Revenue anticipation notes are issued in anticipation of sales tax revenue. Tax-exempt commercial paper finances short-term liabilities. They provide the bond holder with some level of tax preference on their debt earnings (e.g., universities use this form of financing). Grant anticipation notes are backed by expected highway funding.

A special tax bond is paid through an excise tax, which is a tax on specific goods such as gasoline, tobacco, and alcohol. These usually aren't backed by the taxing power of the municipality. A special assessment bond is repaid from the taxes of those who benefit from that specific good. For example, if a bond finances a new road, anyone who buys a home or starts a business on that road pays a special tax levy to pay for the bond that funded the road. The interest is tax free for the residential bond holders. A moral obligation bond is backed by the moral obligation of a state government. Pre-funded municipal bonds have funds set aside to pay them off at their call date. An advance refunding occurs 90 days before the call date. A double-barreled municipal bond has its interest and principal guaranteed by a larger municipal entity. With these bonds, if the revenue from the financed project isn't sufficient, the municipality still backs the payment of the bonds. Certificates of participation (COPs) are where investors purchase a share of lease revenues rather than securing them with the actual revenues. These bonds are dependent on the legislative appropriations process.

Auction rate securities have long maturities so their rate is regularly reset through Dutch auction. A Dutch auction is where the price is lowered until it matches a bid. Municipal bonds and Treasury bonds are sold through Dutch auction.

Early Retirement of Municipal Securities

Municipal bonds have call features similar to those of corporate bonds where the municipality can call the bond back from the investor, usually to reissue the bond at a lower rate. A sinking fund accumulates funds to pay investors when a bond is called. A bond indenture usually states if a sinking fund is required. An extraordinary call is when a bond is redeemed early because there's no longer a source of revenue to pay the interest. An example would be if municipal bonds are issued to build a road or bridge, but the construction never occurs. A partial call occurs when only part of a bond issuance is called by the issuer. A make whole call can occur with municipal bonds just as it can with corporate bonds. On the investor side, there are tender options where the investor offers the issuer the opportunity to buy the debt back (usually at a premium).

If certain conditions occur as specified in the bond's offering documents, municipal bonds can be tendered or put back to the issuer (typically at par value). This occurs when rates rise, and the investor can receive a higher rate of interest with a new investment. This option usually comes with variable or floating rate municipal bonds.

A refunding occurs when the original bonds are escrowed or collateralized by direct obligation guarantees or by actual securities. The maturity schedules of the securities are matched to the scheduled payment on the issued bond, which is called escrow to maturity. Once the match is in place, the bonds are no longer secured by project revenues or the general obligation of the municipality. With advance refunding bonds, the new bonds are sold at a lower rate than the outstanding bonds. The proceeds are then invested and, when the older bonds are called, they're paid with the invested proceeds. Governments do this to postpone a debt payment. Crossover refunding is when the originally pledged revenue stream to service a debt "crosses-over" to pay the interest on the newly funded bonds. In a current refunding, the proceeds from the new debt are used to repay the old debt maturity immediately.

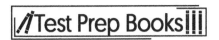

Municipal Bond Marketability

Municipal bonds are rated the same way as corporate bonds. The four basic categories of municipal credit analysis are: the debt burden, the ability of the municipality to properly budget, the availability of tax revenue, and the overall economic environment of the municipality. Municipal bond markets are mostly liquid, so they can be bought or sold with minimal bid-ask spreads. Other factors include quality (rating scores), maturity, interest rate, liquidity for sales in the secondary market, dollar price, issuer name, and credit enhancement.

Municipal Bond Pricing

As with corporate bonds, municipal bonds can be quoted at a percentage of face value, which can be stated as a dollar price. A municipal bond with a par value of $1,000 may be quoted $98 ½ which would be a dollar price of $985. The yield calculation is the same as well. If that same bond had an annual coupon of $10, its yield would be 1.0%. Most municipal bonds pay a regular coupon, typically semi-annually. However, some are zero coupon bonds, which are similar to treasuries with no coupons and offered at a discount to par. Some bonds offer odd coupons, which can occur if a bond isn't issued at the end of a quarter or month. This typically occurs with either the first or last coupon payment, with all of the coupons in between being paid over the standard six-month period. Municipal bonds accrue interest the same way as other bonds.

When a trade is made, the buyer pays any interest accrued on the bond to the seller and then collects the full interest amount at the next payment date. If an investor buys a municipal bond at a premium (i.e., a value greater than par), the investor has the option to amortize the bond premium to reduce the amount of interest in the bond's income. For tax-exempt bonds, as most municipals are, the premium must be amortized. With bonds purchased at a discount, accretion will occur at the implied rate of interest until the bond matures. As with other bonds, the longer the maturity the greater the risk of the bond, so investors are usually compensated with a higher interest rate (which is why the yield curve is upward slopping in normal economic conditions). Investors may want to calculate the tax-equivalent yield of a municipal bond when making an investment decision.

This will help them determine if a municipal bond's yield is comparable to another taxable bond with equivalent risk. Municipal bond investors also may want to calculate the capital gains yield and how much the bond appreciates after their investment, and then back out any fees to calculate a net yield. Municipal bonds are sometimes callable, and the investor may want to calculate the yield assuming the bond is called at its call date (as this yield might be less than the yield to maturity) so the investor will have to consider investing the proceeds at a lower rate than their initial investment. Investors also will want to consider the price value of a basis point (PVPB). This tells the investor how much a bond's value will fluctuate given a change of one basis point (0.01%) in the bond's yield.

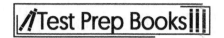

The formula is (the modified duration is required for the calculation):

$$PVBP = Modified\ Duration \times Price \times 0.01\%$$

A municipal bond can also trade "flat" which means that, when the bond trades, no accrued interest is due to the seller. This would be the case if the bond is in default.

Municipal Tax Treatment

As noted above, bonds purchased at a discount will accrete and those purchased at a premium will amortize. An original issue discount (OID) bond will accrete. The interest on most municipal bonds is exempt from tax at the state and local levels, but their capital gains are taxed at the federal level (and their losses are tax deductible). The alternative minimum tax (AMT) applies to municipal bonds. This federal tax ensures that all trusts, estates, and corporations pay some minimal tax. Calculating this tax can be fairly complex. There are certain exemptions, and the rate varies for individuals and corporations. Adjustments are made for corporations so that earnings and profits are accurately reflected. There are also adjustments for net operating losses. For both individuals and corporations, the liability is the greater of either the regular tax rate or the tax rate calculated at the minimum rate. Bank qualified bonds are bonds qualified with tax exempt obligations. This applies to small issues of $30 million or less, and the issuer must meet other activity criteria.

Hedge Funds

The Investment Company Act of 1940 applies to companies that invest or trade in securities, as well as those that issue securities. The act seeks to protect the public interest in investing by eliminating conflicts of interest.

Hedge Fund Structure

Hedge funds can become exempt from the act under Sections 3c1 and 3c7. Under 3c1 the fund can't be owned by more than one hundred beneficial shareholders. Under 3c7 the fund must be owned by qualified purchasers, usually investors with high net worth and high incomes, and less than five hundred investors. Privately placed funds require a private placement memorandum. A "blank check" hedge fund is a fund that has no stated objective or investments yet. These funds invest in highly speculative investments in their seed-capital stage. Hedge funds usually pay the manager a fixed annual percentage, around 1% to 2%, and then a performance-based fee, which is sometimes as much as 20% of the return on the assets managed by the fund. Institutions typically hold anywhere from 1% to 2% in hedge funds or some form of alternative investment. In 2013, hedge fund assets were estimated to be valued at $2.1 trillion collectively. Some hedge funds fall under the regulation of the US Commodity Futures Trading Commission. The Volcker Rule, which limits speculative investment made by banks, encompasses hedge funds (many large investment banks fund hedge funds).

Hedge Fund Characteristics

Some hedge funds have lock-up periods. This means investors can't withdraw their initial investment for a specified period of time. Funds that invest in more-liquid assets like stocks and bonds will have shorter lock-up periods. After the lock-up period, investors still must follow a set redemption schedule. Hedge funds can vary in the strategies they employ. Where most regular mutual funds are long only, hedge funds can employ a long-short strategy where they can profit off of the value of companies going down using derivatives and options for selling shares short. A market-neutral fund will minimize its exposure to the stock market, a strategy that will be profitable when the market experiences downturns. Some funds attempt to profit off of larger global events like changes in currency values. Arbitrage funds attempt to profit off of the mispricing of securities. Distressed funds invest in the debt of companies that are on the verge of bankruptcy and buy their bonds at large discounts.

Hedge Fund Taxation

As the fund manager is compensated from the profits earned on the fund due to hedge fund structure, the fund manager is taxed as return on investment as opposed to at the ordinary income-tax rate. Partners in the fund are taxed as they earn the income, rather than when they actually receive profits (so the taxes are effectively deferred). Hedge funds are taxed at the long-term capital gains rate of 20% due to the longer investment horizon. There is controversy over whether or not this is a sufficient rate, as it is basically half of the marginal income-tax rate, and most fund managers make the majority of their money from the long-term gains of their funds.

Asset-Backed Securities

An asset-backed security (ABS) is backed by the receivables a bank or servicer is owed on loans for everything from automobiles, credit cards, and mortgages to company inventory and student loans. These loans are originated by a bank or finance company and then packaged and sold to investors as ABSs. These securities typically have different tranches with varying levels of risk. The more senior tranches receive interest and principal first while the riskiest, equity-like tranches only receive the residual payment on the riskiest loans. These securities are beneficial to banks and other lenders because they allow them to remove loans from their balance sheets and free up capital, even though it may reduce the incentive for them to make good loans (since most of the risk is passed onto the investor). A collateralized mortgage obligation (CMO) and a collateralized debt obligation (CDO) are riskier, asset-backed securities that have many levels of tranches. Some economists and experts believe these instruments were simply too complex to value and were a direct contributor to the financial crisis of 2007-2008.

Collateralized Mortgage Obligations (CMOs)

Collateralized mortgage obligations (CMOs) are made up of groups of mortgages packaged together to be sold to investors. This type of debt security generates returns for investors based on mortgage payments being made. This enables distributions of principal and interest payments to investors. The details of distributions are based on a set of rules and agreements enumerated in the original deal.

CMOs are structured into a series of tranches, usually based on varying risk levels, that increase in risk and rate of return at each subsequent level. Each tranche has different interest rates, maturity dates, and sizes. By offering a variety of diversified investment options, CMOs can appeal to a wide range of investors. CMOs also appeal to investors who wish to invest in mortgage cash flows without purchasing or originating mortgages. Examples of these types of investors include banks, insurance companies, mutual funds, and hedge funds. Institutions that offer CMOs are able to lower their interest and default risk by transferring debt to investors as structured securities.

CMOs do have certain risks associated with them. Interest rate changes and changes made by the individual homeowners affect CMOs. If for some reason a large number of homeowners in the CMO cannot make payments on their mortgages or even default on them, the CMO will not be able to pay the investors because the capital isn't there.

Collateralized Debt Obligations (CDOs)

Collateralized debt obligations (CDOs) are similar to CMOs in their structure, but a CDO is broader in terms of the collateral of pooled assets. This structured product has bundles of cash flow generating assets usually made up of mortgages, auto loans, credit card debt, and corporate debt. These assets function as collateral for the CDO. CDOs are considered derivatives because their value does not rely on the CDO itself but on the underlying loans.

CDOs are structured into tranches with varying levels of risk. Senior tranches are those that have first priority on being paid back in the event of a default. Therefore, these tranches are considered safer and have a higher credit rating. Riskier tranches, called junior tranches, have higher coupon rates than senior tranches because they carry a higher default risk.

Banks sell CDOs for a couple of different reasons. The banks are able to use the money they receive to make new loans. This also reallocates the risk of default on the loan to the investors instead of the bank. Investors often invest in CDOs because they are able to select a tranche that matches the specific level of risk that they are comfortable taking on.

Because the banks who originated the loans have passed ownership to the individual investors, they have less motivation to collect these loans and enforce strict lending standards. This is one disadvantage of CDOs for an investor. Another disadvantage is the inherent complexity of CDOs. Because the product is made up of a large pool of assets, investors cannot be sure exactly what they are receiving and what value it has.

Characteristics of Asset-Backed Securities

Asset-backed securities (ABSs) set forth in the indenture the terms of the specific security, such as maturity date, interest payment timing, method of interest calculation, and other features, such as callable and convertible options. The indenture is a legal and binding contract or agreement between the parties involved. The maturities of these investments vary. Typically, within one pool of assets, the tranches consist of loans of similar risk and maturity. Assets in this type of security have gone through the securitization process. The securitization process refers to the transfer of ownership of the assets to a special purpose entity or vehicle that is able to package and market them. Principal and interest payments made on the loans pass through to the investors who have invested in the ABSs. Payments are usually made on a monthly basis unless otherwise specified in the original agreement. The payments also include accrued interest on any unpaid principal.

U.S. Treasury Securities

The United States government issues a range of debt instruments including Treasury bills ("T-bills"), Treasury notes, and Treasury bonds. They also issue zero-coupon bonds (STRIPS) and Treasury Inflation-Protected Securities (TIPS). They are backed by the full faith and credit of the U.S. government. Income from these securities is tax exempt at the state and local levels but is taxable at the federal level. Treasury bills matures in 1 year or less, Treasury notes mature in 1 - 10 years, and Treasury bonds mature 10 - 30 years from issuance. Treasury bills are the primary instrument used by the Federal Open Market Committee (FOMC) to regulate the supply of money. TIPS have their principal amount adjusted for inflation as calculated by the Consumer Price Index (CPI). These bonds compensate investors for the inflation that erodes the value of their investment (TIPS typically have a lower yield than comparable Treasury bonds or notes since they're compensated by the inflation adjustment to their bonds). The TIPS breakeven rate (i.e., the difference between the yield on TIPS and regular Treasury notes or bonds) is sometimes used to gauge the inflation that financial markets expect.

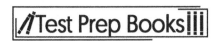

U.S. Treasury Characteristics

Treasury bills are issued in a minimum denomination of $1,000 and then in $5,000 increments. Treasury notes and bonds are quoted on the secondary market at the percentage of par in 1/32 point increments. Bond traders refer to each 1/32nd as a tick, and each percentage point or basis point as a bip. The spread is the difference between the yields of two different Treasury bonds (or any bonds). For example, if the 10-year bond is trading with a yield of 5.0%, and the 5-year bond is trading at 4.0%, the spread would be 1.0% (5.0% - 4.0% = 1.0%). Traders typically look at spreads when deciding which Treasury bonds offer the most value. The advantages of investing in Treasury bonds is that they have essentially zero credit risk, so investors are guaranteed to get back all of the principal. With TIPS, investors are insulated from inflation risk. Treasuries do have a price risk so, if yields increase, the bonds decline in value. There's also reinvestment risk.

After they have been sold at auction by the U.S. government, treasury bonds trade on the secondary market. Treasury markets are highly liquid due to significant trading by both institutional and retail investors in treasury bonds (they are actually the largest security market in the world).

Foreign governments also hold significant quantities of U.S. treasury bonds. Off the run treasuries are treasuries of a particular maturity that were issued before the most recent offering (where the most recent offering is called on the run treasuries). The New York Federal Reserve is the largest holder and trader of U.S. treasury bonds. The minimum amount for primary dealers to trade is $5 million for treasury bills and $1 million for treasury notes and bonds.

U.S. Treasury Accrued Interest

This accrued interest is the dollar amount of interest that's accrued since the most recent interest payment and the bond's sale. The buyer pays the price of the bond plus any accrued interest. For example, if a bond is traded for $1,000, has an interest payment of $100 per year (paid annually), and is traded exactly half a year after a coupon payment, then the bond buyer would pay the bond seller $1,000 plus the $50 in accrued interest (the new bond holder would receive the full $100 interest payment at the next payment date). The number of days since the last payment is the actual unit used to calculate accrued interest, and there are various conventions used to count the number of days.

U.S. Government Agency Securities

Types of Government Agency Securities

There are a number of government agencies that issue debt called Government-Sponsored Enterprises (GSEs). In 1968, the government established the Government National Mortgage Association (GNMA) to expand home ownership in the U.S. Its creation allowed borrowers to find better financing via capital markets and created liquidity in the housing market. The GNMA issues pass-through securities, which are pools of mortgages packaged into tranches, or portions. They "pass" the interest and principal payments of mortgages onto investors in the pass-through securities. These securities are more commonly referred to as Mortgage Backed Securities or Real Estate Mortgage Investment Conduits (REMICs).

There are also the Federal National Mortgage Association (FNMA or Fannie Mae), the Federal Home Loan Mortgage Corporation (FHLMC or Freddie Mac), and the Student Loan Marketing Association (Sallie Mae). Fannie Mae primarily packages mortgages backed by the Federal Housing Administration. Shares of Fannie Mae now trade on over-the-counter markets but previously traded on the New York Stock Exchange. Fannie Mae and Freddie Mac loans are "conforming loans" (i.e., they conform to GSE guidelines, which means loans of less than $424,100, loans with lower loan-to-value ratios, and borrowers with relatively healthy credit scores). Some experts attribute the cause of the 2007-2008 financial crisis to GSEs being unable to compete with larger banks that would write and package loans no matter how risky they were. Initially, Fannie Mae had an "explicit guarantee" that guaranteed principal and interest payments for investors but that became an "implicit guarantee" in 1968. GSEs generally have debt that amortizes (i.e., it pays back a portion of the principal with each interest payment).

All the mortgage backed securities (MBSs) and debt of the government sponsored entities (GSEs) trade on the secondary market. These are bought by institutions, retail investors, and foreign governments. The primary market for GSE securities is when a home buyer obtains a mortgage. The secondary market is when those loans are packaged into mortgage backed securities.

Characteristics of Government Agency Securities

Government agency securities consist of federal government agency bonds and government-sponsored enterprise (GSE) bonds. Federal government agency securities are guaranteed by the full faith and credit of the U.S. government. These securities make regular interest payments and the total face value is repaid at maturity. They offer a somewhat higher rate of interest than Treasury bonds because they are not as liquid as Treasury bonds. They are sometimes callable before their maturity date, which creates a risk to investors that they may be redeemed before maturity. Maturities vary depending on the specific type of bond.

A GSE bond is offered by FNMA, FHLMC, and others, including the Federal Farm Credit Banks Funding Corporation and the Federal Home Loan Bank. These entities were created by Congress to serve a public purpose. Bonds issued by these entities are not covered by the same guarantee as government agency bonds. Therefore, they are subject to credit risk and default risk. Due to the increased level of risk, these bonds have a higher yield than that of Treasury bonds.

In general, agency bonds offer a semi-annual fixed coupon and can be bought in different increments. A minimum investment of $10,000 is typical for the first increment, with $5,000 increments after that. Other agency bonds have a fixed coupon rate, and some have a floating rate tied to a specific benchmark rate. This type of bond is called a floater. Some agency bonds are even offered as no-coupon discount notes (discos) with a short maturity range. These are intended to help with short-term financing demands. The structure, size, and terms of each bond are tailored to different needs and purposes. Government agency bonds are usually quoted in increments of $1/32^{nd}$, as a fraction of their par value.

Government agency bonds are bought and sold through brokers with fees and transaction costs assessed for their services. Investors should consider the yield spread when investing in bonds. This is the difference between a bond with a high yield and a bond with a low yield.

Disclosures for Investment Products

Required Disclosures on Specific Transactions

Material aspects of investments refer to any information that may affect the price of the shares of a publicly traded company. Material information is withheld from the general investment community until it can be disseminated in a fair and transparent matter, so that no party can profit from the information. It is illegal for any party with access to the information to invest or trade and profit from it. They also cannot provide other parties with the information so that they may profit. For example, the CEO, CFO, and other executives at a company have access to earnings information before the general investing public. In theory, these professionals could buy or sell shares in advance of the 10-k or 10-q being filed, to profit or reduce losses before the public and common shareholders.

A statement of additional information is part of a mutual fund prospectus. It is also known as Part B of the registration statement. It is not legally required to be provided unless requested by an investor. According to the SEC, this statement may contain the history of the fund, fund policies, information about executives and managers of the funds, investment advisory functions, fee schedules, tax information, and historical fund performance relative to peers and the fund's benchmark.

Types of Investment Risk

It is important to understand the types of risks associated with investments. Call risk is the risk that an investment can be called away. The term mostly applies to callable bonds but applies to call options as well. When an investor buys a callable bond, they are typically compensated with a higher yield than that of a comparable bond. If interest rates fall, the issuer may call the bond, forcing the investor to invest in a bond at a lower rate than that for the comparable non-callable bond.

Capital risk is the risk that the investor may lose all or part of their initial investment. Equity investors need to understand that there is the potential for the price of their shares to go to zero, should the company be unprofitable or go bankrupt. Bonds have capital risk as well, particularly high yield bonds. Treasury bonds are assumed to have no capital risk, as they are fully backed by the government.

Credit risk is the risk that the borrower won't be able to make payments on his or her debt. Ratings agencies evaluate this type of risk. A company with sufficient earnings and cash in their balance sheet will have less credit risk because they have the funds to service their debt. A start-up company or a company that is unable to generate cash flow has a higher probability of not being able to make interest payments or even return the original principal invested.

Currency risk is the risk of an investment declining in value due to fluctuations in the value of a currency. An investor in the United States may invest in shares of a company that is traded in Euros. If, over the course of the year, the shares increase in value by 10% but the value of the Euro relative to the U.S. Dollar declines by 5%, when those shares are sold and converted back to dollars, the return will be reduced to 5%. This is the risk investors incur when investing internationally.

Inflationary risk is similar to currency risk in that it erodes the value of an investment. If investors choose to hold cash, the value of their cash will be eroded by the amount of inflation. Therefore, if an investor holds $1,000 in cash over a year and inflation is 4%, the value of the cash becomes $960 in inflation-adjusted dollars. Essentially, this means that the original $1,000 value of cash can only buy $960 worth of goods when adjusted for inflation. Bond investors are particularly concerned with inflation risk, as bonds pay a fixed interest rate and do not usually have the potential to appreciate in value. Bond prices can rise, but investors will still only receive the principal invested when the bond matures.

Interest rate risk is the risk that an asset's value – usually a bond or some other type of fixed income security – will decline with an increase in interest rates. The longer the maturity, the greater the interest rate risk because there is more time for interest rates to rise and fall over the life of the investment. Interest rate risk is measured on bonds by calculating the security's duration. This is a measure of the relationship between the amount that an investment's interest rate change will fluctuate and the value of that security.

Liquidity risk is the risk that an asset will not be able to be sold quickly enough, so that the time it takes to execute a sale affects the value of the security. Liquidity risk is minimal for securities that trade on larger and more established exchanges. Thinly traded securities and assets like real estate have liquidity risk. Liquidity risk is measured by the bid ask spread on a security.

Market or systematic risk is the risk that factors that affect the financial market as a whole will impact an investment's value. It is the risk that can't be avoided with diversification and is measured by Beta – the correlation between a security's value and that of the overall market. For example, recession, interest rate spikes, financial crisis and other global events often affect entire financial markets rather than just parts of it.

Non-systematic risk is the risk that can't be shed through a diversified portfolio. Individual companies can face lawsuits, they can develop new products that are unsuccessful, or a company's service may become obsolete due to newer technologies. These are all types of non-diversifiable risk.

Political risk is the risk that decisions made by politicians or government will affect the way business can be conducted. This includes environmental regulations, FDA approval, and decisions made by financial regulators. Political risk also occurs when international countries become unstable and affect a country's financial markets.

Prepayment risk is the risk most often associated with mortgage-backed securities but is applicable to other asset classes. Prepayment risk is the risk that the borrower will repay the loan before it is anticipated to be repaid. This usually occurs when interest rates fall, and the borrower can receive more favorable terms on a new loan. The issuer will not receive the interest payments they would have, had the prepayment not occurred and will, in all likelihood, have to make new loans with that capital at a lower interest rate.

Reinvestment risk is the risk that capital will be reinvested at the lower interest rate. Reinvestment risk comes with call risk as well. If an investor owns a callable bond and it is called, the investor will likely have to invest in a riskier security to receive the same interest rate.

Timing risk is the risk incurred when an investor attempts to buy and sell securities at the most profitable point. Any market participant who invests incurs some form of timing risk. Investors who move into cash risk missing out on any upward movement in the market. Investors who don't want to sell securities incur the risk that the market may move down, causing their portfolio decline, whereas if they had moved into cash, their portfolio would not have lost value.

Investment Returns

Some stocks reward investors for holding their shares by paying dividends. Dividends are paid out of a company's earnings. Any earnings not paid out as dividends are reported on the balance sheet as retained earnings. There are different theories around the importance of dividends. The "bird in hand" theory is that it is better for the investor to have the dividend and decide how to reinvest it, rather than have the company retain that cash and invest it back in the company's operations. Companies typically try to pay a consistent percentage of the stock price as a dividend, as opposed to a percentage of earnings. Companies want to pay a consistent dividend. It is often a sign that a company is struggling if it historically paid a consistent dividend but is now no longer able to do so.

Similar to stocks, bonds pay interest in the form of a coupon. While not all stocks pay dividends, nearly all bonds pay interest, although some bonds (called zeros) pay no interest and simply pay a set discounted amount of principal at maturity. Most bonds pay a fixed dollar rate based on the coupon. This payment is usually made semiannually. The actual interest fluctuates to reflect current market rates due to changes in the bond's value, but the actual coupon dollar amount is the same throughout the life of the bond. Some bonds pay a floating rate of interest based on some index or benchmark. These bonds pay a different dollar amount with each adjustment.

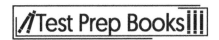

The interest on bonds is taxable, except for municipal bonds, which pay interest that is tax free. Almost all bonds are not taxable at the federal level, and typically when an investor buys bonds issued by the state they live in, they are exempt at the state and local level as well. Investors usually calculate a tax equivalent yield to determine if the net yield they will receive on a taxable bond is higher or lower than a municipal bond of equal risk.

A capital gain is the profit received when assets like stocks, bonds, or real estate are sold. There is a gain if the asset is sold at a higher price than when it was purchased. Interest and dividends are not considered capital gains because they are not returns associated with the sale of an asset. Capital gains in assets held for more than a year are taxed at a long-term capital gains rate, which is lower than the short-term capital gains rate. This encourages investors to invest for the long term rather than just investing for short term profits. There are certain exemptions from capital gains where applicable, usually to increase entrepreneurship and investments in new and growing industries.

Return of capital is when an investor receives all or a portion of their original principal invested. They are not taxed as capital gains. Return of capital occurs on mortgage-backed securities when the investors pay the required portion of principal as dictated by an amortization schedule. Investors and brokers must track investments in a cost basis, so that it is clear what portion of an investment should be taxed at a capital gain and what is simply the return of capital. The calculation is even more difficult when an investment is a partnership. This is usually tracked through each partner's capital account.

Investment Fees

Investors need to account for fees, commissions, and costs when calculating the return on their investment. Investors should focus on the net return when evaluating the potential profitability of a trade. The breakeven rate is the rate at which the investor receives a return of capital plus enough of a profit to recoup only transaction fees. The term applies to regular stock and bond trades, and also to options transactions for which a premium is paid that must be accounted for when calculating a breakeven rate.

Rights of accumulation can be used to keep costs down and lower the breakeven rate for mutual fund investors. This simply assures that funds account for all of an investor's transactions in the aggregate, when processing transaction discounts that require a minimum transaction size.

A Letter of Intent outlines the agreement of two parties who are entering into a transaction before it becomes finalized. This letter is required for mergers and acquisitions, joint ventures, private equity partnerships, and real estate lease agreements. They are typically not binding agreements.

A mark-up is the difference between an investment's lowest current offering price and the higher price the actual dealer will charge an investor. Markups occur when dealers trade with firm capital, not customer accounts. Dealers earn their compensation this way, rather than in the form of a fee. The dealer is assuming significant risk in this type of transaction because the price of the security may go up or down while the dealer has the security in inventory.

Commissions are the fees paid by investors to their broker each time they buy or sell securities. Commissions are commensurate with the dollar amount of the size of each trade. Some brokers use fee-based structures where investors simply pay a quarterly fee. This reduces the incentive for brokers to churn their client's accounts.

A net transaction occurs when a broker receives a customer order and executes the trade with another broker. This must occur with the customer's consent for complete transparency and to ensure the customer receives the best execution and pricing.

Most mutual funds offer a range of share classes, as well as individual issuers of shares of stock. Different share class holders have different rights. For individual shares of stock, this typically means common shares that have voting rights versus preferred shareholders who do not have voting rights. Mutual funds usually list share types alphabetically, A, B, C, D, or I (for institutional).

A non-discretionary fee-based account is an account where the investor still has total control and directs the broker as to what accounts they can trade. The broker does not earn commission but receives a quarterly fee, based on the account's value.

A surrender fee is the fee that the holder of an insurance policy must pay upon cancellation of the policy.

A 12b-1 fee is an operating fee charged by a mutual fund and is considered an operating expense.

Life insurance annuity contracts charge a variable fee called a mortality and expense risk charge. These fees compensate the insurance company for the risk incurred to assure that beneficiaries receive payment throughout the life of the contract.

A soft dollar transaction occurs when an investment manager receives non-monetary benefits from a broker dealer. When an asset manager does large amounts of trading, it generates revenue for that broker, who then rewards the asset manager with soft dollar benefits. These benefits can go unreported as they are not actual hard dollar commission fees. One of the problems with soft dollar arrangements is that the brokerage commissions are higher than they would be for the set fees normally paid on a trade. This effectively erodes the return on the portfolio of investments that the asset manager is managing. With institutional funds that can have assets in the hundreds of millions or even billions of dollars, these amounts can be significant.

There is also the fact that these soft dollar costs are being passed onto the client of the investment manager. The research provided through the soft dollar arrangement can provide excess return to the portfolio that the manager may not have achieved on his or her own. Section 28(e) of the Securities Exchange Act of 1934 covers soft dollars and states that soft dollars actually act to make markets more competitive and pricing more efficient. The guidelines state soft dollars are acceptable if the brokerage provides the advice directly or through written research materials and encompasses economic and portfolio strategy into their recommendations. It also requires that soft dollar agreements and amounts be fully disclosed.

Investments & Taxation

The current estate tax rates range from 18% to 40%. Currently under the Tax Cuts and Jobs Act, up to $10 million, indexed for inflation, can be gifted to receive a lifetime exclusion and exemption from the estate tax rate. A married couple could exclude up to $20 million, indexed for inflation. These amounts are only in effect until 2025. Annual gifts up to $15,000 per recipient are completely tax exempt in 2018. Capital gains can be avoided when a stock is gifted. When a stock is gifted, it is taxed at its current fair market value. Usually it is calculated as the high and low price at which the shares have traded on the date of the gift.

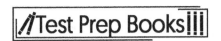

Market Analysis

Advisors use a broad range of tools and theories to speculate and break down financial markets. The Federal Reserve, brokerage houses, banks, data services, and economists all analyze and produce volumes of data that investors can use to analyze investments. There are a number of market sentiment indicators (surveys or groups of data) that investors use to determine the current opinion of the masses. If market sentiment is good, it means people believe economic conditions are healthy, unemployment is low, and earnings will be strong. This is generally perceived as good news for financial markets and investors. Some investors follow the CBOE Volatility Index (VIX) to gauge the market's appetite for risk. The VIX is the implied volatility of the equity markets given how options are currently priced for the market as a whole. A decline in the index means investors as a whole expect lower volatility in the market, while an increase means investors expect more volatility. At the company level, analysts will look at P/E ratios (price-earnings ratios) on individual stocks to determine how much investors are willing to pay for each dollar that company earns. The University of Michigan Consumer Sentiment Index and The Conference Board Consumer Confidence Index are surveys conducted by economists to gauge the public's current opinion on the state of financial markets. The Michigan index contains 50 questions and is answered by 500 people, while the Conference Board index is based on the responses of 5,000 households. The Conference Board also has an index made up of leading indicators. The index is comprised of various indices that measure unemployment, earnings, unemployment claims, consumer spending, capital spending, housing, the yield curve, and the money supply, among others.

The yield curve itself is often used as a predictor of recession. Below is a graphical depiction of the yield curve:

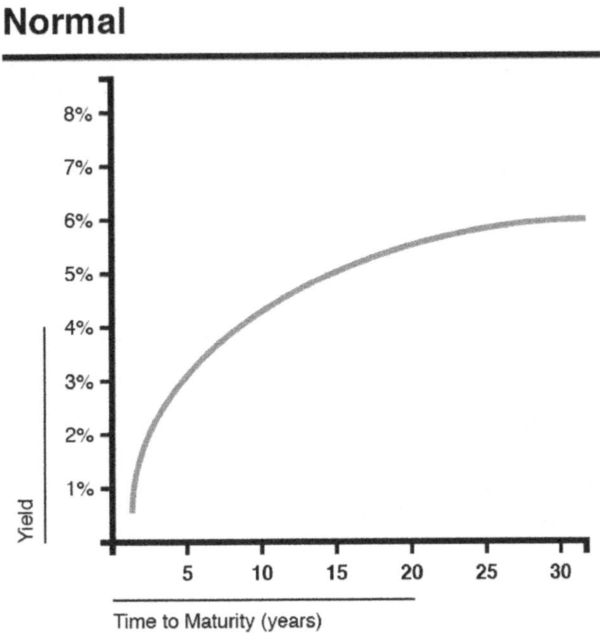

The yield curve typically has an upward slope since investors holding longer maturity securities must be compensated with a higher yield. When the yield curve flattens or becomes downward sloping, it often indicates a recession. There are numerous theories as to why the yield curve takes on different shapes, but the shape exemplified in the image above typically means that long-term yields are declining because there is a reduction in quality in the treasury bond market. Rather than owning equities, high-yield bonds, or securities with more inherent risk, investors buy bonds to endure the downturn in financial markets.

There are also more data-based indicators. Some investment professionals find these more reliable than surveys, which are based solely on the opinions of economists and consumers (since they're prone to human error and the misjudgment of current economic conditions). Available funds are the funds, in aggregate, that can be drawn out of a margin account at a brokerage firm. This is an indicator of how much liquidity is in the system. When the data is trending downward or is low, it indicates liquidity is coming out of the system. In all likelihood, this is because investors perceive the possibility of a downturn in financial markets so they want to keep their money out of the system. The Put/Call ratio (PCR) of an index is another indicator.

A PCR greater than 50% means more investors are betting that the market will decline (since Put options profit from a downturn in the market). A ratio less than 50% means there are more long-term investors. Short interest is another indicator. This is the number of shares investors have sold short but not yet covered or closed out of the trade. Short interest is an indicator of how likely a stock or an index is to decline, and the number usually is evaluated in percentage terms. If a company has 1,000,000 shares of stock trading and 10,000 shares are being sold short, the short interest calculation is 10,000 ÷ 1,000,000 = 1%. Investors often view the trend of this calculation. If the short interest increases to 2% or 3% over the quarter, it indicates that more and more investors feel that the stock will decline and are trying to profit from it.

Research reports are most often issued by investment banks and brokers that issue securities. However, some investment managers and independent research firms also produce research reports. Reports typically provide some form of a buy, sell, or hold recommendation, as well as a price target. Research reports provide financial ratios and other calculated profitability metrics based on a company's financial statements. They also provide an analyst's opinion and discussion as to why that price target has been assigned.

Market Analysis for Municipal Bonds

Just like equities and corporate bonds, there are municipal bond indices fund managers use to benchmark their performance. The Revenue Bond Index has 25 municipal revenue bonds that mature in 30 years and average an A+ bond rating. A fund manager will try to buy similarly rated bonds (with maturities of approximately 30 years) that they believe will outperform the bonds in this index. In addition, the Eleven General Obligation Bond Index consists of general obligation issues, while the Municipal Bond Index has 40 different issues. The Bond Buyer 20 index, or GO 20 Index, is based on 20 general obligation bonds that share a maturity period of 20 years. While corporate bonds are rated from AAA to single A, then to BBB and all the way down to non-investment grade, municipal bonds have just three categories for Moody's ratings services. MIG-1 are the highest quality municipal bonds. They have the lowest probability of default. MIG-2 are high quality municipal bonds, and MIG-3 are considered adequate quality.

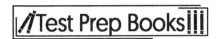

Technical Analysis

While most investors evaluate economic data, opinions of economists, corporate earnings, financial statements, and other financial data when making investment decisions, some investors also use technical analysis when deciding where to invest. Technical analysis is the evaluation of charts and time series to determine the direction of an investment. A trend line is when two parallel lines can be drawn to show the general direction in which a data series is moving. In technical analysis, a saucer is when a stock has trended downward, reached the bottom, and has begun to rise. An inverted saucer is when the reverse occurs.

One of the more complex charts used in technical analysis is the head and shoulders pattern shown below:

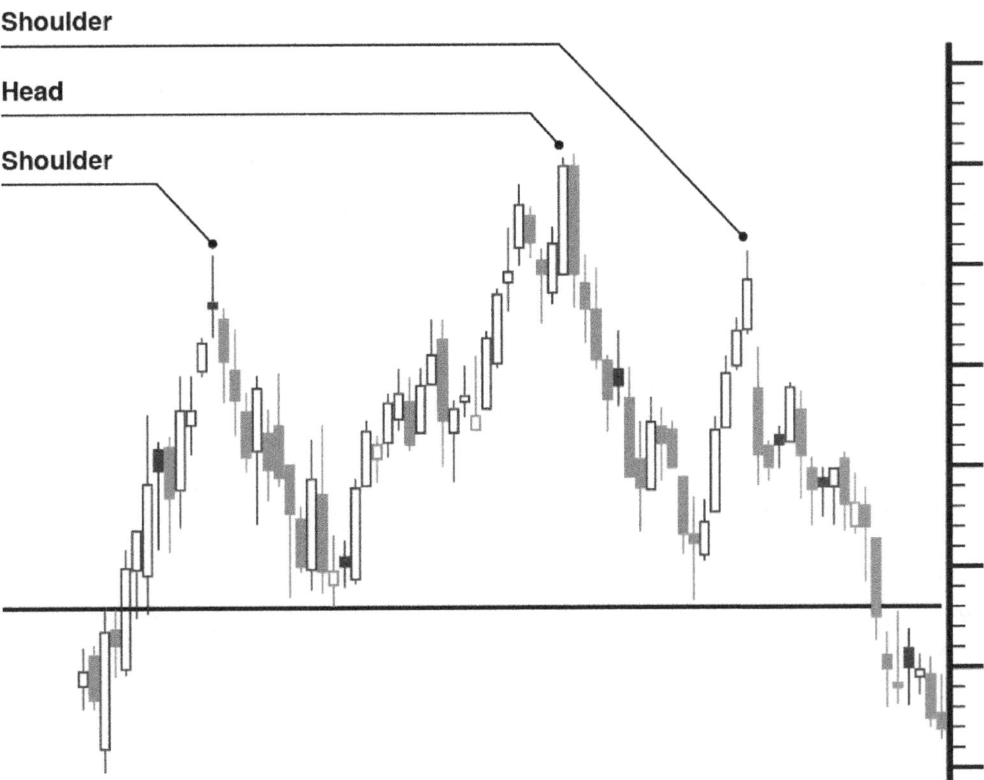

This is what's called a reversal pattern. It indicates that the security is about to reverse against the previous trend. The chart above is a head and shoulders "top" and indicates that, because the trend has breached the neckline on the lower right of the chart, the stock will continue its trend downward. This trend is also called a breakout, which is when a trend moves through a support level and indicates that the prior trend is over. Analysts also use moving averages to find subtle patterns in the price of a stock. By plotting the average price of a security over time, deviations are smoothed out in the data and trends can be uncovered that are hard to identify. Different methods and day counts can be used to calculate moving averages and uncover short- or long-term trends depending on the investor's strategy.

Support levels are another key concept of technical analysis. A support line basically establishes the bottom for a price or trend. If a stock keeps moving up and down but consistently hits a bottom of $51 dollars over a week, there's a support level of $51. Support levels can occur in trends as well. If a line can be drawn straight through a stock price's bottoms over a period of time, this is considered a support line. A support line typically indicates a buy signal for traders wishing to earn short-term profits.

A trading channel is what a stock does between the support and resistance (resistance is when the price tops out at a price that causes a consistent trend line). These channels can be flat or have trends themselves. In technical analysis, consolidation is typically a period when the direction or trend can't be determined. A smart trader will watch a consolidation pattern and won't trade the stock until a clear pattern develops.

Disclosure of Material Events

Material events are key changes made to the status of an issue or to the issuer that must be disclosed to investors when they occur. The following events are examples (but not an exhaustive list) of material events:

- Late principal and interest payments
- Defaults related to non-payment
- Draws on debt service reserves or credit enhancements not previously scheduled
- Changes in credit or liquidity providers
- Adverse tax events that affect tax-exempt status
- Changes to rights of security holders
- Defeasances
- Sale, or other change, to property securing repayment
- Bond calls and tender offers
- Rating Changes
- Failure to supply financial information as required

These disclosures are intended to assist investors in making informed decisions about their investments in municipal bonds. Material events can affect both the value of municipal bonds and/or their tax status. Material events must be disclosed within ten business days of the event. There are certain exceptions to the requirement of disclosures based on the amount of the issue, the number of investors, and the maturity period of the issue. The disclosures of material events are in addition to the required annual continuing information disclosures.

Communicating with Customers

Customer Confirmations

CBOE Rule 9.11 covers options trade confirmations. The rule specifies that the customer must receive confirmation that includes what the underlying security is, the expiration date of the contract, the exercise price, the quantity, the premium being paid or being received for writing the options contract, the broker's fee and commission, the trade date, the settlement date, and whether or not the trade was for a customer's account or with the firm's own capital.

FINRA 2232 addresses customer confirmations. 2232 simply states that customers must be notified when they have purchased an equity security that is a callable security. Most equity shares are not callable, so it should be clear to an investor when shares can be called away by the issuer if certain conditions are met.

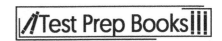

CBOE Rule 9.12 outlines what should be on a customer's statement. The statement must show the customer the value of all open positions, the margin he or she has posted, and funds due to the customer or owed by the customer. The statement should be able to tell the customer exactly what his or her financial position is with that particular account.

MSRB G-15 governs municipal bond trade confirmations. These guidelines require the customer to be notified of all parties involved with a trade and how the broker acted on his or her behalf. The principal, the agent, and any third parties must be included when notifying the customer. More traditional bond metrics must be included as well. The par value, the maturity date, the selling price, and the yield must all be included. The yield must be the lower of the call or maturity date—sometimes referred to as yield to worst.

Rule 10b-10 under the Securities & Exchange Act of 1934 covers disclosures for MBS and ABS securities. Under this rule, the date and time of the transaction must be communicated. This rule specifies that the capacity of the agent or principal must also be included. It must also clarify to the customer that the yield on the asset will be affected by the payments and prepayments on the underlying assets and loans, and it must state if the security is unrated.

Account Information

Information other than total account value that should be included on a customer account statement is purchases, sales, charges or credits, interest credits or debits, transfer activity, dividend payments, securities receipts or deliveries, and any journal entries that relate to the member's securities. Fees related and assessed on the customer's account should also be listed. Gain, or profits, and losses on the account should be displayed throughout the account statement. Both realized and unrealized gains and losses should be presented and classified as long-term or short-term depending on how long the security has been held. Realized gains are recognized when an asset is sold at a higher value than its book value. Unrealized gains are those that can be determined by examining the changes in an account, but no actual cash return has been made, usually because a profitable position has not been closed yet.

Account statements should be sent once every quarter. The statement should also advise customers how to report inaccuracies on their account or material changes in the customer's financial situation.

Withdrawals and Tenders

Broker-dealers are required to communicate with customers at or before undertaking transactions in the customer's account. Written notifications should include the date and time of the transaction. For purchases or sales of securities, the identity, price, and number of shares or units involved must all be disclosed. It should also be disclosed if the broker or dealer is acting as an agent for the customer or some other person. Transactions that include withdrawals from the account also warrant customer notification. A customer must also receive communications if there are any tender offers for any stocks or shares in their account.

There are situations when the broker-dealer can complete transactions without communicating with the customer. Usually this applies to transactions as part of a periodic plan or an investment company plan. Customers under these types of plans can request information, and such information must be provided within five business days from when the request is received.

Account Records

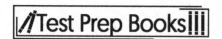

Brokers must have a system in place to maintain customer account records with a high degree of confidentiality. Sensitive information that's stored in paper files or digitally must be kept in a secure place and only be accessible by certain parties. When brokers enter into an agreement with a customer, they assume this liability and must take steps to protect all information. This includes protecting customer contact information, details about accounts, statements, disclosures, and any other information related to transactions and the relationship.

In addition to maintaining accounts with a high degree of confidentiality, it's the broker's responsibility to review customer account details regularly and ensure customers are well-informed about all changes and updates. Communicating this information to the customer by certified mail or private email may be necessary. Account maintenance tasks can include:

- Assessing a customer's changing assets
- Assessing a customer's investment objectives
- Updating a change of address
- Holding customer mail and sending notifications
- Sending notifications to inform customers of risks associated with new or existing accounts

Transferring Accounts

If the customer wants to close their account and transfer it to another broker, they must complete a broker-dealer account transfer form. This form outlines all securities held by the previous broker and the nature of the relationship. It also includes instructions for transferring the funds to the new broker-dealer. The new broker-dealer will send instructions to the previous broker who has three business days to confirm the transfer or request more information if details are missing or invalid.

The account transfer can be coordinated up to three additional business days after the account is validated. In most cases, accounts are transferred through the Automated Customer Account Transfer Service (ACATS), which requires membership in the National Securities Clearing Corporation (NSCC).

Books and Record Retention

Brokers are responsible for maintaining accurate books and records for all financial customer transactions and accounts. Under MSRB Rule G-8, brokers must maintain the following:

- Records of Original Entry: An itemized daily record of purchases and sales of municipal securities, receipts showing transactions, and receipts of cash disbursements. It should also include debits and credits associated with municipal securities transactions and any other cash receipts and disbursements.

- Account Records: Records that reflect purchases and sales of municipal securities, receipts and deliveries of municipal securities, and receipts and disbursements of cash. They also include debits and credits associated with the account.

- Securities Records: These show all positions of municipal securities separately.

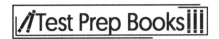

- Subsidiary Records: Records that reflect municipal securities in transfer, municipal securities to be validated, municipal securities borrowed or loaned, and any municipal securities transactions that weren't completed on the settlement date.
- Put Options and Repurchase Agreements: These are records of all written or oral options to sell municipal securities (put options) and any repurchase agreements made.
- Records for Agency Transactions: A memorandum of each agency order that includes instructions for the purchase or sale of securities, terms and conditions of the sale, and any other information related to the transaction.
- Records for Transactions as Principal: This is a memorandum of all municipal transaction securities for a given account. It includes details such as the price and date of execution, the customer's order, and any and all account designations.
- Records of Primary Offerings: Records of the description and aggregate par value of securities, terms and conditions, and all orders received for the purchase of securities by any selling group.

Brokers must also maintain copies of confirmations, periodic statements, and notices sent to customers regarding their account or account status throughout the term of their contract or relationship. Broker-dealers are also responsible for keeping a record of all complaints received from both customers and those acting on their behalf.

Account Closure Procedures

There may be situations where a customer wants to close their account. Customers need to contact their broker immediately to request an account closure and provide their account information. They must advise the broker whether they wish to have their investment holdings sold or transferred to another broker, so the funds can be managed appropriately.

The broker is responsible for closing the account within three business days of the request, and the customer must check their account after it's closed to ensure no funds remain.

Practice Questions

1. What do the horizontal and vertical axis of the capital asset pricing model (CAPM) represent?
   a. Assets, rate
   b. Equities, bonds
   c. Risk, expected return
   d. Volatility, willingness

2. Which of the following would be expected to earn a risk-free rate?
   a. Short-term treasury bonds
   b. Equities
   c. Options
   d. Commodities

3. The S&P 500 return for a time period was 7%. Maggie, a fund manager, had a benchmark in the S&P 500 that returned 9%. What was the Alpha generated?
   a. 2%
   b. -2%
   c. 14%
   d. 9%

4. What are the three areas where investment advisers should consider municipal investment diversification?
   a. Equities, bonds, money market funds
   b. Geographical, type, rating
   c. State, tax yield, government type
   d. Long-term, short-term, mid-range

5. What is the correlation between a stock and the broader market index called?
   a. Alpha
   b. Beta
   c. Delta
   d. Benchmark

6. Which of the following is an account maintenance task that a broker must perform?
   a. Assessing a customer's investment objectives
   b. Sending required disclosures
   c. Identifying employees of a broker-dealer
   d. Sharing customer contact information with other brokers

7. Mary wishes to close her account with her broker. She makes the request on May 22nd, which is a Monday. By what day must the broker close the account?
   a. May 24th
   b. May 29th
   c. May 27th
   d. May 25th

8. Account transfers between broker-dealers are typically transferred through which entity?
   a. National Securities Clearing Corporation (NSCC)
   b. Federal Deposit Insurance Corporation (FDIC)
   c. Automated Customer Account Transfer Service (ACATS)
   d. Securities and Exchange Commission (SEC)

9. Which of the following is NOT included under MSRB Rule G-8?
   a. Records of Original Entry
   b. Annual Reports
   c. Put Options and Repurchase Agreements
   d. Records of Primary Offerings

10. The ratings of a bond provided by the major rating agencies are intended to reflect which of the following?
   a. The issuer's ability to pay the interest and principal
   b. The value
   c. The price
   d. The prepayment risk

11. Research reports include which of the following?

      I. Buy, sell, and hold recommendations
      II. Price targets
      III. Strike prices for options traded on the stock being covered
      IV. The covering analyst's salary
      V. Financial ratios and other metrics

   a. I, II, and III
   b. IV and V
   c. I, II, and V
   d. I, III, and V

12. What is the highest quality rating for a municipal bond?
   a. Mig-1
   b. AAA
   c. Mig-3
   d. Buy

13. The risks associated with a callable bond include which of the following?

      I. Call risk
      II. Reinvestment risk
      III. Credit risk
      IV. Default risk

   a. I only
   b. I, II, III, and IV
   c. II, III, and IV
   d. I, III, and IV

14. By holding cash, an investor increases and decreases their exposure to which of the following risks?
   a. Reinvestment risk and currency risk
   b. Currency risk and default risk
   c. Credit risk and capital risk
   d. Inflation risk and capital risk

15. Which of the following types of risk occurs when an asset can't be sold quickly enough for the security's value to be affected by the trade?
   a. Liquidity risk
   b. Credit risk
   c. Price risk
   d. Prepayment risk

16. Which of the following are examples of political risk?

      I. A new law forces a company to change the way it does business
      II. A currency fluctuates in value
      III. A regulator requires banks to change the way they market loans to customers
      IV. A CEO launders money from the company

   a. I, II, and III
   b. III and IV
   c. I and III
   d. II and IV

17. If a bond is trading above its par value, then the coupon yield will be which of the following?
   a. Negative
   b. What the return of the bond is
   c. Less than the bond yield
   d. Greater than the bond yield

18. Which of the following is an example of return of capital?
   a. When a stock goes from $100 to $150
   b. The amortization of a bond
   c. When a stock pays a dividend of 10%
   d. When a bond makes a coupon payment

19. An arbitrage short selling strategy occurs in which of the following situations?
   a. When an investor owns shares and wants to protect his or her return in case the stock declines in value
   b. When the investor does not own shares and short sells a stock because he or she feels it is overvalued
   c. When the investor uses a straddle
   d. When the investor wants to take advantage of pricing differences in different markets

20. Which of the following is one of the advantages of soft dollar pricing?
    a. It makes markets more competitive and improves pricing efficiency.
    b. It reduces the risk of insider trading.
    c. It does not have to be disclosed.
    d. It can be easily measured.

21. According to MSRB G-15, the yield that must be provided on the customer's written materials is which of the following?
    a. The current yield
    b. The yield to worst
    c. The yield on the par value
    d. The yield to maturity

22. Which of the following may affect the yield on an ABS or MBS?
    a. The trustee's decision on what the yield is
    b. The callability of the securities
    c. Defaults and prepayments on the underlying assets
    d. Their equity value

23. A mutual fund that invests in publicly traded shares of traditional banks would be considered an investment in what?
    a. Money markets, because banks include their short-term loans in money market funds
    b. Foreign currency markets
    c. Capital markets
    d. The bank lending market

24. What is sovereign debt?
    a. Debt issued by companies outside of the U.S.
    b. Debt issued by federal governments
    c. Debt issued by the SEC
    d. Mortgage bonds in a foreign currency

25. Which of these securities is tied to an equity index but guarantees the preservation of the principal invested?
    a. ETFs
    b. ETNs
    c. ELKs
    d. Equity options

26. What are convertible preferred shares?
    a. Shares that convert to debt
    b. Preferred equity that can be converted to common stock
    c. Common stock that can convert to preferred shares
    d. Debt that can be called by the issuing company

27. Which of the following is NOT a rule of an auction market?
    a. All transactions are secret.
    b. The first bid has priority.
    c. Bids and offers must be audible.
    d. New bids are entered when all bids at a certain price have been exhausted.

28. What is the primary market for GSEs?
    a. When the GSE packages the loan
    b. When the originating bank sells the loans to a GSE
    c. When the loan is originated by the commercial bank
    d. When a mutual fund buys the MBS (mortgage-backed security) from the GSE

29. What are the purposes of dark pools?
    a. To prevent downward surges in the market when large blocks of shares are sold
    b. To increase transaction costs for investors
    c. To prevent investors from realizing what they are buying
    d. To allow for smaller increments of trading shares

30. Which of these describes a feature of MOST municipal bonds?
    a. Higher than a comparable high yield bond
    b. Lower than the yield on a comparable corporate bond
    c. Lower than the yield on commercial paper
    d. Negative

31. What is the role of Electronic Communication Networks (ECNs)?
    a. To measure volume of shares traded in exchanges, such as the NYSE
    b. Produce technical charts that are used by analysts to predict market moves
    c. Regulate hedge funds by requiring them to file electronic notices with a network
    d. Facilitate direct trading for investors in an electronic manner outside of the regulated exchanges

32. Which of the following is true about income statements?
    a. It represents changes in the balance sheet.
    b. It lists assets and liabilities.
    c. It calculates a net profit.
    d. It accounts for inventory.

33. What is the complex chart used in technical analysis to examine trends?
    a. Put/Call ratio
    b. Head and shoulders pattern
    c. Moving averages
    d. Breakout

34. EBITDA is useful for measuring and comparing which of the following?
    a. Companies with different tax jurisdictions, debt levels, and methods of accounting for depreciation
    b. Small companies versus very large companies
    c. The cash flow that is needed to fund capital expenditures
    d. The leverage a company employs to produce its net income results.

35. In technical analysis, what is a resistance level?
    a. The average level a stock has traded at in the past 52 weeks
    b. The difference between the highest and lowest point a stock has traded at in the past 52 weeks
    c. The level the stock has traded up to, but not through, multiple times in a short-time period
    d. The point on the chart of a stock that forms the second shoulder in the bearish head and shoulders pattern

36. What is the volume of a stock?
   a. The standard deviation in the bid and ask price over the past 52 weeks
   b. The standard deviation in the stock's 52-week trading range
   c. The number of shares of a particular stock outstanding and not owned by company insiders
   d. The number of shares being traded over a given timeframe

37. Which of the following produces data that advisors can use to analyze financial markets?
   a. Conference Board of Customer Confidence
   b. Minnesota Consumer Sentiment Index
   c. Federal Reserve
   d. The NYSE Volatility Index

38. Which of the following is true of the yield curve?
   a. The yield curve is a predictor of expansion.
   b. The yield curve is part of the index of leading indicators.
   c. The yield curve becomes peaked to indicate a recession.
   d. The yield curve typically has a downward slope.

39. What establishes the bottom for a price or trend?
   a. Reversal pattern
   b. Support line
   c. Inverted saucer
   d. Trading channel

40. Which of the following is NOT one of the sections of the cash flow statement?
   a. Investing
   b. Operating
   c. Financing
   d. Purchasing

41. A company uses the straight-line depreciation method and would like to depreciate a tractor that was recently purchased for $45,000. The salvage value is $6,000, and the useful life is 15 years. What is the depreciation expense?
   a. $3,400
   b. $2,700
   c. $3,000
   d. $2,600

42. Which of the following ratios helps an investor determine how well a company generates cash?
   a. Inventory turnover
   b. Quick ratio
   c. Debt-to-equity ratio
   d. Earnings per share

43. What components are needed to calculate the DuPont identity?
   a. Earnings, Share price, Dividends
   b. Depreciation, Interest, Amortization, Taxes
   c. Net income, Sales, Assets, Equity
   d. Inventory, Liabilities, Debt, Net Sales

44. Of the following securities in a corporation's capital structure, which one has the least credit risk?
   a. Preferred stock
   b. AA-Rated debt
   c. High-yield debt
   d. Commercial paper

45. At the end of the second quarter, if a company has a stock price of $10 and pays a dividend of $0.50 (and has been paying a dividend on a quarterly basis), what is the annualized dividend yield?
   a. 5%
   b. 0.5%
   c. 10%
   d. 20%

46. A company's earnings over the calendar year are $100 million, and the company has 10 million outstanding shares. At the end of the year the company pays a quarterly dividend of $1 per share. What is the annualized dividend payout ratio?
   a. 10%
   b. 40%
   c. 1%
   d. 4%

47. If a company does a reverse stock split for 30,000 outstanding shares trading at $10 per share, what is the market value of the shares at the time of the split?
   a. $60,000
   b. $600,000
   c. $300,000
   d. $150,000

48. A company posts Earnings per Share (EPS) of $2.50 for the full year of 2015. It has 100,000 outstanding shares on December 30, 2015, but the company issues 15,000 shares on December 31, 2015. What is the new EPS if no averaging is needed for the calculation?
   a. $2.50
   b. $2.17
   c. $2.94
   d. $16.67

49. An investor wants to receive some income on their investments without significant price volatility but doesn't want to lose purchasing power from inflation. What type of investment should they make?
   a. Penny stocks
   b. Treasury bonds
   c. Corporate bonds
   d. High-yield bonds

50. What can a company do to reduce its leverage?
   a. Issue bonds and repurchase stock.
   b. Split the stock.
   c. Issue new stock and call their existing debt.
   d. Borrow short-term commercial paper.

51. Which instrument will most likely pay the highest rate of interest?
   a. Short-term commercial paper
   b. Short-term asset-backed securities
   c. Medium-term Treasury notes
   d. Long-term corporate bonds

52. A company has 10,000 shares of Treasury stock and 40,000 shares of outstanding common stock. The company pays a dividend of $90,000. What's the dividend per share?
   a. $1.80
   b. $2.25
   c. $3.00
   d. $0.56

53. If a company believes interest rates will rise significantly, which of the following would be a smart strategy?
   a. Issue floating rate debt.
   b. Repurchase company stock.
   c. Issue long-term fixed-rate debt.
   d. Borrow using short-term commercial paper.

54. Which category below is NOT a common stockholder right?
   a. The right to inspect financial records, systems, and bookkeeping of a corporation
   b. The right to evaluate the assets of a corporation
   c. The right to call and reissue shares at a specified price
   d. The right to receive an equal share of dividends (i.e., pro rata dividends)

55. What are American Depositary Receipts (ADRs)?
   a. Shares of U.S. companies sold on foreign stock markets
   b. Deposits similar to CDs
   c. Shares of foreign companies purchased in the U.S. without having to go through foreign stock exchanges
   d. Stock receipts allowing for the purchase of additional shares

56. What is a fund that accrues a balance for the future redemption of a callable bond by a corporation?
   a. Mutual fund
   b. Money market fund
   c. Sinking fund
   d. Bond fund

57. A rights offering allows which of the following?
   a. A stock issuer to call the stock back for reissuance.
   b. An investor to retire shares when they want.
   c. An existing shareholder to purchase shares at a discount.
   d. A bond holder the right to receive stock dividends.

58. The wash sale rule applies to which of the following actions?
   a. Rolling a put forward with the same strike price
   b. Rolling a call forward with a different strike price
   c. Selling an investment for a loss and repurchasing a substantially similar investment within 30 days
   d. Municipal bond issuers refunding existing bonds with new ones at a lower interest rate

59. If a bond has a par value of $1,000 and the conversion ratio is 20, what is the conversion price of the bond?
   a. $50
   b. $100
   c. $20
   d. $10

60. What's the spread between a 10-year Treasury bond yielding 4.8% and a Treasury note yielding 4.2%?
   a. 4.4%
   b. 0.6%
   c. 1.14%
   d. 1.0%

61. If a bond's duration is 2, what will happen when interest rates rise by 2%?
   a. The bond will double in value.
   b. The bond's value will rise by 4%.
   c. The bond's value will fall by 2%.
   d. The bond's value will fall by 4%.

62. What's the tax-equivalent yield on a municipal bond with a tax-exempt yield of 8% for an individual with a marginal tax rate of 25%?
   a. 2.0%
   b. 6.0%
   c. 0.02%
   d. 10.7%

63. What's the current yield of a bond with a par value of $1,000, a coupon rate of 7%, and a market value of $1,150?
   a. 70%
   b. 7.0%
   c. 6.1%
   d. 11.5%

64. If a callable bond has a yield to maturity of 4.5%, a yield to call of 4.2%, and a coupon rate of 5%, what is the yield to worst?
   a. 4.5%
   b. 4.3%
   c. 4.2%
   d. 5.0%

65. If a bond has a coupon rate of 5% and a current yield of 7%, what is the bond's price in relation to its par value?
   a. The price is at par value.
   b. The price is below the par value.
   c. The par value is below the price.
   d. The price is above the par value.

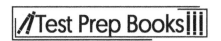

66. What type of security is typically assumed to have no credit risk (i.e., the probability that the full principal will not be repaid is 0%)?
   a. Municipal bonds
   b. Asset-backed securities
   c. Corporate bonds
   d. Treasury bonds

67. If there are two bonds with the same credit risk, the same coupon rate of 5%, and the same maturity date, but one of them has an adjustable interest rate that resets each quarter to the current 10-year Treasury rate, what happens to the two prices of the bonds if the Treasury rate increases by 2%?
   a. Both bonds will increase in value.
   b. Only the adjustable rate bond will increase in value.
   c. The fixed rate bond will decrease in value, but the adjustable rate bond's price shouldn't change by much.
   d. The coupon rate will increase by 2% on both bonds.

68. Which best describes how a puttable bond works?
   a. It grants the issuer the obligation to "put" bonds back to the investor at a lower rate.
   b. It grants the issuer the right to change the rate on the bonds they've issued.
   c. It grants the investor the right to "put" the bonds back to the issuer.
   d. It ensures that the corporation can no longer issue new debt.

69. Which of these is NOT a government-sponsored entity (GSE)?
   a. Securities and Exchange Commission
   b. Freddie Mac
   c. Fannie Mae
   d. Ginnie Mae

70. Zero-coupon Treasury bonds shield investors from which of the following?
   a. Inflation risk
   b. Price risk
   c. Reinvestment risk
   d. Foreign exchange risk

71. Which category below is NOT a part of the credit analysis done by rating agencies for municipal bonds?
   a. The analysis of the ability of the municipality to budget
   b. The analysis of the availability of tax revenue
   c. An analysis of the municipality's population
   d. An analysis of that municipality's economic climate

72. Bonds with an A rating can be described as which of the following?
   a. In default
   b. Having many positive investment qualities
   c. Having speculative fundamentals
   d. Bonds of the highest quality with the lowest risk

73. What is the trade medium used by open-end investment companies?
  a. The New York Stock Exchange
  b. NASDAQ
  c. Over the counter
  d. London Stock Exchange

74. If a mutual fund has a public offering price of 32.56 and a net asset value of 27.18, what is the sales charge?
  a. 19.7%
  b.18.3%
  c. 16.5%
  d. 5.4%

75. Which of the following are taxed at the ordinary income tax rate?
    I. Shares sold after being held for one year
    II. Interest on municipal bonds
    III. Short-term gains on stocks held for less than one year
    IV. Gains due to investing in a foreign currency

  a. III and IV
  b. I and II
  c. II and III
  d. I and IV

76. How are closed-end funds similar to stocks?
  a. They have a CEO and board of directors.
  b. Capital is raised through an IPO.
  c. They file a quarterly 10-Q.
  d. They issue convertible debt.

77. To maintain their tax-free status, closed-end funds must distribute what percent of their income from dividends and interest to investors and what percent of capitalized gains?
  a. 98% of income and 90% of capital gains
  b. 50% of income and capital gains
  c. 98% of income and capital gains
  d. 90% of income and 98% of capital gains

78. How are the deferred sales charges on unit investment trusts paid?
  a. Upon trust liquidation
  b. Annually
  c. Monthly
  d. Up front

79. Which of the below items are examples of riders on variable-annuity contracts?

I. A cost-of-living adjustment
II. A lump-sum payment of principal
III. A positive covenant
IV. A negative covenant

a. I and II
b. III and IV
c. I and III
d. II and IV

80. What does taxation on a LIFO basis mean?

a. Earnings are taxed as ordinary income and any amount over that is taxed from principal.
b. Earnings are taxed as ordinary income and any amount over that is taken from principal and not taxed.
c. Earnings are taxed at the short-term rate and capital gains at the long-term rate.
d. Stocks held less than one year are taxed at the ordinary rate.

81. In reference to REITs, what does DRIP stand for?

a. Dividend repurchase insurance program
b. Divisible retained income purchase
c. Division real estate income plan
d. Dividend reinvestment program

82. Which of the following is the correct sequence when investing in REITs?

I. Rental income is paid to the REIT
II. Investors buy shares
III. Distributions to investors
IV. Acquisitions and capital investment

a. I, III, II, and IV
b. IV, III, I, and II
c. II, I, IV, and III
d. II, IV, I, and III

83. What percentage of income are REITs required to distribute in order to maintain their REIT status?

a. 90%
b. 98%
c. 10%
d. None

84. What is the rate at which qualified dividends are taxed?

a. Short-term rate
b. Long-term capital gains rate
c. Marginal tax rate
d. Ordinary rate

85. What do direct participation programs (DPPs) typically invest in?
a. Real estate, futures, and mutual funds
b. Other private-equity funds
c. Real estate, energy, futures/options, and equipment leases
d. Commercial paper, short-term treasury bonds, and other short-term debt

86. What is the primary risk of DPP land investments?
a. That the land will have unusable oil reserves
b. That taxes on the land will go up
c. That they won't be able to get permits to develop the land
d. That they don't produce any income so the only way to profit is if the value of the land appreciates

87. Which of the following investor information is an inclusion in a DPP subscription agreement?
a. Net worth, income as well as a clear explanation of the risks involved with the partnership
b. Income and tax bill
c. Medical history and criminal record
d. Personal debt and college education

88. Under the Investment Company Act of 1940 Rule 3c1, which of the following would violate the tax-exemption status of a hedge fund?
a. Retain more than 10% of its income
b. Have more than one hundred beneficial shareholders
c. Distribute more than 98% of capital gains
d. Have more than one hundred pension funds investing in their shares

89. Which of the following describes a hedge fund that invests in high-yield debt that has not paid interest in two quarters?
a. Long-short fund
b. Arbitrage fund
c. Distressed fund
d. Global-strategy fund

90. Which of the following is NOT a structured product?
a. CDO
b. CMO
c. ABS
d. Stocks

91. Which of the following represents the investment of a hybrid REIT?
a. Real estate and technology companies
b. Traditional real estate and hedge funds
c. Mortgage debt and commercial properties
d. Convertible bonds and DPPs

92. Where can a listing of expenses and costs be found for unit investment trusts?
a. Their prospectus
b. Their annual report
c. Their 10K filing
d. Through brokers

93. Which of the following is a reason why variable annuities are considered variable?
   a. They may only be offered at certain times of the year.
   b. They vary in the way the contract is written.
   c. They only have tax advantages under certain political administrations.
   d. They have a variable return component that is linked to a portfolio or index.

94. Which of the following is a lock-up provision as it applies to investing in hedge funds?
   a. A period of time that investors cannot withdraw their money
   b. The average duration of the fixed income investments the hedge fund holds
   c. The period of time that the hedge fund has been under investigation by the SEC and cannot perform all of the trades it would like
   d. A period of time that investors can withdraw money, and after the lock-up expires, they will no longer be able to do so

95. What is the primary difference between closed-end mutual funds and open-ended ones?
   a. Closed-end funds are limited to 10 investors.
   b. Closed-end funds do not raise or accept new capital contributions after their IPO.
   c. Closed-end funds invest in fixed income securities while open-ended mutual funds only invest in stocks and ETFs.
   d. Closed-end funds have a different tax treatment of their dividends and returns of capital.

96. When an investor contributes to his or her variable annuity contract, which of the following represents the ownership or value he or she has purchased?
   a. The surrender value of his or her policy
   b. Accumulation units
   c. The rights of value
   d. The implied interest rate

97. Which of the following is an example of a direct participation program (DPP)?
   a. Oil and gas
   b. Leveraged buyouts
   c. Private equity
   d. LIBOR shorting

98. Which of the following will increase the value of a call option?
      I. An increase in the volatility of the underlying asset
      II. A decline in the price of the underlying asset
      III. An increase in the price of the underlying asset
      IV. A decrease in a comparable put option (assuming the discount factor, the forward price, and the strike price in the put-call parity equation are unchanged)

   a. I, III, and IV
   b. I and III
   c. II and IV
   d. I and II

99. When is a *long straddle* most effective?
    a. When markets become volatile
    b. When markets move sideways
    c. When trading volume is low
    d. When volatility is low

100. When does an option writer profit?
    a. When an option is in the money (ITM)
    b. When an option does not reach its strike price
    c. When volatility of the underlying asset increases
    d. When a put exceeds its strike price and a call option does not

101. Assume an American and European option have the same strike price and maturity on the same asset. Which of the following represents the value of these options?
    a. Different in value. The America option is more valuable because it can be exercised at any time before expiration if it is in the money (ITM).
    b. Different in value. The European option will be more valuable because it can only be exercised at expiration.
    c. Equal in value
    d. It depends on the volatility of the underlying asset.

102. When do LEAPS expire?
    a. On a monthly basis
    b. Every two years
    c. The last day of the year
    d. The third Friday of every January

103. Which of the following is NOT a way that an open position in an option can end?
    a. It can be exercised once reaching the strike price.
    b. It can expire worthless by not reaching the strike price.
    c. The buyer of the option can back out of the contract.
    d. An offsetting transaction can be entered so there is zero risk in the position.

104. Which of the following rights are given to the buyer when a put option is purchased?
    a. "Put" the underlying asset to the option buyer at a specified price
    b. "Put" the underlying asset to the option writer at a specified price
    c. Sell the stock short
    d. Buy the asset at the strike price

105. When does an options assignment occur?
    a. When the investor makes the decision to exercise and notifies the broker
    b. When the writer of the contract is assigned the premium
    c. When calls and puts are assigned to a stock
    d. When an analyst is assigned an options industry to cover

106. Which of the following comprise an option's total value?

I. Intrinsic value
II. Exercise price
III. Time value
IV. Strike price

a. I and II
b. II and IV
c. II and III
d. I and III

107. Which of the following is measured by open interest?
a. Value
b. Liquidity
c. Trend
d. Volatility

108. Which of the following is true about the volatility of the underlying assets in options markets and the value of those options?
a. They are negatively correlated.
b. They are inversely correlated.
c. They are positively correlated.
d. They have no correlation, which makes them a good hedging instrument.

109. Which of the following will require an adjustment in options?

I. Stock splits, mergers, and acquisitions.
II. Earnings falling short of expectations
III. Split offs and spinoffs
IV. The stock of the underlying asset falls to zero
V. Extraordinary dividends

a. I, III, and V
b. I, II, and III
c. IV and V
d. II, IV, and V

110. According to Federal Reserve Regulation T, what is the required amount of collateral to trade options?
a. 25% of the amount borrowed to trade
b. 75% of the position's market value
c. 10% of the trade's value
d. 50% of any amount borrowed

111. When does covered option writing and buying occur?
a. When the investor can cover his or her position with cash
b. When the investor owns the underlying asset
c. When the broker can cover the margin call
d. When margin call occurs

112. What is the maximum possible loss a buyer could experience with a put or call option?
   a. The price of the underlying asset times the buyer's position
   b. The risk-free rate of return
   c. The premium the buyer has paid to enter the position
   d. The buyer's loss potential is unlimited

113. What is the largest securities market in the world?
   a. The New York Stock Exchange
   b. The NASDAQ
   c. The market for U.S. treasuries
   d. The derivatives market

114. The repurchase (or repo) market is mostly made up of what type of securities?
   a. Stocks
   b. Corporate bonds
   c. Derivatives
   d. Government securities

115. What type of stock represents the total number of shares ever issued?
   a. Authorized stock
   b. Outstanding Stock
   c. Treasury Stock
   d. Issued Stock

116. What guarantees that an underlying security is held by a bank or exchange and ensures the delivery of the physical asset?
   a. Stock certificate
   b. Endorsement
   c. Holding statement
   d. Escrow receipt

117. Which of the following is NOT a method used to determine cost basis of shares being sold?
   a. Market value
   b. Last in, first out (LIFO)
   c. First in, first out (FIFO)
   d. Identified shares

118. Which of the following is true concerning exchange traded funds (ETFs)?
   a. They typically trade in 100,000 share blocks.
   b. They are highly liquid.
   c. They can only consist of value companies.
   d. They are not permitted in Roth IRA accounts.

119. A mutual fund charges a contingent deferred load charge of 3%. The investor withdraws $12,000 from the mutual fund. What is the amount the investor will receive?
   a. $360
   b. $12,360
   c. $11,640
   d. $8,400

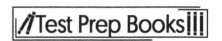

120. Which of these is a fee associated with mutual funds?
   a. Inception fee
   b. Creation fee
   c. Redemption fee
   d. Trading fee

121. Which feature of mutual funds allows investors to exchange shares of the same fund family without incurring a transaction fee?
   a. Exchange Privilege Option
   b. Rights of Accumulation
   c. Rights of Exchange
   d. Transaction Exchange Option

122. Susan is 52 years old. She plans to withdraw funds from her variable annuity to pay for her summer vacation which is going to cost $15,000. What will her penalty be if the full withdrawal is taxable?
   a. $0
   b. $1,500
   c. $750
   d. $1,000

123. What is an option series?
   a. All the options tied to a particular stock or index
   b. A subset of an option class that has the same strike price and expiration date
   c. The time by which the option can be exercised
   d. What determines the amount of the underlying asset attached to some options contracts

124. Which type of debt security is not registered with the SEC and pays principal and interest in U.S. dollars held in banks outside of the U.S.?
   a. Brokered CDs
   b. Commercial paper
   c. Eurodollar bonds
   d. Sovereign debt

125. Which of the following are the riskiest bonds in a corporation's capital structure?
   a. Debenture bonds
   b. Step-up bonds
   c. High-yield bonds
   d. Zero-coupon bonds

126. Which of the following is a factor to consider before investing in a general obligation (GO) municipal bond?
   a. Legal factors
   b. Demographic information
   c. Environmental issues
   d. Operational factors

127. Which of the following is NOT a type of municipal bond?
   a. Special tax bond
   b. Revenue anticipation note
   c. Tax-exempt commercial paper

d. Collateralized debt obligation (CDO)

128. What is the primary instrument used by the Federal Open Market Committee (FOMC) to regulate the supply of money?
a. Treasury bonds
b. Treasury bills
c. Treasury notes
d. Zero-coupon bonds

129. What is the breakeven rate?
a. When an investor receives a return of capital plus enough of a profit to recoup transaction fees
b. The difference between an investment's lowest current offering price and the higher price the dealer will charge an investor
c. When a broker receives a customer order and executes the trade with another broker
d. The net yield on a taxable bond that is equal to the risk of the bond

130. Which of the following must be included on a customer statement?
a. Settlement date
b. Exercise price
c. Value of all open positions
d. Expiration date of the contract

131. What are records that reflect municipal securities in transfer, to be validated, or loaned?
a. Securities Records
b. Records for Agency Transactions
c. Subsidiary Records
d. Records for Transactions as Principal

132. Jason receives stock as a gift from his grandmother. At what value will it be taxed?
a. Current fair market value
b. His grandmother's basis
c. The average value
d. The fair market value 3 business days after the transaction

133. Which fee is an operating fee charged by a mutual fund that is considered an operating expense?
a. Soft dollar fee
b. Non-discretionary fee
c. Surrender fee
d. 12b-1 fee

134. Which of the following is NOT typically included in the statement of additional information?
a. Earnings information
b. Fund policies
c. Investment advisory functions
d. Tax information

135. Which of the following occurs when a bond is redeemed early because there is no longer a source of revenue to pay the interest?
   a. Refunding
   b. Bond indenture
   c. Extraordinary call
   d. Partial call

136. What are the two components of an option premium?
   a. Asset value and volatility
   b. Intrinsic value and time value
   c. Exercise price and time to expiration
   d. Residual income and strike price

137. Which of the following is a fund that invests in securities that pay a consistent dividend?
   a. Value fund
   b. Income fund
   c. Growth fund
   d. Balanced fund

138. Which of the following can be used to adjust asset allocation?
   a. Classes of securities, sectors, and geographical areas
   b. Securities with different standard deviations and variance of returns
   c. Tax-sheltered accounts, taxable account, and tax-exempt accounts
   d. Stocks, bonds, cash, and real estate

139. Which term describes the tendency of a security or index toward highs and lows?
   a. Volatility
   b. Concentration
   c. Diversification
   d. Correlation

140. Which type of debt is backed by collateral?
   a. Secured
   b. Unsecured
   c. Subordinated
   d. Ranked

141. Which of the following is a benefit to investing in debt securities?
   a. Company profits raise the value of the investment.
   b. Investments can be redeemed by investors before their maturity date.
   c. Fluctuations in the market do not affect the interest rate on debt securities.
   d. Companies must repay debt securities even if they go bankrupt.

142. Which term refers to a portion of a CMO categorized by level of risk?
   a. Cash flow
   b. Distributions
   c. Rate of return
   d. Tranche

143. Nearly half of the mortgages bundled together for a CMO are in default. The CMO is unable to make payments to its investors. What type of risk does this illustrate?

a. Liquidity risk
b. Reinvestment risk
c. Credit risk
d. Timing risk

144. Which of the following is a characteristic of a senior tranche in a CDO?

a. Higher coupon rate
b. Higher credit rating
c. Higher default risk
d. Higher number of loans

145. What is one incentive for banks to offer CDOs?

a. To provide a product that doesn't require collateral
b. To offer investments that specialize in one type of loan
c. To move the risk of default on loans to investors
d. To provide a simple type of investment

146. Which of the following could NOT be used as collateral for an ABS?

a. Mortgages
b. Corporate debt
c. Student loans
d. Physical property

147. Which of the following enables the transferring of ownership of assets so that the assets can be packaged and offered to investors?

a. Securitization
b. Indenture
c. Convertible options
d. Accrued interest

148. What is one main difference between federal government agency bonds and government-sponsored enterprise (GSE) bonds?

a. The minimum investment
b. The coupon rate
c. The guarantee
d. The maturity range

149. Joan invests in an agency bond that has a rate tied to the London Interbank Offered Rate (LIBOR). Which type of bond is this?

a. Disco
b. Floater
c. Treasury
d. GSE

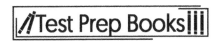

150. Which of the following is NOT a material event that must be disclosed to municipal bond investors?
   a. A defeasance
   b. Issuance of a research report
   c. A tender offer
   d. An adverse tax event

151. Which statement about material events is true?
   a. Material events disclosures are the only disclosures required to be sent to municipal investors.
   b. Material events must be disclosed within fifteen business day of the event.
   c. Material events must be disclosed for every municipal bond issue.
   d. Material events are significant changes to key features of municipal bonds.

152. Which statement about municipal bond trade confirmations is true?
   a. Municipal bond trade confirmations must list all parties involved with a trade.
   b. Municipal bond trade confirmations must show the margin posted.
   c. Municipal bond trade confirmations must describe the customer's financial position.
   d. Municipal bond trade confirmations must include the capacity of the agent or principal.

153. Derek has a stock position with an increase in capital gains, but it has not been closed. How is this type of gain classified?
   a. Recognized gain
   b. Realized gain
   c. Unrealized gain
   d. Open gain

154. When is it NOT necessary to communicate with a customer when undertaking a transaction?
   a. When the customer has requested not to receive notifications
   b. When the broker is acting as an agent on behalf of the customer
   c. When the transaction includes a withdrawal
   d. When the transaction is completed in accordance with a periodic plan

Answer Explanations

1. C: The vertical axis of the CAPM represents the expected return given the amount of volatility, or risk, they are willing to accept which represents the horizontal axis.

2. A: Short-term treasury bonds and highly rated money market funds would be expected to earn a risk-free rate. Equities, options, and commodities experience more volatility in their returns.

3. A: The Alpha is the excess return that fund managers generate against an index benchmark. The Alpha is the return of the fund manager minus the return of the selected index:

$$9\% - 7\% = 2\%$$

4. B: It is important to diversify municipal investments by geography, type, and rating.

5. B: The relationship or correlation between a stock and the broader market index is called the Beta. The Alpha is excess return over an index that is serving as a benchmark. Delta references a change, for example, a change in price.

6. A: Assessing a customer's investment objectives is one of the tasks that brokers must do to maintain a customer's account. Sending required disclosures and identifying employees of a broker-dealer are tasks that should be done when opening an account not during maintenance. Brokers should not share a customer's contact information with other brokers; this information should be protected along with other sensitive client information.

7. D: A broker has three business days to close the account. Three days past May 22nd is May 25th. The other choices do not reflect the three-day rule.

8. C: The Automated Customer Account Transfer Service (ACATS) is the entity that facilitates account transfers between broker-dealers. The ACATS requires membership in the NSCC. The NSCC is regulated by the SEC. The FDIC is not relevant to account transfers between broker-dealers.

9. B: MSRB Rule G-8 describes those records that must be maintained including records of original entry, account records, securities records, subsidiary records, put options and repurchase agreements, records for agency transactions, records for transaction as principal, and records of primary offerings. Annual reports can be furnished to customers along with notices of other corporate actions.

10. A: A bond rating reflects the issuer's ability to pay interest and principal on its outstanding debt. The rating has nothing to do with a bond's value, price, or prepayment risk.

11. C: The analyst's opinion on whether to buy, sell, or hold will be included. Most analysts include a price target as well. Financial ratios and other metrics are included to support the investor's opinion. Information about options traded on the security and the analyst's salary are not included in the report.

12. A: Mig-1 represents the highest rating for a municipal bond (Mig-3 is the lowest rating (adequate) for municipals). AAA is a corporate bond rating and a buy is a recommendation on a stock, not a municipal bond.

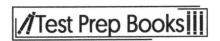

13. B: Although call risk is the risk most associated with a callable bond, callable bonds also have reinvestment risk if the bond is called. They also have credit risk, as there is the possibility that the bonds can go into default and payments will need to be made to the investor.

14. D: By holding cash, investors expose themselves to the risk that inflation will erode the purchasing power of their cash. They have no exposure to capital risk, because cash carries no risk of losing its principal value.

15. A: This situation poses a liquidity risk. If an asset requires a significant reduction in price in order to be sold, the asset or security is said to be illiquid. Credit risk refers to the risk that a borrower cannot pay the interest or principal on debt. Price risk is the risk incurred when a security is purchased that fluctuates in value. Prepayment risk is the risk that a loan will be paid back before its scheduled maturity.

16. C: The introduction of laws and regulations poses a political risk outside of the course of normal business. Currency fluctuations are simply currency risk that investors incur when they invest internationally. The risk of a CEO laundering money is business risk.

17. D: If a bond has a par value of $100 and pays an annual coupon of $5, the coupon yield is 5%. If the bond's value goes up to $120, the bond yield is $5/$120 = 4.2%, which is less than the coupon yield.

18. B: Amortization is when portions of the principal are paid back, which is return of capital. The appreciation of a stock's value, dividends, and interest payments are returns on capital.

19. D: Arbitrage is when an investor wants to sell shares short in a market that has advantageous pricing from a different market. When an investor owns shares and wants to protect himself or herself through short selling, this is known as hedging. Short selling without owning the stock is known as speculation. A straddle uses options, not short selling.

20. A: Soft dollars are thought to make markets more competitive and make pricing more efficient. They do not reduce the risk of insider trading, and they are required to be disclosed. Soft dollars are not as easily measured as regular broker and trading fees.

21. B: The yield to worst must be reported. The current yield, the par value yield, and the yield to maturity may all be overstating the yield if the bond is called.

22. C: The performance of the underlying assets will directly affect the yield the investor receives. MBS and ABS are not callable securities. The trustee cannot change how the payments are passed through—the prospectus outlines how this will happen. MBS and ABS do not have an equity value.

23. C: Just because the investment is in the equity of banks doesn't mean it is not a capital market investment. Investing in the money markets would involve investing capital directly into a money market account. The foreign currency market involves owning options on currency movement or the actual foreign currency itself. The bank lending market is used by banks to trade with other banks and the central bank.

24. B: Debt issued by foreign companies is not considered sovereign debt. The SEC does not issue debt of its own. Mortgage bonds in a foreign country are just an international form of MBS bonds.

25. C: ELKs have their return tied to the performance of an equity index but only provide a percent of the gains or are capped. They guarantee the return of principal. ETNs are an unsecured, unsubordinated debt instrument that does not guarantee the return of principal. ETFs are simply baskets of stocks, so their value fluctuates with the value of those securities. Equity options do not guarantee the repayment of principal and are in fact highly risky as all of that investment can be lost due to the volatility and risk inherent in using options.

26. B: Equity shares can't convert to debt in most cases. Convertible preferred equity are shares that can convert to common stock. Common stock normally can't convert to preferred shares. *Choice* D is referred to as a callable bond.

27. A: None of the transactions in an auction market can be secret. The first bid does have priority. Bids and offers must be audible. New bids occur when all have been exhausted.

28. C: The GSE packages or securitizes the loan before it can be traded on the secondary market. The originating bank sells the loans just after the primary market transaction has happened. The trading of MBSs occurs on the secondary market.

29. A: Dark pools prevent investors from panicking and selling shares when they see a large block of shares of a company being sold on the open market. Dark pools reduce transaction costs. Though dark pools are less transparent, investors still know what company they are buying. Dark pools allow for the trading of large blocks of shares, not smaller.

30. B: A municipal bond will have a lower yield than a corporate bond because it is usually tax free. Municipal bonds typically won't have higher yields than high yield bonds, as they are backed by the tax revenue of the issuer. Municipal bonds yield more than commercial paper because they are longer-term instruments. Yields on bonds are almost never negative. The one situation where a municipal bond may have a higher interest rate than a nonmunicipal bond is when the municipality has defaulted recently or is considered at serious risk of default. The laws governing how and if the municipality can restructure or declare bankruptcy also play a factor in determining the interest rate of municipal bonds that appear risky.

31. D: ECNs are computer systems that facilitate trading between investors and brokers outside of the regulated exchanges, both during and after regular trading hours. All ECNs are required to register with the SEC. ECNs may interact with the market makers on the exchanges and even with other ECNs to increase the likelihood of orders being filled. Some ECNs may be closed and only used for investors to trade between one another. ECNs allow investors direct access to the trading markets instead of going through a stockbroker. This type of direct trading can have advantages in terms of execution speed, but it may be difficult or unnecessary for small retail investors to use.

32. C: The income statement calculates a net profit using revenues and expenses shown over a period of time. The cash flow statement represents changes in the balance sheet. The balance sheet lists assets and liabilities including inventory.

33. B: The complex chart used in technical analysis to examine trends is the head and shoulder pattern. The put/call ratio of an index is a data-based indicator. Moving averages can be used to study patterns but are not usually in the form of a chart. A breakout occurs when a trend goes through a support level indicating that the previous trend is complete.

34. A: EBITDA is useful for comparing companies because it excludes debt payments, amortization, depreciation, and taxes. This shines a light on how well a company can produce at a high margin and the expenses involved with operating the company. Cash flows can be analyzed by using a metric such as free cash flow (FCF). Leverage impact can be measured using the DuPont method for measuring return on equity (ROE).

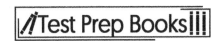

35. C: A resistance level is a price level that a stock has failed to break multiple times and will likely provide future resistance, if the stock trades up to that level again. If a stock breaks through a resistance level, it is often seen as a bullish sign that the rise will continue. Other options include a trading range, the 52-week average price, and part of a head and shoulders trading pattern.

36. D: Volume is the number of shares being traded. Many stock quotes will list the volume for the current day and also the average volume over the past 90 days for comparison. Volume can be used in technical analysis to confirm or reject stock moves as true or false. Standard deviations in bid and ask price, as well as trading ranges, are measured by other technical indicators or not measured at all. Shares outstanding are referred to as the float of the stock.

37. C: The Federal Reserve, brokerage houses, banks, data services, and economists provide and analyze data useful to market advisors. Other information can be found by studying the CBOE Volatility Index, the Conference Board Consumer Confidence Index, and the Michigan Consumer Sentiment Index.

38. B: The yield curve is measured and included in the Conference Board index. The yield curve is a predictor of recession. The yield curve flattens to indicate a recession and typically has an upward slope.

39. B: A support line establishes the bottom for a price or a trend. A reversal pattern shows that a security is about to reverse against the previous trend. An inverted saucer happens when a stock has trended upward, reached the top, and started to go back down. A trading channel describes when a stock is between the support and resistance.

40. D: The cash flow statement represents cash flows from investing, operating, and financing activities. Together with the amount of cash on a company's balance sheet, the cash flow demonstrates how solvent a company is.

41. D: Straight-line depreciation is calculated by taking the cost of the asset less the salvage value and dividing by the useful life in years:

$$(\$45{,}000 - \$6{,}000) \div 15 \; years = \$2{,}600$$

42. A: The inventory turnover ratio indicates how quickly a company can turn over their inventory. A quick turnover usually leads to increased net income. The quick ratio helps determine liquidity. The debt-to-equity ratio can indicate how likely a company is to go bankrupt. Earnings per share measures the amount of earnings on a per share basis which helps determine the value of company's stock.

43. C: The DuPont identity separates return on equity (ROE) into its components. The calculation involves net income, sales, assets, and equity.

44. D: Preferred stock has a residual claim to the corporation's assets. AA-Rated debt has some credit risk. High-yield debt is below AA debt in the capital structure, so it has a greater credit risk. Therefore, commercial paper has the least credit risk.

45. D: The dividend yield formula calls for dividing the annual dividend by the current stock price. The company has been paying a quarterly dividend of $0.50, so the annual rate is $2.00, which is 20% of $10.

46. B: The dividend payout ratio relates the amount of dividends to the total net income of a company. The earnings number is already annualized.

$$(\$1 \times 4\ quarters) \times 10\ million = \$40\ million$$

$$\$40\ million \div 100\ million = 40\%$$

47. C: The market value of $\$10 \times 30{,}000 = \$300{,}000$ will be the same before and after the stock split.

48. B: The first step is to find the amount of earnings. The earnings per share formula can be used to solve for earnings:

$$\$2.50 = \frac{Earnings}{100{,}000} \rightarrow Earnings = \$250{,}000$$

The new earnings per share after the issuance of the additional stock is equal to:

$$\$250{,}000 \div 115{,}000 = \$2.17$$

49. C: Penny stocks have a fair amount of volatility and are often delisted. Treasury bonds provide income, but inflation can erode their value. High-yield bonds often trade like equities and have significant volatility. Therefore, the correct answer is corporate bonds.

50. C: A leverage ratio is the ratio of debt to equity. Calling debt reduces the numerator of the equation; is50suing stock increases the denominator resulting in less leverage for the company.

51. D: Short-term instruments typically pay a lower interest rate. Medium-term Treasury notes pay a lower interest rate because they have a shorter maturity than long-term corporate bonds, and corporate bonds also pay a premium to investors in the form of a higher rate because of their credit risk.

52. B: Treasury stock does not receive a dividend. Therefore, the dividends per share can be calculated as follows:

$$\$90{,}000 \div 40{,}000 = \$2.25$$

53. C: If the company issues floating rate debt, it will increase their interest expense when rates go up. When rates rise, it typically has a negative effect on stock prices, so the company would be spending cash to buy stock that'll be cheaper at a later date. Issuing short-term commercial paper would just mean they'd have to keep reissuing it as rates rise. Therefore, the smart strategy is to issue long-term fixed-rate debt.

54. C: The right to call and reissue shares at a specified price is a company's right when issuing a callable bond. It is not a common stockholder right.

55. C: American Depositary Receipts (ADRs) are shares of foreign companies purchased in the U.S. without having to go through a foreign stock exchange.

56. C: A sinking fund accrues a balance that's used to redeem bonds or preferred stock. Mutual funds are investment vehicles used by investors. A money market fund has short-term investments. A bond fund is a portfolio of individual, fixed-income securities.

57. C: A rights offering can be one way for a company to raise capital as it encourages existing shareholders to purchase additional, newly issued shares at a discount.

58. C: The wash sale rule prevents investors from selling a security for a tax-deductible loss and then buying back that same security. The investor must wait 30 days before buying a similar security in order to be eligible to deduct the loss. The other options are strategies that will not apply the wash sale rule because any derivatives are not applicable for the wash sale rule. In addition, municipalities cannot deduct investment losses from their taxes because they do not pay taxes but rather collect them.

59. A: The conversion ratio formula is:

$$conversion\ ratio = \frac{Bond\ par\ value}{Conversion\ price}$$

By substituting the bond par value and the conversion ratio, the conversion price can be found:

$$20 = \frac{\$1{,}000}{Conversion\ price} \rightarrow Conversion\ price = \$50$$

60. B: The spread between two bonds is the difference between their yields:

$$4.6\% - 4.2\% = 0.6\%$$

61. D: Duration is a measure of the inverse relationship between a bond's value and its yield. $2 \times 2\% = 4\%$ and, because there is a rise in interest rates, there will be a decline in price of 4%.

62. D: The calculation is the tax-exempt yield (8%) divided by 1 minus the marginal tax rate (25%) or:

$$\frac{8\%}{(1 - 25\%)} = \frac{0.08}{0.75} = 10.7\%$$

63. C: The coupon rate of 7% equates to an annual payment of \$70. Substituting \$70 for the interest and \$1,150 for the price, the current yield can be found:

$$\frac{\$70}{\$1{,}150} = 6.1\%$$

64. C: The coupon rate is irrelevant. Here, the worst-case scenario would be for the bond to be called away from the investor on the call date prior to its maturity, which is the yield to call of 4.2%; therefore, 4.2% is also the yield to worst.

65. B: Assuming the bond was issued at par, the current yield would have initially been the same as the coupon rate. If interest rates rise, the bond's value would decline to reflect the higher interest rate environment. Therefore, the bond's price is below the par value.

66. D: Municipal bonds may not have principal paid in full if there isn't a significant tax base in that municipality. Asset-backed securities have credit risk because borrowers may stop paying their loans. Corporate bonds have credit risk because companies can go bankrupt and not have enough assets to pay back all of their creditors if liquidated. Treasury bonds are usually assumed to have zero credit risk since they're backed by the full faith of the U.S. government.

67. C: Since rates have risen, the fixed rate bond will decrease in value, but the adjustable rate bond's price shouldn't change very much. The adjustable rate bond won't have the same price volatility because its coupon now pays a rate that reflects current levels.

68. C: A puttable bond grants the investor the right—not the obligation—to "put" the bond back to the issuer.

69. A: The SEC (Securities and Exchange Commission) is not a GSE (Government-Sponsored Entity) even though it is a government agency.

70. C: Zero-coupon Treasury bonds are still affected by inflation and still fluctuate in price. There's no influence of foreign exchange risk on them. Thus, zero-coupon Treasury bonds shield investors from reinvestment risk.

71. C: When rating agencies perform a credit analysis for municipal bonds, they do evaluate the ability to budget, tax revenue streams, and the economic climate. They do not analyze the municipality's population.

72. B: Bonds in default have the lowest rating, which is a D. Bonds that are speculative are considered non-investment grade and are rated less than BBB. Bonds with the highest quality are AAA rated. Bonds with an A rating have many positive investment qualities.

73. D: Open-end investment companies use the London Stock Exchange.

74. C: Using the sales charge formula, the public offering price and the net asset value can be substituted:

$$Sales\ charge = \frac{(Public\ offering\ price - Net\ asset\ value)}{Public\ offering\ price}$$

$$\frac{(32.56 - 27.18)}{32.56} = \frac{5.38}{32.56}$$

$$0.165 = 16.5\%$$

75. A: Short-term gains on securities held for less than one year and gains from investing in foreign currencies are taxed at the ordinary rate. Gains on shares held for longer than one year are taxed at the long-term rate. Municipal-bond interest is tax free under most conditions.

76. B: They raise funds through an IPO just like a traditional company that issues stock to raise capital. They do have managers but not the typical management structure of a company that issues stock. Closed-end funds do not file a 10-Q (though they do file reports with the SEC), and they do not issue convertible debt.

77. D: To maintain their tax-exempt status, closed-end funds must distribute 90% of income and 98% of capital gains to their shareholders.

78. C: Deferred sales charges are paid monthly.

79. A: Cost-of-living adjustments adjust the payments to assure the investor is receiving payments to cover his/her cost of living, usually adjusted by an inflationary index. Lump-sum payments assure principal will be returned in its entirety. Disability riders assure payment should the owner of the annuity become ill. Positive and negative covenants apply to bonds, not annuities.

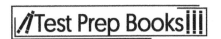

80. B: Earnings are taxed as ordinary income, and the excess amount is taken from principal (and not taxed). Earnings are not taxed at the short-term rate. Capital gains are not part of the LIFO tax basis. The term applies to variable annuities, not stocks.

81. D: DRIP stands for dividend reinvestment program. Under this plan existing shareholders can purchase more shares when a dividend is paid at a discount to the current share price.

82. D: Investors buy shares in an IPO, the REIT acquires and invests in properties, tenants pay rent to the REIT, and a percentage of that money is distributed back to the shareholders in the form of dividends.

83. A: REITs are required to pay out 90% of their income to maintain their tax status as a REIT.

84. B: Qualified dividends paid out by REITs are taxed at the long-term capital gains rate.

85. C: DPPs invest in real estate, energy, futures/options, and equipment leases (as well as oil and gas). They do not invest in mutual funds. Funds that invest in other private-equity funds are funds-of-funds. Money-market funds invest in short-term debt instruments.

86. D: DPPs typically invest in land purely to speculate, which is significantly risky. While they do develop land for oil drilling, they do not do this with specific land investments. Taxes on land can go up, but this is not a significant risk. DPPs do not develop land, so getting permits for development is not a risk.

87. A: Net worth and income are provided to assure the investor has sufficient financial resources to make a risky investment. The investor's tax bill, medical history, criminal record, personal debt, and college education are not relevant information.

88. B: To maintain their tax-exempt status hedge funds cannot have more than one hundred beneficial investors. REITs can't retain more than 10% of income (they must distribute 90% of income to maintain their REIT status).

89. C: This would be considered a distressed fund. Long-short funds buy stocks and sell others short. Arbitrage funds try to take advantage of the mispricing of securities. Global-strategy funds seek to gain profit from events in international markets, such as emerging-market debt or large currency movements.

90. D: CDOs, CMOs, and ABS are all types of structured products that have tranches and some level of financial engineering or structuring to create several products with different levels of risk. Equities are not considered a structured product, as equity holders simply have the right to residual cash flows.

91. C: Hybrid REITs invest in mortgage debt and traditional commercial real estate. REITs typically do not invest in tech companies, hedge funds, convertible bonds, or DPPs.

92. A: UITs list information on expenses and costs in their prospectus.

93. D: Variable annuities are variable because the amount of the annuity stream in the future is dependent on the performance of some component of the contract that is linked to an investment. The better that an investment performs, the higher the future cashflow, although the contract will likely have an assumed or projected rate. The other options are not features of annuities, since they can be purchased any time of the year and have existed for decades.

94. A: A lock-up provision prevents investors from withdrawing any money from the fund. These provisions allow the hedge fund to pursue its strategy without redemptions interfering. This is important, since many funds pursue strategies that take several years to play out and see results.

95. B: A closed-end fund is closed because after its initial public offering, no more capital will be contributed to the fund. The investments inside the fund are not rolled over and once expired, the profits, losses, and capital will be returned to investors. Due to this lack of liquidity, if demand for the fund wanes, it can begin to trade below NAV. Closed-end funds are not restricted on their number of investors, nor must they only buy fixed income securities. Private placements and some business structures have a limit on how many investors can be involved, but mutual funds of any type do not have such a restriction.

96. B: Accumulation units (AUs) are what an investor receives when paying his or her variable annuity premium. These rights represent the stake in the underlying investment funds and determine how much the investor will receive when he or she cashes out or the annuity begins its payments. AUs are used instead of the actual paper value of the investments, since these can fluctuate widely. The surrender value only applies if the investor gives up the policy.

97. A: The three types of direct participation plans (DPP) are oil and gas, real estate, and equipment leasing. Leverage buyouts and private equity are investment strategies practiced by hedge funds and other institutions. Shorting the LIBOR (London Interbank Offered Rate) is an investment that hopes the LIBOR will decrease from its current levels. None of these strategies are available as a DPP.

98. B: An increase in volatility increases both the value of the call and put contracts on an asset because it increases the likelihood of each contract reaching the exercise price. An increase in the underlying asset's value increases the value of the call option because it pushes the value closer to the strike price (or over the strike price, putting it even further into the money). A decline in the asset's value has the opposite effect. A decrease in the put's value, assuming the discount factor is held constant, means the call option's value would decline by that same amount.

99. A: A straddle is a strategy that buys both put and call options, both of which are positively correlated with volatile markets. When markets trade sideways it means neither puts nor calls are likely to hit their strike prices. Low trading volume is usually consistent with low volatility, both of which mean it is unlikely a long straddle will be an effective strategy.

100. B: The writer of the contract profits when he or she collects the premium paid to write the contract, and the option goes unexercised. If an option is in the money, the option is exercised, and the writer will incur a loss of (approximately) the difference between the strike price and the asset price. Volatility increases the value of the option contract for the buyer (and increases the likelihood the position will be unprofitable to the seller). If a put exceeds the strike price, the option will be incurred, and the writer will incur a loss on the position.

101. A: The American style option is more valuable because it can be exercised at any time over the life of the contract. The asset could exceed the strike price and then no longer exceed it at the time of expiration. The option would expire worthless on the European contract. The American style option could be exercised at any time, so it is more valuable.

102. D: LEAPS expire on the third Friday of every January and have expiration dates up to three years.

103. C: An option contract is binding on both sides — buyer and seller/writer. If an option reaches its strike price, it can be exercised (but is not required to be). It will expire worthless if the strike price is not reached. An offsetting position can be taken to have zero risk in a current open position.

104. B: It gives the buyer the right to put the stock to the option writer (not the buyer). Puts profit when an asset price decreases, but it is not actually short selling. A call option is when an investor can buy an asset at the strike price.

105. A: The assignment occurs when the investor makes the decision to exercise the option and notifies the broker.

106. D: An option's total value is comprised of its intrinsic value, usually the value if the option were to be exercised immediately, and its time value, which is derived from the probability it will exceed the strike price before expiring.

107. B: Open interest is a measure of the amount of liquidity in the market.

108. C: Option values and volatility of the underlying asset have a positive correlation, since volatility increases the likelihood that the asset will reach the strike price and the option can be exercised.

109. A: Stock splits, mergers, acquisitions, split offs, spinoffs, and extraordinary dividends all require options traded on those shares to be adjusted. Adjustments do not occur for poor earnings or if the stock price goes to zero.

110. D: The required amount of collateral is 50% of any amount borrowed; 75% is required for LEAPS, simply due to the length of the trade's life; 10% of the value is required for interest rate options.

111. B: Being covered means the investor owns the underlying asset whether buying or writing the option.

112. C: The maximum amount buyers of put or call options can lose is the premium they have paid, regardless of whether they own the underlying asset. Options traders who write positions without owning the underlying collateral are exposed to potential unlimited losses.

113. C: The U.S. treasury market is the largest security market in the world. Choices *A* and *B* refer to two of the largest regulated exchanges in the U.S. stock market. Choice *D* refers generally to all derivative instruments such as options and credit default swaps. *D* is the smallest market of the four due to the illiquid, complex, and risky nature of derivatives.

114. D: Stocks are found in mutual funds or ETFs (or are held on an individual basis). The same is the case with corporate bonds. Derivatives are instruments used to speculate on specific securities or hedge the risk of a particular investment. Government securities are what are actively traded in the repo market.

115. D: Issued stock represents the total number of shares of stock that have ever been issued. Authorized stock is the number of shares a company is allowed to sell. Outstanding stock represents the shares currently being traded on the market. Treasury stock are shares that have been repurchases by the company.

116. D: An escrow receipt guarantees that an underlying security is held by a bank or exchange and ensures the delivery of the physical asset when the contract is exercised or expires.

117. A: Identified shares, LIFO, and FIFO are all different methods that can be used to determine the cost basis of the shares being sold. Market value is used to determine the initial cost basis of shares that are inherited or gifted.

118. B: Exchange traded funds (ETFs) are highly liquid. They typically trade in 50,000 share blocks and can include large cap, small cap, growth, or value companies. ETFs are permitted in Roth IRA accounts.

119. C: The contingent deferred sales load is deducted from the withdrawal. The charge is:

$$\$12{,}000 \times 0.03 = \$360$$

Therefore, the withdrawal amount after the charge is:

$$\$12{,}000 - \$360 = \$11{,}640$$

120. C: Mutual fund fees may include up-front fees, redemption fees, management fees, and distribution fees. Inception, creation, and trading fees are typically associated with unit investment trusts (UITs).

121. A: An exchange privilege option is sometimes offered to allow the investor to exchange shares without having to pay a transaction fee if the funds are in the same family.

122. B: Funds withdrawn from a variable annuity before the policyholder is 59 ½ must be assessed a 10% penalty tax. The $15,000 withdrawal will have a penalty of $\$15{,}000 \times 10\% = \$1{,}500$ because Susan is not yet 59 ½.

123. B: A subset of an option class that has the same strike price and expiration date is an option series. An option class is all the options tied to a particular stock or index. The exercise date is the time by which the option can be exercised. The multiplier is what determines the amount of the underlying asset attached to the options contracts.

124. C: Eurodollar bonds are not registered with the SEC and pay principal and interest in U.S. dollars held in banks outside of the U.S. They usually have lower costs and less regulatory issues.

125. C: High-yield or junk bonds are rated below Baa/BBB and are the riskiest bonds in the capital structure of a corporation.

126. B: General obligation (GO) municipal bonds should be analyzed by considering certain factors including demographic information, unemployment rate, operational and management capabilities, the current debt profile, and the tax base. Choices *A*, *C*, and *D* refer to factors that should be considered before investing in revenue bonds.

127. D: A collateralized debt obligation (CDO) is not a type of municipal bond. Municipal bond types include special tax bonds, tax anticipation notes, tax-exempt commercial paper, bond anticipation notes, and revenue anticipation notes.

128. B: Treasury bills are the primary instrument used by the Federal Open Market Committee (FOMC) to regulate the supply of money. Treasury notes, Treasury bonds, and zero-coupon bonds are other types of debt instruments issued by the federal government.

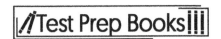

129. A: The breakeven rate occurs when an investor receives a return of capital plus enough of a profit to recoup transaction fees. The difference between an investment's lowest current offering price and the higher price the dealer will charge an investor is the mark-up. A net transaction is when a broker receives a customer order and executes the trade with another broker. The net yield on a taxable bond that is equal to the risk of the bond is not an actual financial concept.

130. C: The customer statement must include the value of all open positions, the margin the customer has posted, and funds due or owed by the customer. The other three choices should be included on options trade confirmations.

131. C: Subsidiary Records are records that show municipal securities in transfer, municipal securities to be validated, municipal securities borrowed or loaned, and any municipal securities transactions that weren't completed on the settlement date.

132. A: When stock is gifted, its tax is calculated based on its current fair market value. This is found using the high and low prices of the shares on the date of the gift.

133. D: A 12b-1 fee is an operating fee charged by a mutual fund and is considered an operating expense.

134. A: Earnings information is considered a material aspect of investment. This information is not released to the general investment community until it can be done in a fair and transparent matter.

135. C: An extraordinary call is when a bond is redeemed early because there's no longer a source of revenue to pay the interest.

136. B: An option premium is comprised of an intrinsic value and a time value. As an equation, this means *Option Premium = Time Value + Intrinsic Value*. The other choices reflect factors that affect the premium of the option.

137. B: An income fund invests in securities that pay a consistent dividend. The other funds listed have different goals and objectives.

138. D: Asset allocation involves adjusting investments among asset categories such as stocks, bonds, cash, and real estate. Choices *A*, *B*, and *C* relate to other portfolio analysis strategies, so they are incorrect.

139. A: The highs and lows, or fluctuations, of a security or an index are referred to as the volatility. Concentration means investing in a large percentage of similar securities from the same company or sector. Diversification is the opposite of concentration. Correlation concerns whether stocks move in the same direction or not.

140. A: Secured debts are those backed by collateral. Unsecured debt is not backed by collateral. Subordinated bonds are those with a lower payout priority. Ranked debt is not a relevant term.

141. C: Debt securities pay a set interest rate, so fluctuations in the market do not affect the interest rate. Company profits raise the value of the investment (Choice *A*) for equity securities, not debt securities. Choice *B* is incorrect because investments can be redeemed by the issuer, rather than the investor, before their maturity date. If a company goes bankrupt, there is a chance that the debt will not be repaid, so Choice *D* is incorrect.

142. D: A tranche is a part of a pooled group of securities that is separated based on characteristics such as risk, rate of return, interest rates, maturity dates, and sizes. Cash flow and distributions are associated with the rate of return for an investment, so Choices *A*, *B*, and *C* are incorrect.

143. C: Credit risk is the risk that a company won't be able to make payments on its debt. In this case, the CMO is unable to return the principal that was invested. Liquidity, reinvestment, and timing risk are not relevant to this situation.

144. B: A senior tranche has a higher credit rating but a lower coupon rate and a lower default risk. The number of loans does not vary directly from tranche to tranche.

145. C: Banks offer CDOs because they can move the risk of default from the underlying loans onto the investor. Choice *A* is incorrect because CDOs are backed by collateral. The collateral is made up of mortgages, auto loans, credit card debt, and corporate debt, so Choice *B* is incorrect. Choice *D* is not correct because CDOs are a complex investment due to their structure.

146. D: Mortgages, corporate debt, and student loans are all cash-flow generating receivables that can be used as collateral for an ABS. Physical property is not used as collateral for an asset-backed security because it requires active behavior to generate a return.

147. A: Securitization enables the transfer of ownership of assets so that the assets can be packaged and offered to investors. Indenture refers to a contract or agreement. Convertible options are sometimes included in an indenture agreement. Accrued interest is part of the payment received on an investment in an ABS.

148. C: Federal government agency bonds are guaranteed by the full faith and credit of the U.S. government, whereas GSE bonds are not. The minimum investment, coupon rate, and maturity range varies for both types of bonds, but the differences are not based on whether the bond is a federal government agency bond or a GSE bond.

149. B: An agency bond that has a floating rate tied to a benchmark rate like the LIBOR is called a floater. Disco bonds are no-coupon discount notes. A Treasury bond is a debt instrument issued by the U.S. government. A GSE bond can have a variety of coupon rates.

150. B: Issuance of a research report is not a material event that must be disclosed to municipal bond investors. A defeasance, a tender offer, and an adverse tax event are all material events that should be disclosed, so Choices *A*, *C*, and *D* are incorrect.

151. D: Material events are significant changes to key features of municipal bonds. Material events are not the only disclosures that must be made to municipal bond investors, so Choice *A* is incorrect. Choice *B* is incorrect because material events must be disclosed within ten business day of the event, not fifteen. Choice *C* is also incorrect because there are exceptions to the requirement of disclosures.

152. A: Municipal bond trade confirmations must list all parties involved with a trade and how the broker acted on their behalf. Choices *B* and *C* discuss requirements for a customer statement. Choice *D* is typically provided in the disclosures of a mortgage-backed security (MBS) or an ABS.

153. C: Because the position has not been closed yet, this is a gain on paper, or an unrealized gain. If the position was closed and the cash received, it would be a realized gain. Recognized gain and open gain are not actual types of gains.

154. D: If a transaction is completed in accordance with a periodic plan or an investment company plan, the transaction can be completed without customer notification. A customer request does not necessarily remove the requirement for notifications. Customers must be notified when a broker is acting as an agent and when a withdrawal has been made.

Processing Customer Purchases and Transactions

Providing Current Quotes

Orders, Offerings, and Transactions

An order provides instructions from an investor to a broker or firm to buy or sell a security for the investor. Orders can be given over the phone or by using an online trading platform. Offerings are made when a company issues their stock in order for it to be purchased by the public. Investors choose to invest in offerings for a variety of reasons and should be aware of risks associated with this type of investment. A transaction is any activity in a customer's account that facilitates the buying and selling of financial instruments.

Trade Execution Activities

There are several governing bodies with rules regarding spreading market rumors. NYSE Rule 435(5), NYSE Rule 476, FINRA Rule 6140(e), and FINRA Rule 2010 address market rumors. NYSE Rule 435(5) makes a general statement, in that investors and market participants must not circulate rumors that can influence the market. This includes "unsubstantiated" rumors, even if they appear in the main stream. Circulation and the sources of these rumors should be reported by market participants. FINRA Rule 6140 is more specific about guidelines around rumors. Part (a) of this rule states trades cannot be made at prices to induce the market to trade on poor price information. Essentially this means participants cannot inflate the price of a stock for their own benefit. The rule also states syndicates and margin accounts can't be used to artificially influence prices.

Front running occurs when a broker takes advantage of the market for their own benefit while their customers' orders are pending. In such situations, a broker may purchase blocks of shares to drive up prices before executing the trade for a customer. The broker could then sell the new shares at the artificially inflated prices to reap a short-term profit. Traditional front running is more easily detected because regulators can simply compare paper records between a broker and client, but when front running is carried out via computer, it is much harder to detect. In 2001, the SEC changed the pricing of stocks from 1/8 increments to pennies to deter front running by reducing the incentive.

Churning occurs when a broker or salesman executes trades simply to increase their commission. If caught, all commissions and fees must be repaid, as well as any losses incurred on the investment. Fines can be assessed, and licensing can be suspended. SEC Rule 15c1-7 addresses churning. Frequent in and out purchases and high turnover are often indicative of churning. Most mutual funds turn their portfolio over about once a year, so monthly turnover can be evidence of churning. Reverse churning can also occur; this is when infrequently traded accounts are put into fee-based accounts to maximize the commission.

Commingling of funds occurs when an advisor mixes their own funds with those of a client. Commingling makes it difficult to determine to whom specific funds belong. This increases the potential for fraud. If commingling is identified, any losses are allocated to the advisor and any gains are allocated to the client. Unauthorized transactions are prohibited on most exchanges. This occurs when trades are executed without the permission or authorization from the client. There are some exceptions; a broker may be able to sell a client's securities if a margin call is made, and the client does not have sufficient cash.

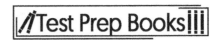

FINRA Rule 2010 covers unauthorized transactions. Advisors and brokers are prohibited from making guarantees that gains or losses will occur. FINRA Rule 2150(b) states advisors cannot make a statement guaranteeing that there will be no losses on any securities purchased.

SEC Rule 206(4)-3 covers referral fees. This rule states that an advisor cannot pay a cash fee unless specific conditions are met. If there is a written agreement or if the client is notified in advance that the solicitor is being compensated with a fee, it is legal. An advisor who violates these rules can lose his or her registration license.

Broker must have a reasonable basis for recommending the purchase or sale of a security. When making a recommendation, brokers must consider their client's income, net worth, portfolio, investment objectives, liquidity, experience, investment horizon, and their total portfolio. It is also important to have a conversation about a client's ability and willingness to take risks.

Types of Security Quotes

Most securities are traded with a bid and ask system. The bid refers to the price that buyers are willing to pay for a bond or a share of stock, and the ask refers to the seller's asking price. The difference between the two amounts is known as the bid-ask spread or simply as the spread. If the ask is $25 and the bid $24, then the spread is $1.

The bid and the ask are constantly changing as buyers and sellers enter and exit the market. If the market is made up of one buyer and one seller with an ask of $25 and a bid of $24, either no trade will occur, or the two parties will move their amounts up or down until the two are equal. This means the parties agree on the price of the security, and the trade will be executed. On electronic exchanges, thousands of these trades are executed instantly. A firm quote guarantees the bid or the ask up to the amount quoted. This is different from a nominal or subject quote where neither the amount nor the quantity of the trade is set. These types of quotes are made to test the market for a security's value. A not held quote is used for a trade that an investor wants executed on a best efforts basis, which allows the broker or trader to buy or sell without a limit.

Municipal bonds have specific rules as governed by the Municipal Securities Rulemaking Board. Rule G-13 clarifies the specific language around a quote. A quotation is any time an indication of a bid or offer transpires. G-13 also clarifies that any time a quote is communicated, it is distributed or published. The rule states that when a quote is published, it is a bona fide quote, meaning it is not subject to a price change. Thus, when investors see a published or distributed quote, they can have confidence going into the trade that it will be executed at the price they are expecting. The rule also states that nominal quotes are for informational purposes only and will not have a trade executed when a nominal bid or ask is given. Brokers must also use good judgment when valuing a municipal bond trade. A workout quote is the price at which it is believed a security will be traded in the market within a set period. Fast markets are markets in which there are large lots of trades and significant price volatility. This is often the case in IPO markets.

Types of Orders

A buy order takes place when an investor wants to purchase stock he or she does not own. A sell order occurs when an investor owns a security and wants to sell it on the open market, usually because he or she believes the stock is overvalued. To sell short means an investor wants to profit from a decline in the value of a security, and simply selling the stock does not accomplish this. The investor is actually selling a stock he or she does not own and is agreeing to repurchase the stock at a later date.

For example, if an investor wants to sell one share of a company trading at $100, brokers typically require a margin account of 50% of the capital—which in this case is $50. This ensures the investor has funds to cover the loss if the trade goes bad. The broker then borrows the shares from one of his or her clients, his or her own inventory, or another broker dealer. The shares are then sold on the open market for $100, and the proceeds are put in the short sellers account for a total of $150 in the margin account. If the stock rises by $10, it means the required margin goes up by $10, so he or she is required to add $10 to his or her margin account for a total of $160 in the account. If the stock goes down $10 to $90 per share and the short seller decides to close the account, he or she would see a $10 profit from being able to buy the shares back at cost of $90.

To sell shares short, the price the short seller wants to sell shares at must be higher than the previous transaction. This is called an uptick rule. This essentially means a stock must have upward momentum for an investor to sell shares short. This prevents short sellers from piling in when a stock is in decline. A market order is simply an order that is executed at whatever the market price is. In a limit order, the investor has more control, and the order is not executed if the market price does not fall within the limit range. A stop order means the trade is only executed when the price surpasses a certain point. A day order expires if criteria is not reached for a trade to occur during that day. A good-til-cancelled (GTC) order means the order is in place until executed, unless the investor cancels the order.

Certain types of orders are also strategies in options trading. When option traders buy or sell to open, they are essentially opening a position on a stock, bond, or index. A buy-to-close or sell-to-close order closes a trade that has been opened, and the investor will incur a loss or gain from his or her trade. This basically eliminates the exposure he or she had when the trade was opened. In a spread strategy with options—not to be confused with the bid-ask spread—an investor enters into multiple options transactions, with different strike prices and expiration dates. This enables the trade to be more diverse than compared to one trade that has a single-strike price and exercise date. A straddle is an options trading that involves an investor simultaneously buying a put and a call of the same underlying stock with the same strike price and expiration date. An investor who expects significant volatility in the price of a security will set up this type of strategy. It is only when the security has significant ups and downs that an investor will profit from this type of transaction.

A diagram of the strategy and potential payoff is below:

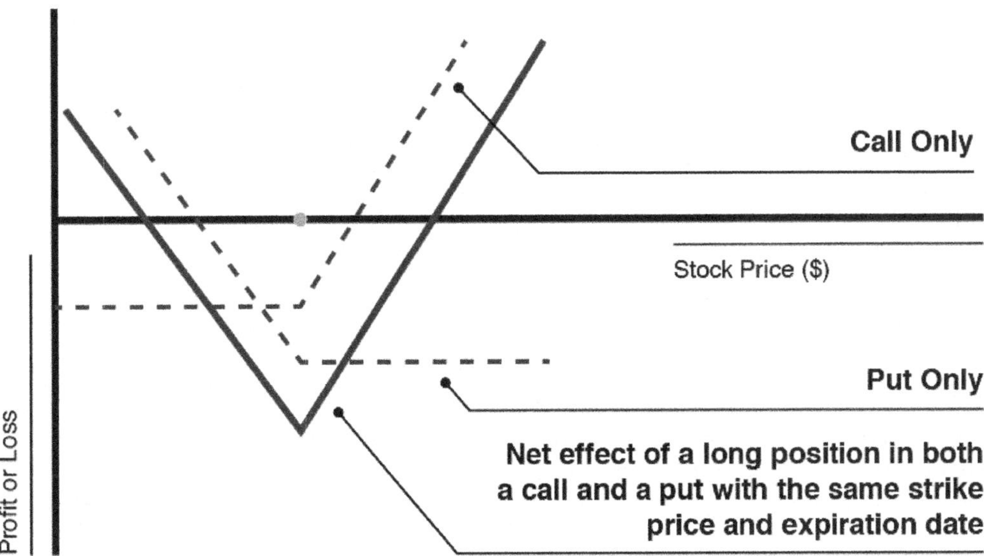

Options securities orders can be structured to profit off of any movement in a stock that an analyst might forecast. In a reversal straddle, a trader sells both the put and call positions on the same stock. In this case, the investor receives the premiums for selling the positions and profits when the stock stays within the strike prices. This is basically selling volatility—e.g., profiting from the market or the stock not going anywhere. This is more of a highly speculative and highly risky investment position. If the stock goes way up or way down, the seller of the position has almost unlimited exposure.

In an all or none order, the broker must execute the trade completely—i.e., all shares must be sold, or none sold at all. For example, if there is not enough supply for an order of 10,000 shares to be bought, the order is cancelled. In a fill or kill order, if the order cannot be filled right away, it is cancelled or killed. In an immediate or cancel order, part of a trade can still be executed if it cannot be filled in its entirety. However, the portion of the trade that is not able to be filled immediately must be cancelled. In a not held trade, the investor gives the broker discretion in trading and will not hold the broker responsible if trades are not executed at the ideal price. A market on close order is executed as close to the end of the trading day as possible.

Short Sale Requirements and Strategies

FINRA Rule 4320 outlines the requirements for short sales. The rule specifically addresses failure to deliver situations. This is when the broker or dealer on the sell side of the contract—the short seller—has not delivered the securities to the buyer. If this occurs, the seller will not receive payment if the trade is profitable. This is the credit risk associated with this type of transaction. Most firms do due diligence to prevent this type of situation from arising, but because of the risk inherent in short-selling, these situations do arise. The rule states any failure to deliver position outstanding for more than 35 days requires the participant to close the position by purchasing a similar security. The rule also applies if only a portion of a trade fails to deliver, simply to the balance of what has not been delivered.

Typically, short sales must be order marked so that it is clear that the investor is not actually in possession of the underlying security in the transaction, that the shares are actually borrowed either out of a broker or customer account, and that margin has been posted. In short sales, allocation occurs when a broker approves a short sell to be executed.

Regulation SHO took effect in 2004 and requires the documentation of what has transpired for the allocation to occur. According to this rule, the actual securities do not have to be borrowed and in possession of a trustee. As long as a security is easily attainable—usually a liquid security that is actively traded on a market on a daily basis—the allocation requirement is considered to be fulfilled. If a security cannot be borrowed, this would be considered a naked short.

Though the idea of a short sale is pretty straightforward—an investor wants to profit from the decline in a security's value—there are more dynamic strategies that can be undertaken. An investor may simply notice that a stock is highly overvalued. Perhaps the price/earnings (P/E) ratio is significantly higher than similar stocks, or perhaps an investor believes a company's growth estimates are not realistic. If an investor does not own the stock and wishes to profit from a short sale, this is speculation. Speculation is different from investing in that there is more inherent risk in the trade than in a traditional long position. An investor that believes the security may be overvalued can hedge his or her position through a short sale. This may be less costly than selling the shares outright. It also allows investors to protect themselves from a price decline if they feel it is short-term or temporary and still retains shares as a long-term investment.

Investors may or may not have complete hedge in place. A fully hedged position would mean that a gain or loss on the shares the investor owns is directly offset by his or her short position. A hedge ratio is usually calculated so that the investor can quantify the exposure from both positions. Another strategy with short sales is arbitrage. An investor may utilize this strategy if he or she feels different markets are pricing the same security differently. The strategy here is to take advantage of the mispricing by buying the security on one market—at a lower price—and then selling the security on the other market at a higher price. The chart below shows the potential payoff of a put option versus short selling the stock.

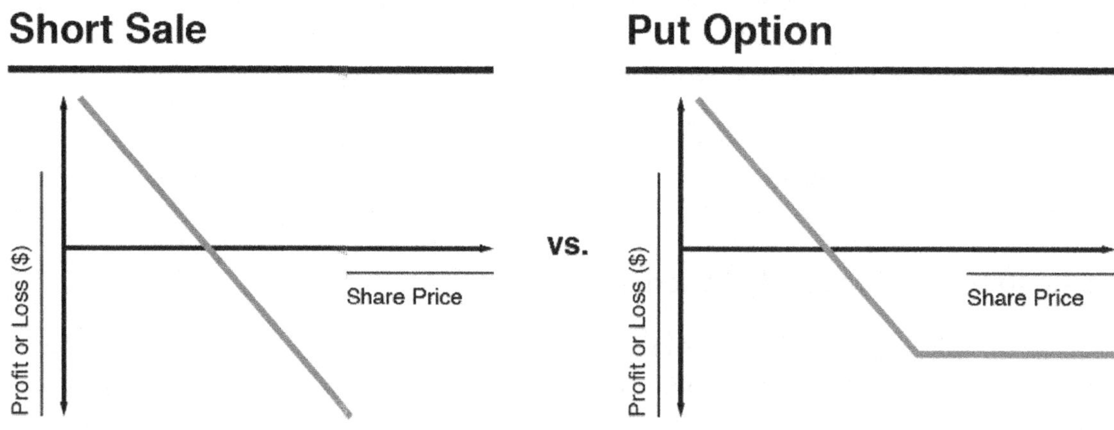

Securities Lending

In securities lending, there are typically two types of securities: easy to borrow and hard to borrow. Easy to borrow securities have delivery assured. These are typically highly-liquid, heavily-traded shares on established exchanges. Easy to borrow securities do not require a locate (the required approval from a broker prior to an equity security short sale) to occur with a broker as there is a high probability the securities can be borrowed easily. This is also referred to as a blanket assurance.

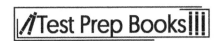

A hard to borrow security is an illiquid security. These are securities with small amounts outstanding and are sometimes privately-placed securities. A broker usually will not approve a short sale with these types of securities, unless the shares are placed with a trustee before the proceeds can be placed in the short seller's account, and they will have exposure to the trade. As discussed earlier, a failure to deliver occurs when the securities cannot be delivered to the short seller's account.

Federal Reserve Regulation T has guidelines around required margin amounts and how much credit brokers can extend to customers. This is the regulation that requires the initial margin of 50%, and with this regulation, the Federal Reserve has the authority to change that amount if it seems that markets are at risk of becoming too volatile. Section 220.103 addresses the specifics of borrowing securities. The rule states brokers cannot borrow securities simply to have them on hand; they must be tied to an actual short sale.

Best Execution Obligations

FINRA Rule 5310 has specific guidelines around the best execution of trades. It assures that brokers will complete due diligence and always attempt to find the best price when executing a trade. The broker must consider security price, liquidity, and historical volatility when trading a security, which is usually incorporated with the client's ability and willingness to take risk and the understanding of what his or her overall investment goals are. The broker and client must consider the complete dollar amount of the trade. A broker should evaluate the different markets a security is trading in and how frequently quotations and information about the security becomes available. The rule states no third party should have any influence on the broker to execute a trade using his or her best efforts. The guidelines make clear a brokerage must have adequate staff and resources to attain best execution for clients. A broker's broker must be used if best execution cannot be obtained. The same rules apply when the broker is trading as a principal, not just for customer accounts. Investors can use various types of stop and limit orders to reduce the chances of not receiving best execution, but they cannot eliminate that risk entirely. These guidelines provide investors with some assurance that they will receive the best price available.

The SEC Regulation NMS also covers best execution. This rule addresses competition, efficiency, and transparency in markets. Within this regulation is an order protection rule. It basically means if there are two different prices quoted on different exchange, the broker is required to execute at the price more favorable to his or her customer. The rule basically eliminates risk if there is some incentive for the broker to trade at the unfavorable price—e.g., a higher sales commission or a new business. The regulation also has an access rule. This rule requires better communication among exchanges and lowering costs associated with investors obtaining pricing information. The regulation also allocates revenue to exchanges and brokers that promote self-regulation for best execution.

Delivery Obligations and Settlement Procedures

Information Required on an Order Ticket

Different exchanges have different rules around the information required for a trade. CBOE Rule 6.24 specifies the criteria for options trades. The rule makes clear that all trades on the CBOE must be executed electronically and must be systematically traded. This includes buy orders, sell orders, modifications to trades, and cancellations of transactions. Orders can still be called in by telephone, but the trade must be entered electronically on the broker's end of the transaction—whether it is by the broker or by the broker's assistant. The required information in the system includes the option symbol, the month and year that the trade expires, the strike price, whether the position is long or short, the quantity of the trade, and the permit holder. There are procedures to be followed in the event of a system failure. The same required information must be transcribed in written form and transmitted to a floor trader. In the event of a cancellation, the time the order is brought to the floor must also be recorded.

Market Making Activities

Most secondary markets have a designated market maker (also known as "specialists"). They maintain fair and orderly markets and make sure there is sufficient liquidity for specified firms that are traded on an exchange. This helps to reduce volatility in the stock price. The maker is a point of contact for the company and keeps them informed as to who has been trading the stock and what trading conditions have been like for the company's stock.

The maker is usually required to provide quotes for a specific percent of the time. Makers must have adequate capital to be approved to trade and provide quotes on an exchange. The primary difference with makers is that they have access to information only after a trade has been placed, so they have the same information as floor brokers, as opposed to having inside information. Makers can't trade for their own account when they have an open order for the same security at the same price on their book. The SEC prohibits broker dealers from using manipulative or deceptive devices to effect short sales (this is where an investor can profit from the decline in a stock's price) or influence swap agreements for their own profit.

Equities that don't trade on an exchange are traded over the counter (OTC). These stocks are traded through a telephone and computer network rather than on an organized exchange. Smaller companies typically trade OTC because they do not meet the criteria to be listed on an exchange. OTC markets are regulated by the National Association of Securities Dealers (NASD). An example of an OTC market is what is known as the "pink sheets." These markets usually have daily bid quotes published. Bulletin board stocks are another example of an OTC market. Thinly traded micro-cap and penny stocks trade on this exchange.

A NASDAQ market maker executes both principal trades (which are for its own account) and agency trades (trades for its customers). These market makers aren't in the exchange, as they are for the New York Stock Exchange (NYSE). They are required to quote both sides of a trade (bid and ask). A bid wanted announcement occurs when a seller wants to entertain bids on securities. In this transaction, the response does not need to be specified, as the price may be negotiated. On the other side, an offer wanted can occur. The SEC order handling rules state market makers must display customer limit orders that are priced better than the market maker's quote or add to the size associated with the market maker's quote when the market maker is at the best price.

Like the NYSE there are listing requirements for the NASDAQ. Some of the requirements include a minimum of $1.25 million shares trading, a minimum bid of $4 per share, and three market makers. A company must also have aggregate pre-tax earnings of $11 million over three years, aggregate cash flow over the same time of $27.5 million, or a market capitalization greater than $850 million (along with some other requirements).

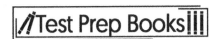

Use of Automated Execution Systems

The automated execution system is used to help facilitate trades without having to manually input them into the system. This allows trades to be entered faster and more efficiently than in the past. A system of technical markers and trading algorithms alert the computer when to enter trades so that they can be made even when the trader is not present, such as at night. This system is also used to buy or sell large orders simultaneously during the day in situations where the trader might not otherwise have been able to execute them. Metrics used to signal buying and selling of shares include price, volume, and other criteria useful to the trader.

Automatic execution is particularly useful to foreign exchange traders because these markets trade 24 hours a day. Automation helps ensure these traders do not miss out on profitable opportunities. It is also useful in today's society in which information is disseminated rapidly and using manual entry to trade based on this information is not effective.

The automated execution system does have drawbacks. The rapid entry of trades can cause the market to cease to function properly at times and even undergo anomalies. At other times changes in market conditions may not be reflected in the particular set of indicators used to set up the automatic system. The system will continue to trade unless the trader intervenes.

Regulatory Reporting Requirements

Brokers and other members of the investment community are required to submit regular reports to regulators. FINRA created an Order Audit Trail System (OATS). The system is used to recreate events as they occurred and monitors the trading practices of all member firms. FINRA Rule 7440 outlines the procedure for how the system acquires and processes information. Trades are recorded down to the second that they occurred. Additional information that is reported includes each person that receives the trade order from the customer, the broker or trader who executes the order, and the specific department associated with the order. The security specific information recorded by OATS includes the security symbol, where the order originated, the quantity of shares traded, whether or not the order is a buy or sell transaction, whether or not the order is a short sale, the type of order (limit, stop, etc.), the expiration of the trade, the size of the block if it is a block trade, special handling instructions, and if the trade is a program trade or an arbitrage trade, if applicable.

FINRA also has the Trade Reporting & Compliance Engine (TRACE). This system is used for the bond market to provide better transparency. The system flags which bond transactions should and should not be recorded. It also analyzes data and makes the information available to the public. TRACE eligible securities include dollar-denominated securities that are corporate bonds—including high yield bonds—issued both in the U.S. and internationally. They must be securities-registered with the SEC. Mortgage backed securities, asset backed securities, collateralized mortgage obligations, and money market securities are not eligible for the TRACE system. All qualifying trades must be reported within to TRACE one hour of being executed by member firms on each side of the trade, if applicable.

FINRA also has a Trade Reporting Facility (TRF). FINRA has separate TRFs at NASDAQ and the New York Stock Exchange. Under this facility, trades must be reported within ten seconds of being executed. Any reporting that occurs after ten seconds is considered late. The standard transaction data is reported on this system as well. This includes the stock symbol, the number of shares or bonds traded, the price of the transaction, and whether or not the trade is a buy, sell, or short sale. Trades may not be aggregated on the system. Each trade is reported individually. The system also processes cancelled and reversed trades.

The Municipal Market Access system is a repository for all trading information on municipal bonds. It includes not just pricing information, but credit rating information as well. More specifically, the information found on the Electronic Municipal Market Access (EMMA) includes offering documents, credit ratings, financial reports, and disclosures on municipal issuers, prices, yields, interest rates, and other statistics.

Finally, the Real-Time Transaction Reporting System (RTRS) is used to report all transactions in municipal securities. This system is operated by the Municipal Securities Rulemaking Board (MSRB). All such transactions must be reported within fifteen minutes of execution between the hours of 7:30 AM and 6:30 PM, Eastern Standard Time. If these types of transactions take place outside of RTRS's business hours, then they must be reported within the first fifteen minutes of the system's opening on the following business day.

Good Delivery

In investments, a good delivery means that a certificate has all of the proper endorsements and requirements—the signature of the guarantor, proper denomination/currency, etc.—to ensure that the title can be transferred to the buyer of the security or certificate. The broker is required to accept the transaction when it is considered a good delivery.

A certificate must also be in good physical condition and not mutilated in any way. If the certificate is in the name of two persons, both owners are required to provide authorization to sell the shares. If the owner of the stock certificate is deceased, the stocks pass to the beneficiary if one was designated. If not, the ownership of the stock is decided in the probate process. The following terms relate to good delivery:

- Due bills: These are financial instruments that list a stock seller's obligation to deliver any pending dividends to the new owner or a stock buyer's obligation to deliver pending dividends to the previous owner. The receipt of the dividend is determined by the ex-dividend date.

- Stock or bond powers: These are legal forms that authorize ownership transfers of a registered stock or bond. A stock power form is generally only used when physical possession of stock certificates is needed. A bond power form takes the place of endorsing the actual bond certificate.

- Delivery versus payment (DVP) and receive versus payment (RVP): These are both settlement procedures that require a payment to be made before a transfer of securities can occur.

- Book entry securities: These are securities with ownership recorded in the books of a financial institution. They are recorded electronically without paper certificates.

- Bearer form: This form has no written record of ownership. Physical possession of the security is the only way to determine ownership.

- Registered form: This form calls for the firm that issues the security to keep a record of ownership. The name and address of the owner is usually engraved directly on the certificate.

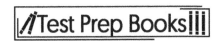

- Registrar: This is a bank or trust company that maintains records of bondholders and shareholders.
- Direct Registration System (DRS): This is a service provided by the Depository Trust Company (DTC) that gives registered shareholders the option of holding their shares in the records of a transfer agent in book entry form rather than holding a physical stock certificate.

Settlement of Transactions

NYSE Rule 133 covers non-cleared transactions. This rule requires a duplicate form of each seller to be sent to the buyer on the same day of the transaction. Rule 135 covers differences and omissions. When the recipient of a confirmation does not have knowledge of a trade, the trade ticket will be stamped "Don't Know" and returned to the seller, effectively making any transaction assumed null and void. These trades must be reported to the floor broker by noon of the following day. Rule 136 covers transactions excluded from a clearance. The transactions shall be subject to Rule 133.

The settlement of transactions refers to the process and period from the time of the trade date to the settlement date. The trade date is when the order is executed, and the settlement date is when the trade is final. During this period, the buyer provides payment for the shares, and the seller delivers the shares. The current settlement period is two business days. Some specific security categories have different settlement dates, such as CDs and commercial paper, which settle on the same day as the trade execution. Extensions of the settlement period are sometimes allowed if needed because of issues with market mechanics. Settlements that are negotiated have terms that are agreed upon by the two parties to the transaction. Options are considered settled when they are exercised or assigned by the options holder.

Transactions that have a risk of being cancelled, such as stock splits and new issues of stock, trade on a *when, as, and if issued basis*, usually shortened to "when issued basis." This means they are conditional trades that have been announced but not issued yet. Shares of stock can be traded without rights because they have already been exercised, transferred, or expired. This is known as ex-rights. If a stock is trading as ex-dividends, then the stock does not include the value of the next dividend payment. This is usually because the stock was purchased after its ex-dividend date.

Resolution of Errors and Complaints

Erroneous Reports, Errors, Cancels & Rebills

Not every trade is executed correctly. Numbers can be mis-keyed, the wrong share class could be purchased, or the incorrect tranche of a bond may be traded. These are mistakes that must be accounted for, documented, and reported when necessary. According to CBOE Rule 6.52, if a trade is executed in error, the trade is not a binding agreement and may be voided.

FINRA Rules 11892 and 11893 also address errors. Rule 11892 is in regard to exchange traded securities. This rule provides numerical guidelines classifying erroneous trades. A security quoted anywhere from $0 to $25—but that has a trade executed at an amount greater than or less than 10% of that quoted price within normal trading hours—will be considered an erroneous transaction and is subject to being voided. This means if brokers and exchanges are quoting a share of a stock at $20 and the broker buys shares for a customer for $23 (15% of the stock's value), this trade shall be considered erroneous. The threshold is 20% outside of trading hours as securities will be less liquid during that time, and traders can expect to not get the best execution. The percent threshold is 5% and 10% for stocks up to $50 and 3% and 6% for stocks of more than $50. These guidelines assure brokers will not trade shares excessively outside of where they are being quoted. The guidelines also address misinformation during issuance of securities. Rule 11893 addresses over the counter securities. Under this rule, FINRA reserves the right to use an entirely different price other than the reference price during time of extreme market volatility. When a trade is considered erroneous or executed in error, a rebill or a cancel and rebill will occur. This sometimes occurs when a trade is posted to the wrong account. The rebill will require confirmations on both the buy and sell end of the trade, and the rebill requires signing off by the principal of the broker.

Addressing Customer Complaints

All complaints to the Financial Industry Regulatory Authority (FINRA) must be submitted in writing. FINRA may use a formal or informal process to handle customer complaints depending on the customer making the complaint.

Formal proceedings occur when the customer pursues them to resolve a complaint, and the issue is resolved according to FINRA's code of procedure. In this case, the District Business Conduct Committee (DBCC) has first jurisdiction over the complaint. If the customer is dissatisfied with how the issue is handled, they can appeal the outcome to the FINRA Board of Governors or take the case up to the Supreme Court.

Informal proceedings: This is when a complaint is resolved according to FINRA's code of arbitration. At least two arbitrators participate in an informal hearing, and the decision is binding (not open to appeal). Arbitration can be pursued by customers as well as members of FINRA. Mediation is also an option for these types of complaints.

Arbitration, Mediation, and Litigation

The arbitration process is initiated when a party files a Statement of Claim. The other party has 45 days to respond to the complaint. If both parties are still in disagreement, a hearing is scheduled, and a mediator may be called in to come up with an acceptable solution. If the issue is still not resolved, a hearing will take place with several arbitrators from both inside and outside the securities industry. At this stage, the ruling is final.

Simplified arbitration is used in cases of less than $50,000, and a single arbitrator—not a panel—makes the final decision on the case. Disputes between a customer and a member of FINRA, or between two FINRA member firms, are handled directly through arbitration. When one party files a claim, the other party has 45 days to respond. However, the two parties can reach a mutually acceptable settlement with the help of a mediator before the case moves forward to a panel of arbitrators who would make a final decision.

Form U4

Employees involved with securities or investment banking for a Financial Industry Regulatory Authority (FINRA) member firm must register with FINRA. Employees who work in a FINRA member firm in clerical or administrative positions that do not interact with clients or customers may not have to register.

Form U4 (Uniform Application for Security Industry Registration or Transfer) is filed electronically via the Central Registration Depository by the firms that employ representatives of investment advisors and broker-dealers to register them with FINRA and with the states.

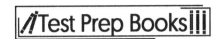

Individuals must pass a Qualification Exam for Principals before they are allowed to register. Principals are employees, directors, sole proprietors, partners, or managers of the member firm who train, solicit, or otherwise engage in or support securities activities or investment banking.

Registered persons must complete what is known as the Regulatory Element on the second anniversary of their registration, and again three years thereafter as part of their continuing education. The content of the Regulatory Element is determined by FINRA.

Registered persons may be required to take the Regulatory Element outside of this timeframe if they break certain securities laws and/or are subject to certain fines or disciplinary action(s).

Each member organization has a responsibility to annually evaluate and assess all employees who directly interact with customers or clients to ensure their securities knowledge is accurate and up-to-date. Written plans must be developed when considering the size, scope, and nature of the member firm's business to ensure the plan is appropriate.

This training plan, at a minimum, must cover the following topics:

- General investment features and associated risk factors
- Suitability and sales practice considerations
- Applicable regulatory requirements
- Training in ethics, professional responsibility, and the requirements of Rule 2241 for registered research analysts and their immediate supervisors

The member firm must administer the written plan it develops and document both the plan and its implementation.

Addressing Margin Issues

Characteristics of Margin Accounts

Customers who purchase securities using borrowed money are classified as margin accounts. The broker must approve these accounts since they're dealing with high-risk customers that typically provide securities and cash as collateral. Most brokerage firms have restrictions on which accounts can be margin accounts and what kinds of securities can be purchased in them.

Since there's a higher risk involved in margin trading, a certain portion of the account must be owned by the customer, so they can deposit more cash in the account or sell securities if the value of a stock drops. Customers are approved for these accounts based on their credit history and must use at least $2,000 for their first purchase on a margin account.

Brokers must furnish disclosures outlining the risks involved with margin accounts and day trading accounts. This ensures that the customer is fully aware of the risks and can approve their account for various types of trading. Disclosures, typically in the form of written letters and notices, are either mailed or emailed to the customer. The customer is required to review and sign each disclosure as their agreement to proceed with the transaction and relationship.

When a customer opens a margin account, they must receive a letter (in writing) every year informing them of the risks involved. The letter must reference that the customer may lose more money than they have in their account at any given time, and that:

- Margin calls must be met immediately.
- Borrowing rules are subject to change at any time.
- The brokerage firm chooses which stocks are sold to meet a margin call.

Brokers who specialize in setting up and managing day trading accounts must also provide a statement to customers outlining all of the risks involved and how the accounts are managed. This statement must outline all risks involved with day trading. The customer either needs to approve the account for day trading or sign a form confirming that they don't intend to use it for that purpose.

Key Terms

- Credit Balance: The amount the customer has contributed to or received in their brokerage account to date.

- Debit Balance: The amount the customer has borrowed from the brokerage firm to date.

- Exempt Securities: Securities that are not registered under the Securities Act of 1933. These include: securities issued by the federal government or its agencies; municipal bonds; securities issued by banks, savings institutions, and credit unions; public utility securities; and securities issued by nonprofit, educational, and religious organizations.

- Hypothecation: The practice of using stocks as collateral for a loan. Stock market investors must sign a margin agreement to give the brokerage firm permission to do this.

- LMV (Long Market Value): This refers to the current value of the stock the investor bought on margin. It's important to note that this may be different from the value of the stock at the time of purchase.

- Loan Value: This is the difference between the margin requirement of an account and the total cost of the account.

- Margin: The amount borrowed and then used to purchase securities.

- Margin Calls: When the equity in a margin account falls below the maintenance level, the brokerage firm issues a margin call asking the investor or customer to deposit more funds or stocks to reach the minimum level. If they fail to do so in a timely manner, the brokerage firm can sell the stocks out of the account to raise money. Most brokers issue a margin call when the investor's position falls below 25%, but many brokers have higher maintenance level requirements.

- Marginable Securities: These are securities that can be used as collateral for margin trades. An example would be stocks listed on the New York Stock Exchange and the NASDAQ exchange. In some cases, over-the-counter (OTC) stocks can also fall into this category. Mutual funds and newly issued stocks can't be bought on margin, but they can be used as collateral after 30 days. Options (except for LEAPS) and many OTC stocks can't be bought on margin or used as collateral and, therefore, are non-marginable securities.

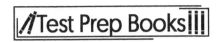

- Portfolio Margin: An analysis of a portfolio's risk used to determine margin requirements; essentially a risk-based margin policy. It usually results in lower margin requirements. Regulation T states that the portfolio margin can be six to one or more, whereas the regular margin can only be leveraged twice.
- Rehypothecation: The practice of using the same stocks as collateral for a bank loan. Unless the brokerage firm has written consent from both customers, the practice of combining stocks from two different customer accounts is prohibited. Customers who allow rehypothecation are typically compensated with a rebate on fees or charged a lower cost of borrowing. The brokerage firm is not permitted to pledge more than 140% of a customer's debit balance at any given time.
- SMV (Short Market Value): The current price of the stock a short seller has sold. Since it's based on the current value of the stock and not the stock price at the original transaction, it's constantly fluctuating.
- Special Memorandum Account (SMA): SMAs are margin accounts used for calculating Regulation T requirements on brokerage accounts. An SMA also calculates unrealized gains so the customer knows the actual market value of their portfolio.

Product or Strategy Specific Requirements

Certain types of investment products and strategies with margin accounts are subject to additional requirements and restrictions. Per Regulation T, since mutual funds are part of a continuous public offering, they can't be purchased on margin. However, if they're purchased and held for at least 30 days, they can be used as collateral for a margin purchase of other securities. Low-risk securities (such as U.S. Treasury Bonds) are not subject to these same restrictions.

Calculations

Initial Margin

The initial margin requirement is the amount the customer must contribute before the broker can set up a margin account. Under Regulation T, this amount is 50%. However, brokerage firms have the right to establish initial margin requirements higher than this percentage. For example, if someone wants to buy 1,000 shares of a company at $2 per share, they would need to make a $2,000 purchase. If they only have $1,000 available, they would then borrow the remaining $1,000 from the brokerage firm. If the shares drop by a certain percentage, the brokerage firm may issue a margin call. When this occurs, the customer must deposit more cash to make up for the difference, thereby reducing the risk that they will default on the loan.

Maintenance

Customers have two options with margin accounts: borrowing money to buy securities (long margin account) or borrowing securities directly (short margin account). Long margin accounts involve using a combination of the customer's money and money the broker lends to make a profit. The customer then pays back the broker. These are well-suited for bull markets where security values increase.

Short margin accounts involve selling the security (or securities) borrowed from the broker, waiting for a price decrease, and then buying the security at a lower price. They then return the security to the broker and pocket the extra cash. These are well-suited for bear markets where security values decrease. Since short sales involve selling stocks that the investor doesn't own, they're subject to stricter margin requirements. Under the Federal Reserve Board's Regulation T, the initial margin requirement for short sale accounts is 150%. This includes the value of the short sale (100%) and an additional margin requirement of 50%.

The following is the equation to use to calculate a short margin account:

$$SMV + EQ = CR$$

SMV is the short market value, EQ is equity, and CR represents the credit balance.

Special Memorandum Account

Special Memorandum Accounts (SMAs) refer to the purchasing power of an account. It is created when the value of stocks purchased on a margin account increases. Based on the 50% margin requirement, $0.50 of SMA is created for every dollar stock price increases.

SMAs function much like lines of credit. The customer uses the value of their SMA to purchase additional stock or withdraw cash without selling the original stocks bought on margin. In addition, investors have the freedom to increase their SMA simply by depositing more cash in their account.

Other Margin Accounts

Two other types of margin accounts are:

- Portfolio Margin Account: Where the initial margin requirement is based on the risk of the portfolio. These accounts may have a lower initial margin requirement of 15% or 20% (not Regulation T's minimum 50%), but the customer must have a higher absolute amount of equity (usually $150,000 or more). The margin for these accounts is calculated using Options Clearing Corporation's (OCC's) Customer Portfolio Margin system.
- Day Trading Account: Considered less risky, these accounts are used to make multiple trades per day. The value of these accounts fluctuates significantly based on the daily price of a stock. As a result, these high-risk accounts are subject to different rules than other margin accounts. The customer must have at least $25,000 in equity in the account or they're not permitted to day trade. The buying power of a day trading account is four times the equity in the account above the 25% maintenance minimum. This amount is defined as the maintenance margin excess.

Practice Questions

1. Which of the following forms is used to terminate the registrations of representatives with a specific self-regulatory organization or jurisdiction?
   a. Form U4
   b. EMMA
   c. Form U5
   d. TRACE

2. When must registered persons first complete the Regulatory Element?
   a. Before they are allowed to register
   b. On the first anniversary of their registration
   c. On the second anniversary of their registration
   d. On the third anniversary of their registration

3. Which of the following is true of continuing education for registered persons?
   a. There are three elements: regulatory, firm, and personal.
   b. Organizations who employ registered persons must evaluate members' securities knowledge biannually.
   c. Organizations must document their written plan and its implementation.
   d. FINRA details specific points that must be covered in the training plan.

4. What is hypothecation?
   a. The practice of using stocks as collateral for a loan
   b. The difference between the margin requirement of an account and the total cost of the account
   c. The amount the customer has borrowed from the brokerage firm to date
   d. The amount borrowed and then used to purchased security

5. Assuming an initial margin requirement of 50%, how much would an investor need to deposit as an initial margin if they wish to purchase 5,000 shares of stock priced at $8 a share?
   a. $20,000
   b. $40,000
   c. $2,500
   d. $10,000

6. Which type of account involves selling securities borrowed directly from the broker?
   a. Special Memorandum Account
   b. Maintenance Account
   c. Long Margin Account
   d. Short Margin Account

7. What is the minimum amount of equity a customer is required to have in an account to participate in day trading?
   a. $150,000
   b. $2,000
   c. $25,000
   d. $100,000

8. Which of the following is an example of an exempt security?
   a. Coca-Cola common stock
   b. A high-yield junk bond
   c. A closed-end mutual fund investing in commercial paper
   d. A U.S. Treasury bond

9. If a portfolio with assets of $200 Million does $400 Million in trades in one quarter, what is the annualized turnover rate?
   a. 800%
   b. 200%
   c. 50%
   d. 25%

10. Under what condition can a broker sell a client's securities even if they are unauthorized to do so?
   a. If the markets become volatile
   b. If a trigger is about to be reached and the markets will halt trading.
   c. If a margin call on a client's account occurs, and they do not have cash or securities to cover the amount required
   d. If a stock declines by more than 10% in value

11. What is the benefit of the TRACE system?
   a. It generates fees from investors and brokers who use TRACE.
   b. It provides transparency to boost investor confidence in OTC trading.
   c. It prevents insider trading.
   d. It allows for faster trade execution.

12. Reverse churning can occur with which of the following?
   a. Commission-based brokers
   b. Fee-based brokers
   c. Investment bankers
   d. Research analysts

13. The bid-ask spread of a stock that has a bid of $25 and an ask of $26 is which of the following?
   a. $1
   b. $25.50
   c. $26
   d. $0.50

14. Assuming the required margin is 50%, what is the dollar amount in the client's margin account immediately after $1,000,000 worth of Microsoft stock is borrowed and sold for a short sale?
   a. $1,000,000
   b. $500,000
   c. $750,000
   d. $1,500,000

15. Assuming the required margin is 50%, what is the dollar amount in the client's margin account immediately after $1,000,000 worth of Microsoft stock is borrowed and sold for a short sale, and the value of the shares then increases by 50%—to $1,500,000?

a. $3,000,000
b. $1,000,000
c. $500,000
d. $0

16. If an investor wishes to profit from a position in a stock she feels will not go up or down, which of the following is the position she should take?

a. Buy a straddle
b. Buy put and call options
c. Sell a straddle
d. Buy the stock and sell it short at the same time

17. What happens when a failure to deliver occurs with a short sale?

a. The broker for the short seller is unable to locate securities to deliver to the buyer.
b. The stock fails to decline in value.
c. A stock fails to tick upward before a short sale can be executed.
d. A bond fails to convert to equity.

18. Which of the following systems is used to report all transactions in municipal securities?

a. Trade Reporting & Compliance Engine (TRACE)
b. Trade Reporting Facility (TRF)
c. Order Audit Trail System (OATS)
d. Real-Time Transaction Reporting System (RTRS)

19. If a broker is executing a sale for 1,000 shares for a client and can either sell the shares on one exchange for $20 per share and receive a $500 commission or sell them on another for $19 on a different exchange and receive a $1,000 dollar commission, what is considered the best execution?

a. Sell the shares for $19 to increase his commission
b. Sell the shares for $19 and split the commission with the client
c. Sell the shares for the $20 price
d. Wait until the prices align

20. According to FINRA Rules, an exchange traded stock must be traded within what percent of the quoted price for a stock valued at $100 that is trading during regular trading hours?

a. 20%
b. 10%
c. 5%
d. 3%

21. A "good delivery" refers to which of the following?

a. A security that has all of the proper endorsements and requirements
b. An investment that has been profitable
c. A trade that has been executed with best efforts
d. Bonds that have the correct yield

22. In the event of an order cancellation, which of the following additional pieces of information must also be recorded?
   a. The reason for the cancellation
   b. The month and year the trade expires
   c. The time the order is brought to the floor
   d. The strike price

23. Which of the following terms describes a trade that is only executed when the price surpasses a certain point?
   a. Day order
   b. Stop order
   c. Market order
   d. Good til cancelled order

24. In short selling, a locate occurs in which of the following situations?
   a. When stock goes down in value
   b. When the broker approves the execution of the short sale
   c. When the shares go up in value
   d. When the broker locates an investor interested in short selling

25. What is a fill or kill (FOK) order?
   a. A type of order that will execute at the price specified and has unlimited duration
   b. A type of order that will attempt to fulfill the entire trade, or cancel the trade if a portion is unable to be filled
   c. A type of order that will fill portions of the order that are able to be filled while leaving the unfilled portions open to be filled later in the trading day
   d. A type of order that will never be executed but is used to test how such an order will affect the bid/ask spread in a particular security

26. Which of the following is NOT true regarding customer complaints?
   a. Complaints cannot be resolved using mediation.
   b. Complaints must be submitted in writing.
   c. Complaints can be solved using a formal or informal process.
   d. Complaints are submitted to the Financial Industry Regulatory Authority (FINRA).

27. When a party files a complaint in the arbitration process, how many days does the other party have to respond?
   a. 30
   b. 60
   c. 45
   d. 75

28. Simplified arbitration is used in cases involving less than how much money?
   a. $50,000
   b. $25,000
   c. $10,000
   d. $15,000

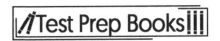

29. Where are stocks NOT listed on a regulated exchange, such as the NASDAQ or NYSE, traded?
    a. On an over the counter market
    b. On a private exchange, available only to company insiders
    c. In a specific ETF that only owns unlisted stocks
    d. They do not trade

30. An equity market maker does NOT perform which of the following?
    a. Keep trading in a security liquid
    b. Reduce market volatility
    c. Take advantage of mispricing in the market
    d. Keep fair and orderly markets

31. Which regulation calls for an initial margin requirement of 50%?
    a. Regulation A
    b. Regulation T
    c. Regulation D
    d. Regulation SHO

32. Which of the following is a listing requirement for the NASDAQ?
    a. Minimum of $1.25 million shares trading
    b. 4 market makers
    c. Minimum bid of $5 per share
    d. Market capitalization greater than $750 million

33. What must be stamped on a trade ticket when the recipient does not have knowledge of the trade?
    a. Null and Void
    b. Cleared
    c. Return to Seller
    d. Don't Know

34. Which of the following can be considered a possible disadvantage of the automated execution system?
    a. An automated execution system enters trades when a trader is not present.
    b. An automated execution system can buy and sell large orders simultaneously.
    c. An automated execution system continues to trade based on preprogrammed indicators unless someone intervenes.
    d. An automated execution system executes trades based on a variety of metrics.

35. What is a security with ownership recorded electronically by a financial institution and without a paper certificate?
    a. Due bill
    b. Bearer security
    c. Stock power
    d. Book entry security

Answer Explanations

1. C: Form U5 is used to terminate the registrations of representatives with a specific self-regulatory organization or jurisdiction. Form U4 is used to register representatives. EMMA is the system that tracks information about municipal securities. TRACE is the system by which all broker-dealers must report the information pertaining to trades involving certain fixed income securities that are traded over-the-counter, on the secondary market, or not on a regulated exchange.

2. C: Registered persons must complete what is called the Regulatory Element on the second anniversary of their registration and then every three years following that. A qualification exam must be passed before anyone can register.

3. C: Member organizations must document their written plan and its implementation. Continuing education includes two elements, regulatory and firm. Organizations must assess employees' knowledge annually. FINRA provides a minimum number of topics that must be covered in training plans but not specific points.

4. A: Hypothecation describes when a client uses stocks as collateral for a loan. Choice B is the definition of loan value. Choice C references the debit balance. Choice D defines margin.

5. A: To find the initial margin requirement, the initial margin percentage of 50% is multiplied by the total cost of the stock. In this case, the stock price is $8 for 5,000 shares:

$$\$8 \times 5{,}000 = \$40{,}000$$

The initial margin that needs to be deposited is:

$$\$40{,}000 \times 0.5 = \$20{,}000$$

6. D: Short margin accounts refer to when customers sell securities borrowed from the broker and then wait for the share price to go down before they buy them back. A special memorandum account simply means the purchasing power of an account. A maintenance account is not an actual account dealing with securities. A long margin account occurs when a customer borrows money to buy securities.

7. C: Customers who wish to day trade must have at least $25,000 in equity on any day that the customer day trades.

8. D: Exempt securities are those that do not have to be registered with the SEC. Most exempt securities are issued from the U.S. federal government. In this example, the only exempt option is a U.S. Treasury bond. The other funds, stocks, and bonds must all be registered and are non-exempt. All the other options are non-federal government securities and thus must be registered.

9. A: $400 Million in trades in one quarter is equivalent to $1,600 Million in trades per year. $1,600 divided by $200 equals 800%. This is evidence of "churning" a brokerage account.

10. C: If a margin call occurs and the client has insufficient funds or no securities that can be used as collateral, the broker can sell securities in the client's portfolio to cover the call without permission. Volatile markets and market triggers are not sufficient circumstances for a broker to trade without their client's permission.

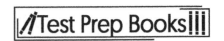

11. B: It provides improved transparency in OTC trading as these transactions would otherwise go unreported. Additionally, investors have better insight as to where these securities are trading.

12. B: Reverse churning occurs with fee-based accounts, where brokers have no incentive to trade for a customer because they are simply earning a fixed fee. Commission-based brokers have the incentive to churn, not reverse churn. If commission-based brokers do not trade for customers, they earn less money.

13. A: The spread is the difference between the bid and the ask price. In this case, it is $26 less $25, which is $1. The average of the two numbers is $25.50, and $26 is simply the asking price.

14. D: The initial margin is 50% of $1,000,000 or $500,000. That amount will increase by $1,000,000 once the shares are borrowed and sold and the proceeds placed in the customer's account.

15. B: The stock going up will cause the short seller's position to go down by $500,000. Therefore, the account that had $1,500,000 will now have a balance of $1,000,000. This essentially will cause the investor to lose his or her entire initial investment—the initial margin—of $500,000. However, the value could increase if the value of the stock goes back down and if he or she still has his or her short positions.

16. C: By selling a straddle, the investor is selling both call and put options and collecting a premium from the party buying the contract. If the stock does not move outside of the strike prices for the put and call contracts, the option will not be exercised, and the seller will simply collect her premiums. Buying a straddle would cause a loss for the buyer as she has paid the premium but cannot exercise the options. Buying the stock and selling it short would not be profitable as she is not getting a return from the stock itself, and the short sale position would not be profitable either.

17. A: This is when the broker is unable to find shares that have been sold short. The result is naked short selling. The delivery has nothing to do with the change in the stock's value or if a bond converts to equity. When a stock does not tick upward, it cannot be short sold, but this is the uptick rule.

18. D: The Real-Time Transaction Reporting System (RTRS) is used to report all transactions in municipal securities. The Trade Reporting & Compliance Engine (TRACE) system is used for the bond market to provide better transparency. The Trade Reporting Facility (TRF) has separate systems at NASDAQ and the New York Stock Exchange. Under this system, trades must be reported within ten seconds of being executed. Finally, the Order Audit Trail System (OATS) is used to recreate events as they occurred and monitors the trading practices of all member firms.

19. C: Selling the shares for their maximum value would be the best execution. Increasing the broker's commission would not be the best execution as this is in the broker's best interest, not the client's best interest. Splitting the commission is not an option. Waiting for the prices to align is not best execution as the share price might fall even further.

20. D: 3%. FINRA Rule 11892 provides numerical guidelines for classifying erroneous trades. An erroneous transaction is subject to being voided, such as a security quoted anywhere from $0 to $25 but that has a trade executed at an amount greater than or less than 10% of that quoted price within normal trading hours. If brokers and exchanges are quoting a share of a stock at $20 and the broker buys shares for a customer for $23 (15% of the stock's value), then this trade is considered erroneous. The threshold is 20% outside of trading hours as securities will be less liquid during that time, and traders can expect to not get the best execution. The percent threshold is 5% and 10% for stocks up to $50 and 3% and 6% for stocks of more than $50. These guidelines assure brokers will not trade shares excessively outside of where they are being quoted.

21. A: A "good delivery" means that a security has all of the proper endorsements, requirements, and guarantees.

22. C: In the event of an order cancellation, the time the order is brought to the floor is the additional piece of information that must also be recorded. The reason for the cancellation does not need to be recorded. The month and year the trade expires and the strike price are pieces of information that are already required on an order ticket.

23. B: A stop order is a trade that is only executed when the price surpasses a certain point. A day order expires if criteria is not reached for a trade to occur during that day. A market order is simply an order that is executed at whatever the market price is. Finally, a good til cancelled order (GTC) means the order is in place until executed, unless the investor cancels the order.

24. B: In short selling, a locate occurs when the broker approves the execution of a short sale.

25. B: Fill or kill (FOK) orders are filled in their entirety or cancelled. No partial orders are executed using this order type, so it is a good choice if an investor wants a particular position size but will not accept a partial position for whatever reason. Other options include an immediate or cancel order, a limit order, and an order type that does not exist.

26. A: Complaints can be solved using mediation if it is an informal proceeding. Complaints are submitted to FINRA in writing and are solved using either formal or informal proceedings.

27. C: In the arbitration process, after one party files a Statement of Claim, the other party has 45 days to respond to the complaint.

28. A: Simplified arbitration, where only a single arbitrator makes a final decision, is used in cases involving less than $50,000.

29. A: Stocks not listed on an exchange trade on one of the over the counter markets like the "pink sheets" or the bulletin board. There is no private exchange available only to company insiders. ETFs must be linked to an index and there is no index that only tracks stocks not listed on a regulated exchange, although there are indexes that track a basket of medium and small market capitalization companies.

30. C: Market makers maintain liquidity, try to keep stock price volatility down, and keep markets fair and orderly when trades are executed.

31. B: Regulation T regulates required margin amounts and has the power to change the amount of margin required depending on certain situations.

32. A: NASDAQ listing requirement include a minimum of $1.25 million shares trading, a minimum bid of $4 per share, and three market makers. They also require companies to have market capitalization greater than $850 million.

33. D: If the recipient of a confirmation does not have knowledge of a trade, the trade ticket should be stamped "Don't Know" and returned to the seller. This will cause the transaction to be assumed null and void.

34. C: An automated execution system continues to trade based on preprogrammed indicators unless someone intervenes. This can be a disadvantage to the automated execution system if conditions in the market change and those conditions are not part of the preprogrammed indicators. This could result in trades being made that are not beneficial to the customer.

35. D: A book entry security is a security with ownership recorded electronically with a financial institution; it does not have a paper certificate. A due bill relates to the payment of pending dividends. A bearer form security has no written or electronic record of ownership. Stock power is a legal form to authorize the transfer of ownership of a stock.

Dear Series 7 Test Taker,

We would like to start by thanking you for purchasing this study guide for your Series 7 exam. We hope that we exceeded your expectations.

Our goal in creating this study guide was to cover all of the topics that you will see on the test. We also strove to make our practice questions as similar as possible to what you will encounter on test day. With that being said, if you found something that you feel was not up to your standards, please send us an email and let us know.

We have study guides in a wide variety of fields. If you're interested in one, try searching for it on Amazon or send us an email.

Thanks Again and Happy Testing!
Product Development Team
info@studyguideteam.com

Interested in buying more than 10 copies of our product? Contact us about bulk discounts:

bulkorders@studyguideteam.com

FREE Test Taking Tips DVD Offer

To help us better serve you, we have developed a Test Taking Tips DVD that we would like to give you for FREE. **This DVD covers world-class test taking tips that you can use to be even more successful when you are taking your test.**

All that we ask is that you email us your feedback about your study guide. Please let us know what you thought about it – whether that is good, bad or indifferent.

To get your **FREE Test Taking Tips DVD**, email freedvd@studyguideteam.com with "FREE DVD" in the subject line and the following information in the body of the email:

a. The title of your study guide.

b. Your product rating on a scale of 1-5, with 5 being the highest rating.

c. Your feedback about the study guide. What did you think of it?

d. Your full name and shipping address to send your free DVD.

If you have any questions or concerns, please don't hesitate to contact us at freedvd@studyguideteam.com.

Thanks again!